KT-197-524

THE ILLUSTRATED GUIDE TO WINE

THE ILLUSTRATED GUIDE TO

WINE

BY CHRIS FOULKES

Executive Manager	Kelly Flynn
Editorial Manager	Susan Egerton-Jones
Art Editor	Ruth Levy
Editorial Assistant	Fiona Thomas
Production	Peter Phillips

This edition produced exclusively
for W H Smith

Edited and designed by the Artists House
Division of Mitchell Beazley International Ltd.
Artists House
14–15 Manette Street
London W1V 5LB

"An Artists House Book"

ISBN 0 86134 093 0

Typeset by Hourds Typographica Limited, Stafford.
Reproduction by La Cromolito s.n.c., Milan.
Printed in Italy by Poligrafici Calderara. s.p.a., Bologna.

INTRODUCTION

Wine is a long-term pleasure. No-one who drinks and enjoys it ever stops learning. Elderly connoisseurs make as many discoveries as young enthusiasts.

It's with some trepidation therefore that I have written my first book after a mere ten years of tasting, studying and writing about wine. If I have crammed a lot into those years it is due to the openness and generosity of the wine world. And if I've learnt anything it is due to the experience of working with some of the most talented of wine writers. I thank them, especially Hugh Johnson, for their friendship and guidance. Thanks also to Duncan Baird and Kelly Flynn for asking me to write this book, to Ruth Levy, Peter Phillips and Susan Egerton-Jones for turning it out so handsomely, and – most of all – to Carrie for proving that closeness and candour can go hand in hand. This book is for her.

Chris Foulkes

CONTENTS

Chapter Three

MAKING WINE

Chapter Four

WINE MASTERCLASS

FOREWORD

At some unmarked moment within the last two or three years we crossed an invisible frontier. Wine, from being considered an exotic beverage by the majority of us, began to be accepted as a familiar friend, a normal part of life — if not everyday life, at least every week, or every month: a pleasure without affectation that makes meals taste better, and friendship warmer. When the great moment came the old bugbears of mystique and snobbery faded into the background. Most of us today consider ourselves wine-drinkers, more or less.

Now, having crossed the Rubicon, we have a bit of boning up to do. Wine (life, too, so they say) is like a bucket. The more you put in the more you get out. If you limited yourself to Liebfraumilch you will never know one hundredth of the varied tastes and pleasures that wine offers: a wider range in its way than your butcher, fishmonger, grocer and greengrocer all combined. For wine varies not just from place to place, but from year to year and from maker to maker.

Wine keeps moving on, surprising us with new sensations, offering moments of pleasure that range from exquisite cool refreshment to a deeply satisfying, cockle-warming glow.

To make the most of it must be the aim of every practical person, especially as experience tempts us to experiment beyond the cheap but scarcely cheerful basic levels. We soon find that there are swigging wines, and there are sipping wines. There are down-the-hatch wines and wines that stop you in your tracks the moment you pull the cork and let the genie out of the bottle. To know which is which, and how and when to buy and serve them, is what the practical person needs to know. It is what this book sets out to relate, in suitably unfussy terms — the terms of a practical person who has edited many wine books — some of my own included — and who has learned from other authors' extravagances just what is, and is not, essential information to the newcomer to wine.

To be practical is one thing. To be fresh, original and stimulating on a subject as old and tried as wine is another. Chris Foulkes is all these things. He demystifies without bathos, explains without talking down, and writes with the freshness of someone who makes new discoveries every day.

The book starts where we all start, with the decisions we have to make in choosing wine. It goes straight to the practicalities of buying, and puts food and the sort of occasion where they belong among the priorities. On wine with food there is much good and original advice — leading on to a closer look at wine and its flavours, how they vary and why, how different sorts of wine are made and where the best and most typical of each kind come from.

Chris Foulkes starts with the wine in your glass, and leads you back through its story to a better understanding of why it is that way, and how it is best enjoyed. "Enjoyed" is the key word. A wine that is not enjoyed has failed in its sole purpose. The same, come to that, goes for a wine book. I guarantee you'll enjoy this one.

Hugh Johnson

Chapter One

WINE IN THE GLASS

WHY WINE?

Wine is for pleasure. It's as simple as that. Wine is one among many alcoholic drinks, yet with its great range of styles and strengths it can please more people, suit more occasions and (speaking for myself) give more pleasure than any other. The aim of this book is to introduce the fun, enjoyment and interest that wine offers.

For many, the reason why wine brings them pleasure is because of its variety. Alone among drinks it is always changing. It is a natural fluid, the product of the very basic chemistry of yeast and fermentation. Even after being bottled, a wine can change: a good wine will mature, developing flavours undreamed of in its raw youth. And wine is the product of many factors: the weather in the year of its making, the skill or otherwise of the person who made it, the environment of the vineyard where the grapes were grown. All this means every bottle is potentially different, a new experience just waiting for a corkscrew.

The pleasure to be had from wine can happily be increased to a very large extent by a relatively small amount of knowledge. Because of its subtle variety, there is more to know than about spirits, or even beer (a drink as complex in its way as wine). Knowledge about styles and tastes lets us fit wine more enjoyably into our lives, choosing the right bottle for different occasions. A little background about the place a wine comes from, and how it is made, adds to the interest when you're drinking it. Some basic skills in choosing, storing, decanting and so on make sure you get the best from what you buy.

One of the reasons why wine finds a place in so many people's lives is that it goes so well with the food. No other drink, alcoholic or otherwise, partners food in such a rewarding way. Much of the first chapter of this book is devoted to suggesting how to exploit this partnership to the full. The fact that we usually drink wine with food has a bearing on health, making wine less potentially harmful than other alcoholic drinks. We should not overstress the benefits of wine, as the French, with their fixations on their livers, tend to do. But there is no doubt that wine has useful properties, aiding digestion at the very least.)

But wine is not medicine, it is pleasure. Drunk in that spirit — and in moderation — it will do you nothing but good.

It used to be taken as read that when starting to learn a bit about wine, you set out first to learn about the regions where it is made, then how it is put together, with an apologetic bit at the end on actually drinking the stuff. This book works the other way round. It's a statistical probability that you drink wine already, even if only occasionally.

So I start by looking into the kinds of wine you're finding in your glass, and the various ways it can be enjoyed. This chapter progresses right through the different kinds of meals, and dishes, and parties, suggesting styles of wine for each. It then talks about taking wine more seriously: enjoying it for its own sake, rather than as an adjunct to family and social life.

The second chapter is about the world of wine. Each bottle comes from *somewhere*, and the factors that prevail there are what form the taste of the wine. So the chapter starts off by describing these key influences, and then looks around the world of wine to see how they apply in different places. These days we can buy wine from every continent, from places as diverse as Oregon and China. The wines of each have a story to tell, and a subtle variation of taste to contribute to our enjoyment.

Wine may be natural, but it is man-made, so the third chapter describes how people go about turning grapes into a drink. It looks at the importance of different sorts of grapes, and at the varying techniques both traditional and modern. Together with the world round-up, this should arm you with the general background of the bottle you're about to enjoy.

Wine is not cheap, especially good wine, so it is worth mastering the simple skills that will get it to the glass at its best. These skills are the subject of the last chapter, a "masterclass" that describes the handful of common-sense tricks needed. It also talks about the ancillaries that add to the enjoyment of wine: glasses, decanters and the like.

When all this is said, the very best introduction to wine is a corkscrew. This book hopes to add a little to your pulling power.

All wine starts in the vineyard — and wine country is some of the most charming, and peaceful, anywhere. Peace there may be, but there's hard work too: the vineyards must be tilled and grapes must be picked.

THE KINDS OF WINE

The wine in every bottle there is stems from grapes. But that's about all wine has in common. Its variety is both exhilarating and bewildering.

The wine colourchart would over-excite an interior decorator: there are hues from barely gold-tinged clarity, water-like in the glass, through to opaque purple-black. Colour is just one facet. Tastes range from tart to succulent. Weight and intensity vary from feather-light to hammer blows. The touch on your tongue can be velvet or glasspaper. It can be hard to remember that these varied drinks actually have a common source: grape juice.

With so many sorts to try, where to begin? But once begun, the beguiling choices open up until you realise there is a lifetime's worth of tastes to be tried.

Most of us stop far short of that. For many wine drinkers, it's enough to know a few styles, or even a few examples of these styles. Everyone finds his or her point to stop along the way. Picking up a vocabulary of wine styles is, however, worthwhile. It makes the use of wine, to enhance our meals and enliven our entertainments, easier and more assured. And it leads to the pleasure in discovery that is what makes wine worth writing about.

To bring order to the chaos of styles and varieties, it's helpful to divide wines into three groups. These are, first, table or light wines, then sparkling ones, and finally, fortified wines. Light wines are the most natural in the sense that Man has done least to them. Later chapters describe the way they are made, and explore the reasons why they taste the way they do. Enough here to say that they are the straightforward fermented juice of grapes. Sparkling wines are natural too, but made in such a way that they contain carbon dioxide, which when the bottle is opened escapes as bubbles. Fortified wines have a little spirit — brandy, perhaps — added to strengthen and stabilize them. They are wines to sip rather than gulp.

Wine varies in taste and also in status, or price, which rises with status on a roughly parallel scale. There are ordinary wines, good ones and great ones. There are wines which never leave their place of origin, and others which are as widely traded as any other staple commodity. Some wines are perhaps more famous than great, some the reverse: finding these, and paying bargain prices for them, is one of a wine-lover's fondest pleasures.

The scale of prices depends on where you buy: France has no tax on wine, as befits a country that makes a living from it. Britain and Scandinavia view it as a luxury, even a vice, and tax it accordingly. But the basic price of various wines, as they leave their producers, indicates the scale of values the world applies. Everyday "jug" wine, from a big modern plant in southern France, Italy or the Central Valley of California, costs at the time of writing about £2.00 in the UK after tax, but only about £0.30 at the winery gates. Call this winery price one unit per bottle. Up the scale, a slightly better wine from a small French château or an Italian farm costs twice or three times the basic: two or three units. At the top, the famous bottles from top vineyards can cost twenty, thirty or more times the base price.

Unlike a bottle of Scotch or vodka, wine varies dramatically in price. A millionaire anxious to reduce his bank balance can easily pay fifty times as much for his wine as you or I spend on a perfectly drinkable bottle. He would find it hard, impossible, to find a whisky with such a price tag: the best malt Scotch will cost perhaps four times as much as the ordinary blended whisky. The Cognac people would perhaps oblige him with something rare, old and expensive. But then they're selling distilled *wine,* and the wine pricing habit it obviously catching.

Wine choice is based on two main factors: status and style. Within those are the variations. My guideline is to start with the job I want the wine to do, and take it from there.

Right: *all wine starts as grapes. It ends up as anything from the lightest, softest dry white through to sweet, rich, almost black dessert wines. The choice lies with the maker, guided by sun, soil, rain and custom.*

Far right: *the drinker's choice is rather harder to make . . .*

WAYS OF ENJOYING WINE

Wine shop managers are used to the customer who comes in with a purposeful look, combs the shelves, quizzes the staff on what to drink with what — and eventually leaves with a familiar brand of Portuguese Rosé, Liebfraumilch or Lambrusco. In other words, safety conquers imagination under the pressure of choice. Butchers have the same experience: people come in with notions of exotic cuts of meat, quail under the choice and leave with lamb chops. In this part of the book I hope to harden your resolve, arm you with alternatives and force the branded wine people to work harder for their living . . . and for you.

There's nothing wrong with brand-name wines. It's just that there is more wine, more various wine, in the world than ever got behind a famous label or in a TV commercial. Use is the key to picking your wine, and as meals, mood, company and season change, let your choice range across the spectrum. If wine is not various, it is grocery, and you are wasting time reading about it.

Start with when. When will you enjoy your next bottle? With food, or in the garden on a warm evening, or at a party with 20 friends? Wine drunk on its own needs to be light in taste, good rather than ordinary (quality stands out clearly, bereft of masking food flavours) and low in alcohol. A meal of spicy food calls for a robust, clear-tasting wine in copious quantities (and therefore cheap).

There are two ways of matching occasion and bottle. One is for me to list the wine types, and suggest when to drink them. The other is to list uses and suggest the right wine. Here you get both options. First, the wines.

It's either red or white, still or sparkling. (Or a combination of those — ever tried *red* sparkling wine?) Red and white natural, or still, wines have much in common. Some whites are closer in taste and feel to some reds than they are other whites. Frequently the first decision is not "white or red?" but "heavy or light?"

You have to know a bit about wine to decide on style, for labels rarely tell you the character of the wine inside, though it's easy to see the colour. The label does, however, have a lot to say for itself. It just needs translation, the use of that basic vocabulary of styles and tastes. The wine business has woken up to the need for more information, and many labels now carry a description of the contents. Some merchants are better at this than others, and one has to judge from the tone whether the marketing department or the wine experts came out on top in the label-writing committee.

A more objective guide to basic wine taste is the dryness/sweetness rating system recently adopted by the British wine trade (and likely to be used elsewhere). Each white wine is given a rating on a scale from 1 (dry) to 9 (sweet). This helps a lot when you're faced with an unknown bottle. The system lacks subtlety, however, and furious arguments break out between merchants (and wine critics) as to whether a given wine is a 3, a 4 or even a 5. Also the decision on a wine's number is often arbitrary: a store will decide all German wines are grade 5 when they can of course vary widely, from 3 to 9.

What is meant by "dry" and "sweet"? Taste is detected by the tongue, which is supposed to know only four sensations: sweetness, sourness, bitterness and saltiness. The combination of these factors is the taste of anything, from wine to the glue on the back of a stamp. We can judge sweetness — it's one of the four basic tastes. Relative sweetness is the key to a "sweet or dry" judgement, though sourness and bitterness, as expressed by the acidity in wine, have something to say too.

However we come to the conclusion, there's a pretty wide agreement on whether wine is sweet or dry. A lot of wine drinkers stop right there and decide they like sweet white wine, or dry, and don't try much else. Which is a pity, for in matching bottles to occasions the sweet-dry spectrum is of tremendous use. The fashion for dryness has blinded a lot of sophisticated people to the charms of softer, sweeter wines, and has condemned them to stand through many a party sipping a tart, dry wine when something a notch sweeter would be far more fun. Equally, sweet-wine drinkers miss the refreshing taste of dry wine with food.

Sweetness in white wine should be natural: it comes ideally from the sugar produced by the sun shining on a bunch of grapes. If it is, then the sweetness will be matched by a natural fruit tartness to give all the pleasure of a good, garden-grown apple. Sadly a lot of wine has sugar added in its manufacture. There's nothing illegal or dishonest about this, but sweetened (rather than naturally sweet) wine always shows its origins in a certain sugary artificiality, most noticeable on the aftertaste.

Dryness comes from letting the wine go on fermenting until all the grape sugar is used up. This *should* leave plenty of fruity flavours to complement the tartness, but a lot of cheaper dry wines lack this, and end up empty of taste: astringency and alcohol and not much else. The best value in everyday whites is rarely the driest or the sweetest, but something with a touch of the natural sugar left to give it body and interest.

White wine styles

Stepping beyond sweet and dry, white wines divide into broad stylistic groups. There is a discernable "French" kind of white wine, and a "German" kind. France aims for dryness, freshness and strength, Germany for sweetness and elegance. (Neither set of adjectives are exclusive, of course.) It's interesting that when other countries make wine for the world's markets they imitate either or both styles. Bulgaria's big wine industry makes sweetish Riesling (in the German mould) and dry Chardonnay (in the French).

Besides these two kinds of white wine there are the variations due to latitude. It is harder to make fresh, elegant white wine where the summers are very hot. Technology is challenging this rule, and it's possible, with money, for it to win. But most Mediterranean whites, for instance, show their origins in a weighty, ponderous flatness. They can be very enjoyable, especially with their local food, but they are neither fresh and crisp nor refined and elegant.

There are, too, white wines made so badly, or (more usually today) from uninteresting grapes in boring places, that they taste of very little and have no distinct style. These wines have their place — usually mixed with mineral water or soda on a hot day. Or in a stew. Much ordinary French and Italian and Spanish wine is like this. The new world of California and Australia is luckier: at the everyday level, their whites are frequently better made and have more taste than do European ones.

Another down-market perversion of a fine style is cheap German wine. The tendency is to produce drinks with a taste which owes more to sweetness than grapes: "sugar-and-water" wines for people who don't like the taste of wine at all, really. The difference between these drinks and "real" German wine is enormous, far bigger than the price gap. The pages on Germany offer clues to which is which.

What do you get when you pay a lot for a great white wine? Intensity. Whatever the style, be it a dry Burgundy or a sweet Sauternes, what you get is more of the same. More tastes per sip, to put it baldly. The smell, the taste, the aftertaste that lingers long after you swallow, all have more to them, more

triggers for thoughts and metaphors and memories. Some winelovers argue that this makes great wines cheaper than ordinary ones, because each swallow generates so many sensations. Don't concentrate too hard – let the wine charm you. To drink wine with too much single-mindedness is rather like listening to Beethoven on headphones — a solitary and dismal pleasure. Wine is really only fun when shared: choose your company carefully when great wines are on the table.

Truly sweet white wines are a minority taste today, despite the efforts of wine writers and merchants, most of whom love them. But even their fans have to admit that sweet wines are harder to enjoy because there is a limited range of uses for them. The conventional time to open a sweet bottle is at the end of a meal, with dessert. This is fine in theory, but in practice the bottle of Sauternes or whatever will be jostling for attention beside the last of the red wine left from the main course. There will perhaps be an embarrassment as to whether to turn to the cheese before the pudding (in the French fashion) or after (as in the Anglo-Saxon). Some sweet things do not suit sweet wine: chocolate always seems wrong, as does anything with strong citrus-fruit flavours. No, good sweet wines are best drunk alone. Once their taste is tried and enjoyed, the occasions will make themselves: in a sunny garden, as an aperitif (very cold), with cake in the afternoon, instead of a pot of tea . . .

Red wines

Whites are enjoyable without food, reds less so. Some reds, those on the lighter side, are readily quaffed. But at a party when both are on offer, six glasses of white will be asked for to one of red.

Red wines are harder to split into styles than whites. Weight is one key quality of a red wine, another is softness or harshness. There have been efforts to devise red wine scales on the lines of the 1-9 system for whites, but they tend to confuse because sweetness is not really the point: nearly all red wines are technically dry. They differ in harshness or softness, and in solidity and degree of alcohol — weight. Usually a severe, bitter flavour in a wine is tannin (like in strong tea), which will disappear with maturity to be replaced by smoothness. But some red wines are always hard and harsh. Do not dismiss them, as is easy to do: abrasive reds have their place as do velvety ones.

Age is a key factor with a red, both the age it is and the age it is intended to be. While nearly every white wine is ready to be drunk within two or three years of the harvest, quite a lot of reds are designed to mature in bottle. It is a quirk of the wine business to sell customers a product not quite ready for use, but the practice will not die out. Some red wines improve so dramatically after a period in the bottle that it is worth the buyer's patience. And it is cheaper to buy wine young and keep it yourself than pay a merchant's price for a mature wine. Thus it's possible to buy reds that although good are not ready to drink. They will be few and far between in the average wine shop or supermarket, but they will occur. If you come across excess harshness in a red wine, ask yourself (and the wine merchant) if it is too young yet. It may be just bad wine, of course, but harshness on its own is no fault.

Just when is a red wine "ready"? Different palates give different answers. The French accuse their British customers of keeping wines too long, of hoarding bottles until the contents are faded and sad. The British counter with charges of infanticide: French drinkers miss out on the subtle nuances of a mature wine, they say.

Nine red wines in ten are ready to drink when you buy them. They may well get better, but they'll be ready. It is often possible to soften the taste of an astringent, earthy wine by keeping it for an extra six months or so: more on this later.

The north-south division, useful in classifying wines, works with reds too. Southern reds are typically high in alcohol and weighty in taste. That is not so with the cheaper Spanish and southern French reds, which, like the whites, combine an emptiness of flavour and a fierce alcohol level. Go up the quality scale a notch, however, and you find the solid, tasty reds of the Rhône or Rousillon, Rioja or Piedmont. Farther north, red wines such as Burgundy, Chinon and most Bordeaux are lighter and softer in flavour and alcohol. One immediate qualification: red Bor-

deaux's style depends almost entirely on status. Everyday claret is light, soft and ready young. The good Bordeaux wines have more structure and weight and need time. Latitude means that nearly all California and Australia reds are "southern" rather than "northern" in style.

The very best red wines are made in the northern rather than southern latitudes, though as with whites new techniques can and do conquer the problems of over-ripe grapes and overheated fermentations. Great red wines are multi-faceted liquids: they change remarkably in their long lives, and they reflect in colour, smell and taste all the ingredients of soil, sun and skill that go into them. Luckily, the taste of maturity and quality is to be found in very many wines which are far from dear.

So if in whites you look for dryness or sweetness, in reds the search is for gentle softness or brisk astringency, lightness or weight: with reds there are more dimensions to juggle with and, most experienced wine tasters would agree, more interest and pleasure to be had.

Sparkling wines

The taste of fizz depends on the wine the maker started with: the effect, which is far more important, varies far less. Wine with bubbles is a fast-acting boost to the mood, the party spirit, the sense of fun. This is not imagination; it happens because the bubbles speed the absorption of alcohol into the blood. I would like to be able to say that there is therefore no magic in champagne, just practical science. But every time I drink a bottle of really good champagne, I believe in magic.

With sparkling wine, it's hard to escape from the fact that you get what you pay for. The best way to make it, the way that gives the most and the longest-lasting bubbles and the subtlest taste, is intricate, time-consuming and, not surprisingly, the most costly. (Cheap fizz is known in the business as "bicycle-pump" because that, on an industrial scale, is how the bubbles get in.) The other expensive bit is the basic wine. Good fizz comes from clean, fruity, well-balanced wine. It's no accident that the key grape varieties grown in Champagne are those used to make the superb still wines of Burgundy.

Most sparkling wines are dry, some excessively so. Assume this unless the label says different (see chapter two for specifics) or unless the wine is suspiciously cheap. It's well worth noting that cheap fizz can be a very nasty liquid indeed.

Fortified wines

Most corners of the Mediterranean long ago devised a sweet, strong wine, often made from half-dried grapes. They still exist, but some have been elevated from peasant status into industries, and have been copied world-wide. The good thing about a fortified wine is its consistency. Year after year, bottle after bottle, the makers of sherry and Madeira follow their house styles. Each firm will have a range, from dry to sweet, with several degrees of quality too.

All fortified wines show in their weight the extra alcohol added to them. They are therefore drunk in smaller amounts than light wines. The dryness to sweetness scale used for white wines works well with them, though because of their weight no dry sherry ever matches the astringency of a really dry light wine. Harshness is a quality totally lacking in fortified wines. This is because they are always mature when bottled and sold (vintage port is an exception). The ageing takes place in barrels at the maker's premises.

Fortified wines are among the most versatile – and the easiest – to keep and serve. Fashion neglects them today: don't be a slave to fashion.

ON WINE DECISIONS

What wine with dinner tonight? For the lucky, the choice is made in a cool cellar, stacked with bottles many and various, something on hand for every occasion. Most of us are forced to a decision in a crowded shop, with hazy ideas countered briskly by a harassed assistant. Even worse, the options can be bald names on a restaurant wine list, with a waiter and his pen ready to make absolute our hesitant haverings.

It takes about 20 years and a seriously large income to build up a top-class personal cellar. So until you make it, wine decisions will always be with you. The way to scale the problem down to size is to match use with style. The trick is to define the use the wine is to be put to, select a style of wine that suits, and then to snatch out of the air (or out of your memory) one of the many wines that match.

The first point to establish about any occasion is who you are trying to please. If it's just you, or just family whose tastes you know, the choice is easier. Friends, or strangers, limit the options. However self-confident, the matching of claret with crab will take some carrying off – whatever they do in Bordeaux. Some people, happy people, are unaware of what others think (and presumably also have blinded taste-buds) but that sort need no advice. Also, certain people demand a certain status. It's no use ignoring the unhappy fact that snobbery is rife in wine. The especial snobs are those who know very little, just enough to have fixed ideas. You can't give these blockheads unusual wines. Your explanations that Chile, or the Lebanon, or Sicily, make superb wines these days will go unheard. They want their wine familiar, and preferably French.

This sort of snobbery crops up in surprising places, and among people clever enough to know better. You may think you don't know any; you will be surprised. The makers of Chablis, and Pouilly Fuissé, and blended clarets, have made a handsome living from the snobs for years.

So, while people fence in your choices, keep the experimenting to yourself until word gets around that you're knowledgeable on wine. The snobs will then begin to batten onto your enthusiasms and you'll be a leader of fashion.

Occasions vary in seriousness. A hilarious party is no place for a Grand Cru, which would just get in the way of the jokes. Large formal affairs are also bad environments for great wines: the varied company, the talk, the cigar smoke all distract and detract. Keep the best bottles for small gatherings of people who are prepared to let the wine get a word in.

Price is the key constraint. Wine, good wine especially, is not cheap. There will be occasions when lots of people must be catered for, and then a good ordinary wine must do. The trick is to find one that's interesting as well as inexpensive. The research can be fun.

Food makes a lot of decisions for us, though the next few pages show that the choices can be wide and the obvious is escapable. Some "rules" are best dealt with quickly. Red with meat, white with fish? It's advice rather than an order — advice anyone who has tried the opposites tends to give. Try it for yourself, and see if you don't find that fish gives a metallic taste to red wine. It is sometimes said the oil in fish does it, but other kinds of oily food respond well to red wine. Some fish goes well with some red wines, but the general advice is still sound.

White wine with red meat is by no means unpleasant, just a bit of a waste. Whites go best with poultry, pork or cold meat. Red beef or lamb, especially if hot or served with strong flavours, demands red wine for optimum enjoyment. Whites are overwhelmed by the opposing tastes.

Most of the time, one wine per meal is enough. There is much pleasure, though, in trying two or more at different stages in a meal. The advice is: white first, then red; young wines before old; dry ones before sweet. This is only today's convention: a study of Victorian menus shows that they enjoyed a heavy glass of sweet sherry at the start of a meal, with soup, and thought nothing of following a sweet champagne with claret (which was drunk like port, after dinner). But they had tougher digestions, and harder heads, in those days.

Right: *food and wine can be matched, the style of the wine suiting the fare and the occasion.*

WHAT TO DRINK WHEN

White wine styles

Enough of generalities, let's get down to cases. What do you drink with shellfish, or curry, or at a barbecue party? Here we take some examples of occasions, dishes and meals and suggest some wines to suit them. The white wine sweetness scale of 1 to 9 is used as an additional pointer to the style of wine that might do.

In the following pages on food and wine numbered bottle symbols in the captions give an indication of the kind of white wine suggested to go with a given dish. The driest wines are labelled 1, the sweetest 9.

It's a rather one-dimensional approach, for dryness-sweetness is only one facet of a wine's character. The numbers should be considered in conjunction with the notes alongside them, which discuss other wine characteristics and make specific suggestions.

The 1 to 9 scale shown below is however an invaluable starting-point. It was drawn up by the British Wine Development Board, a body set up by the drinks trade to encourage knowledge and appreciation of wine (and of course to encourage people to drink it). Several retailers had previously worked out their own scales, but, like videotape or computer formats, they all had different structures and were incompatible. The Board's scale is voluntary, but most people who sell wine in Britain agree with it and an increasing number of shops use it.

The scale, or something like it, seems set to spread to other wine-drinking countries. The European Common Market Commission has amended its strict labelling laws to allow the numbers to be printed on wine labels. The British government has backed it as official, and American retailers are showing interest in it.

It is possible to analyze a wine in a

White Wine Sweetness Scale

1

Bergerac
Muscadet
Touraine
Saumur
Chablis
Entre-deux-Mers
Pouilly Blanc Fumé
Sancerre
Champagne
Manzanilla Sherry
Tavel Rosé

2

Graves
Riesling d'Alsace
Frascati Secco
Orvieto Secco
Verdicchio
Soave
Chardonnays
Méthode Champenoise, Cava & Sekt
Dry Vouvray
Trocken German wines
White Rioja
White Burgundy
White Rhône
Spanish Dry White
Fino Sherry
Dry Sherry types
Dry Montilla
Sercial Madeira

3

Pinot Blanc d'Alsace
Brut Sparkling wine
Muscat d'Alsace
Halb-Trocken German wines
Hungarian Olasz Riesling dry
Grüner Veltliner Austria
Gewürztraminer d'Alsace
Dry Amontillado Sherry
Medium Dry Montilla
Medium Dry Vermouth
Dry White Vermouth
Dry White Port
Anjou Rosé

4

Vinho Verde
Chenin Blancs
Moselle Kabinett
Other Gewürztraminer
Rhine QbA
EEC wines
Moselle Deutscher Tafelwein
Moselle QbA
Rhine & Nahe Kabinett
Yugoslav Laski and Hungarian Olasz Riesling medium dry
Australian, New Zealand, and Bulgarian Rieslings
Full Amontillados
Medium Dry Sherry types
Portuguese Rosé
Orvieto Abbocato

5

Rhine Deutscher Tafelwein
Moselle Spätlesen
Vouvray Demi-Sec
Austrian Spätlesen
Liebfraumilch
Rhine Spätlesen
Medium British Sherry
Verdelho Madeira
Medium White Port

6

Demi-Sec Sparkling and Demi-Sec Champagne
Tokay Szamarodni Sweet
Spanish Medium
All Golden Sherry types

7

Asti Spumante
Moselle Auslesen
Rhine Auslesen
Tokay Aszu
Ières Côtes de Bordeaux
Monbazillac
Pale Cream Sherry
Montilla Cream
Bual Madeira
Rosso, Rosé and Bianco Vermouths

8

Moselle Beerenauslesen
Austrian Beerenauslesen
Rhine Beerenauslesen
Moselle Trockenbeerenauslesen
Spanish Sweet White
Moscatels
Sauternes
Barsac
Dark Cream Sherry
Cream and Rich Cream Sherry types

9

Rhine & Austrian Trockenbeerenauslesen
Eiswein
Malmsey Madeira
Muscat de Beaumes de Venise
Marsala
Brown Sherry
Moscatels

laboratory and show how much sugar it contains. But what matters to the drinker is *perceived* sweetness: the taste, not the chemical formula. Thus a wine's place on the 1 to 9 scale is decided by expert tasting. It is a guide, not a code, for no one individual has quite the same impression of the taste of a wine as another.

Every such scale has its weaknesses. For instance, some wines come in varying degrees of dryness or sweetness depending on the vintage and/or the maker. Some, such as Tokay, are made in a range of sweetnesses.

But even after all the ifs and buts, the scale is a major step forward in choosing wine. To use it, simply apply your own experience: if you enjoy a level 3 wine in a given setting or with certain food, the odds are that another "3" will give the same pleasure. The lists of wines have a strong European bias, partly because Europe's classics have over the years established styles which they stick to. New World wines are more volatile in character. To check the number of a wine not listed, search the lists for the one which most closely matches it in style.

Red wine styles

The experts on the Wine Development Board tell me that they are working on a red wine style scale. But they have a rather glum look as they say it, for red wine is far harder to pin down. As discussed elsewhere, it is weight rather than dryness or sweetness which makes the difference. In the next few pages I talk about "light" and "heavy" red wines, which is as far as the consensus of taste goes. That apart, one must have reference to specific wines with a distinct style.

Before the meal

Wine not only goes well with food, it will sharpen up the appetite beforehand. Top chefs urge customers at their restaurants to drink wine as an apéritif rather than spirits, for they know wine will aid the diner's enjoyment. Bad chefs, with more to hide than display, might give the opposite advice.

For a wine to work as an appetizer it must be fresh, relatively light in alcohol and clean to the taste. Dry sherry is the classic choice, though it is not particularly thirst-quenching and it can be too weighty: sherry is after all 50 per cent more alcoholic than ordinary wine. If you choose sherry, pick a dry one (even people who say they like "medium" often enjoy a really good, cold *fino* with a dish of olives and radishes . . .). Serve it cold. And serve it fresh: dry sherry does not, contrary to widespread belief, keep for ever, either in bottle or after being opened.

Dry white wine is the currently fashionable apéritif. The trap is to choose one that's too dry: dryness can quickly become astringency without accompanying food. It is the acidity which is appetising, so go for a wine with acidity but also balancing body, even sweetness. German wines can work well in this rôle. Pick a good one – perhaps a Moselle Kabinett, or even a Spätlese; not an everyday bottle, which can taste flabby without food.

I tend to avoid Sauvignon wines as apéritifs. They are either too tart or too strong and obvious in taste, or both. Keep away too from over-powerful Chardonnays which, with their mouth-filling tastes and abundant alcohol can numb the palate rather than titillate it. Chenin Blancs, drier Rieslings and good Italian whites are all worth exploring.

Sparkling wines come into their own as apéritifs. They excite the appetite, sharpen the wit and turn a meal into a party. Serve them very cold, and don't let the anticipatory drinking last too long, or the social bubbles will go flat.

If you offer people bits and pieces to eat as well as a drink, match one to the other. German wines are out of place with Mediterranean tastes like salami and anchovies, but go beautifully with creamy, fishy delicacies. Strong-tasting foods overwhelm subtle wines: if the appetizers are Greek houmus, vinegary stuffed vine leaves and black olives, drink a strapping southern white wine with them, not a soft Loire white.

Soup

The Victorians drank sherry with soup. These days we tend to put the sherry *in* the soup rather than drink it. There's a natural aversion to drinking anything much with a liquid, but the old habit had its points. Solid, farmhouse-style soups, the ones that are a meal in themselves, work well with a light red wine, Beaujolais, perhaps, or a Vin de Pays. Clear soups, consommé and the like, are pleasant with sherry; a good fino, served less cold than when it's used as an apéritif. Richer soups demand sweeter sherrries, or Madeira, Fishy soups are a problem; white wines fail utterly — stick to dry sherry or nothing at all.

Vegetables or Fruit

First courses cover a wide range of tastes. One currently fashionable kind of dish is the sort that combines vegetable and fruit flavours; mushrooms and fruits, perhaps, or chestnuts, in the Chinese style. Nouvelle cuisine relies for some of its effect on such combinations. Wines to partner such dishes need to emphasize the fruity element. The Germans are making a successful counter attack on the French domination of the table with medium-dry Rhine wines that go well with this kind of food. Vouvray and other mid-Loire whites are French equivalents. The new wine regions are making fruity, heady wines of this sort in quantity. If white wine seems inappropriate, a chilled light red such as a Gamay or a light young claret can be fun.

With this kind of food, analyse the dominant flavour and match the wine to it. If sourness is dominant, choose a drier wine; if fruit, err on the sweeter side.

Charcuterie

The whole delicious universe of cold meats — pâtés, salami, hams, potted meats, terrines — are versatile partners for wine. The natural choice is a fresh, young red — from the Cabernet Francs of the Loire to a Zinfandel — but medium to dry whites go well too. East European and Alsace whites, the more solid among the Germans — Franken or Rheinpfalz rather than Mosel — and New World whites such as New Zealand Gewürztraminer, all work well. The point is that most of these foods contain a high percentage of pork, which is a rich meat with a fairly high fat content; a substantial wine works best.

When cold meats are the foundation of a meal, rather than just a first course, the same rules apply. A salad and charcuterie lunch is a good occasion for a rosé, preferably a dry example such as a Provence, a Californian or one from northern Spain.

Shellfish

Cooks find dozens of different things to do to shellfish, so the wine must match the cuisine as well as the ingredients. Plain shellfish demand a sharp, clean white wine; Muscadet is the current choice, since Chablis got too expensive. The weightier white burgundies are too assertive in taste, though a Mâcon would do. Outside France, look for wines made in the image of Chablis — every wine country has one, and some of them are even *called* chablis, to the fury of the French. The trick is to find a relatively low-alcohol wine with brisk acidity. New Zealand Chardonnays and Chenin Blancs do well, as do many of the white wines of the USA's Pacific Northwest.

When the shellfish are treated in a more elaborate way, or when they are the richer-tasting sorts like crab or lobster, turn to a more solid white wine. Alsace Riesling or Pinot Blanc, burgundies, California Chardonnay, the better whites of Northern Italy and Spain, certain dry Rhine wines (but choose carefully; dryness is important).

FISH

Fish: plain grilled

If fish is served in a straightforward way, plain grilled or plain fried, it is the taste of the fish itself that is intended to dominate. Wines to go with it should be good, but not too assertive. White, almost certainly, and dry, though not too acidic. Fish equals light, dry white wine is an equation that does not always work: a certain amount of fullness of flavour is necessary with denser, stronger-tasting fish. White burgundy fills the bill, as do dry white Bordeaux and Mosels of Kabinett quality — they will be rounded yet still have refreshing acidity — dry Rieslings and Sauvignons from other parts of the world, good Italian Soaves and Pinots from the north-east. Alsace wines keep cropping up in these lists — but they do go well with food. Try a Riesling with plain grilled fish. Choose Chardonnays with care; the stronger-tasting, oaky ones seem to work less well with fish than do lighter, more austere wines. Avoid white wines which are too bland — the more ordinary Muscadets, QbA Mosels, and many southern French wines. Fish has definite, if delicate, tastes and needs a wine up to its weight.

Fish in sauces

A whole tradition of cookery is based around fish served with subtle sauces — sole and plaice, mostly. This kind of cuisine uses butter, cream and other rich ingredients. Such dishes are fine partners to really good white wines. Top white Graves, with its dry yet intense flavours; fine Rhinegau wines of Kabinett status, the best white burgundies, all live happily with sauced fish dishes.

Some fish, such as salmon, call for stronger tastes: with these, scale the wines down a little. Keep the best white wines for the subtler dishes — or serve them with plain poached fish. The dish pictured, poached Scottish salmon with cream and prawn sauce, would be decidedly on the rich side. Montagny or Rully Burgundy, mid-weight New World Chardonnay would work well.

Sea fish

Sea fish, such as the grilled sea bass shown left, have powerful assertive flavours. Bass, like herring, mackerel and tuna, is a dense-fleshed, oily fish. Balance these qualities with a brisk powerful wine. It should be dry, to counter the oiliness, yet not too delicate. A good estate-bottled Muscadet qualifies, though ordinary Muscadet does not have the length and power. Sancerre, Pouilly Fumé and other tart, flavoursome Sauvignons work well, though the more southern Sauvignons (Bordeaux, California) usually lack the necessary bite. Light red wines, served cool, are enjoyable with salmon and can work with other fish; try Loire Saumur, or Beaujolais, or a Gamay from elsewhere. And try it — it's a matter of personal taste and sometimes works very well, despite the general truth about red wine and fish.

Elaborate fish dishes

Fish and shellfish are often used in more elaborate dishes such as vol-au-vents, pies and terrines. These recipes will also include cream, butter, wine, herbs and other flavourings as well as the fish. Such dishes are a good excuse to drink stronger-flavoured white wines such as Gewürztraminers, the unusual wines of southern Germany (Rülander, Weissburgunder and Silvaner are grape names to try), and — a drier alternative — Rhône whites. Looking further afield, try Hungarian white wines of the traditional sort (*not* Welch Riesling), Austrian Gumpoldskirchners and Wachau Rieslings, white Riojas of the old-fashioned aged-in-wood kind. The assertive, fatty Chardonnays of California and Australia, and Australian Semillons, also work well. This dish consists of plaice stuffed with prawns, the whole in a strong, tangy sauce. Fight back against the sauce with a brisk, flavoury wine.

Beef

Plainly-cooked beef, in the form of grilled steaks and roasts, is a fine partner for really good red wines. When beef is cooked in casseroles, pies and other dishes, it usually has a richer, warmer taste and then more robust and weighty red wines are suitable.

The more refined Cabernets, the more "earthy" clarets (St-Emilion and Pomerol rather than Médoc), and medium-priced burgundies are good choices for plainly-cooked beef. Choose relatively high-quality wines, ones with a taste and character distinct enough to match the flavour of the beef. With casseroles, look to Rhône and Spanish reds, Australian Shiraz, the more robust of the New World Cabernets, Italian Barolo. Few red wines fail to go well with beef; the trick is to match the stature of the wine to the character of the meat; light, soft reds get swamped.

Lamb

The classic partner for plain roast lamb is claret, especially the subtle, somewhat austere wines of the Médoc and Graves. The partnership of tender, rather sweet meat and tannic, finely-balanced wine works beautifully. You'll get the same general effect with good, lighter-weight Cabernets from California and elsewhere in the New World of wine. Other wines to go with roast lamb or lamb chops and cutlets are fine burgundies, quality Chianti and other Italian wines, Spain's Rioja *Reservas*, Pinot Noirs from New Zealand or the Pacific Northwest. The aim is a red wine with some acidity and fruit; it should not be bland. Lamb casseroles tend to be rich and aromatic, so go for younger, more robust wines, such as Southern French reds, Zinfandel, East European and Australian Cabernets (but save the really good ones for a roast), good Valpolicella and Barbaresco.

Pork and Veal

Pork is fattier than beef or lamb. It asks for a fairly powerful wine, which can be red or white. Alsace whites and dry Rieslings from Australia and California work well, as do the more unctuous and robust Chardonnays (i.e. not Chablis or a wine in the Chablis style, but a commune Côte d'Or type, or an Australian or Californian in the same mould). Red wines need a certain amount of "cut"; oaky Rioja, brisk Chianti, the younger styles of Pinot Noir. Pork is often served with a strong-flavoured stuffing, or in casseroles; scale down the quality of the wine when matching these dishes, but follow the same principles. When it is cooked or served with rich sauces, drink either a young, fresh red or a solid white with some fruit and perhaps sweetness; Rheinpfalz Kabinett, east European Riesling, or — for a drier taste — white Rhônes.

Veal is a more delicate meat, and one much used by chefs as a foil for subtle sauces. Match your wine to the sauce, or, with plain roast veal, go for a soft fresh red such as a young Beaujolais, a Cabernet Franc or a young Claret.

Bacon and Ham

Cured pork, served hot or cold, has a smoky, salty flavour which demands a different kind of wine than straightforward pork. It should be thirst-quenching, uncomplicated and brisk. Red or white will do, and this is one of the few mealtime excuses for a good dry rosé. Reds such as young Zinfandel and Gamay (including Beaujolais); Italian Rosso Cónero, Merlot or Valpolicella, all suggest themselves. White choices might be white Rioja, fleshy New World Sauvignons, East European Chardonnay. The places to look for good rosé include Spain (especially Rioja), California and the Rhône.

If ham is baked with a sweet, spicy glaze (as in the picture), the above advice applies — only more so. The wine needs a bit of extra stuffing; try southern Germany's Baden wines, or Hungarians, or Vouvray from the Loire.

POULTRY AND GAME

Poultry

Birds vary in strength and robustness of taste, and provide the basis for innumerable dishes. Thus the choice of wine depends very much on the taste of the bird in question and what has been done to it. Most poultry is dry, like chicken and turkey. Duck and goose, however, are richer and much fatter. With dry, delicate birds choose light red wines. They can be good ones: roast birds are fine partners for the best wines, including good dry or medium-dry whites as well as fine reds such as claret and good burgundy. Duck needs a rich, tasty white wine with some acidity (German Kabinett or Spätlese, New World Rieslings or Australian Semillons) or a fairly powerful red such as young burgundy or Zinfandel.

When poultry is used as the basis of a dish, or is served with sauces, match the wine to the treatment: creamy sauces go well with German wines (the drier ones) or Chardonnays. Spicy southern dishes can be matched with light, tasty reds such as Côte du Rhônes and ordinary Italians.

Game

Game birds are stronger-tasting than poultry, and usually drier. When simply roasted, choose a good red wine, with more weight and taste than when matching poultry. A good Rhône, a substantial St-Emilion, *Gran Reserva* Rioja, Barolo or Vino Nobile di Montepulciano. The same advice applies to casseroled game birds: the wine can be less special but no less substantial. Furred game such as venison, hare and rabbit are also rich, strong meats. Again they ask for solid, earthy reds: good Rhônes, the bigger Cabernets, Barbaresco.

CHINESE AND INDIAN

Wine can be enjoyed with just about any kind of food, even dishes from cultures where wine is unknown. The choice of wine, as always, depends on the intensity of the flavour of the food. Very strong or spicy tastes will, however, overwhelm wine, which can be reduced to a rather unsatisfactory thirst-quencher. On the other hand, all cuisines offer some light and very subtle dishes which are truly complementary to wines.

Chinese food

Chinese food has a galaxy of flavours, but the underlying sweet-sour contrasts and the stress on the taste and texture of ingredients accord with modern Western ideas on eating. White wines of light, slightly sharp character drink well with Chinese dishes, perhaps because they have little character of their own. Champagne is also very enjoyable, especially one of the lighter *blanc de blancs* ones. Other sparkling wines work with Chinese food, as do the sort of fresh young reds which are pleasant chilled: Beaujolais and other Gamay wines, Nouveaus of all sorts, Loire reds, young Zinfandels. Some Chinese food, such as the hot Szechuan dishes, go better with beer or tea than wine.

Indian food

Few Indian dishes can really be said to go well with wine. Those that do are the milder dishes of North India, especially Tandoori baked meat and poultry. I find a soft, fairly ordinary red wine can add a pleasant fruity, dry note to the spicy richness of this kind of food. With stronger-tasting Indian dishes, cold white wine with some sweetness and taste (Gewürztraminer, Riesling) can work, though beer is best. If you drink wine, have water on the table as well: spicy food excites a thirst which wine will not quench.

Much the same advice applies to other Eastern cuisines. Many Eastern dishes are less hot than legend portrays; these can be matched with simple, clear-tasting wines.

Mexican food

Anything cooked with chilli needs lots of soft, quaffable red wine – and water. Subtler Southern dishes should be matched with wine according to the suggestions under meat and poultry.

PASTA AND VEGETARIAN

Pasta, Rice and Beans

Pasta and other dishes based on a non-meat ingredient and a flavoured sauce can be matched to a wine according to the sauce, be it meat, fish or vegetable. It is sensible to bear in mind where the dish comes from and choose an appropriate wine; Italian with pasta, or a Spanish red with paella (despite the fish). Fish sauces suggest white wines (though it's not a rule) and meat, vegetable or tomato sauces better accompany red ones. Match the weight of the wine to the lustiness of the sauce.

Bean dishes usually end up rich and powerful. Drink a young, brisk red with them to counteract and complement the heaviness.

Salads

Salads are fine, but some of the dressings they attract do not go well with wine. Anything with a lot of vinegar in it attacks the taste of wine. Serve a sharp white, such as a Chenin Blanc or young Sauvignon, or if you prefer red, a young earthy one like a Vin du Pays. Today's more imaginative salads, using beans and pulses, or fruit, as well as greenery, offer more scope. A young red wine would go well — nothing grand, just a Gamay, Cabernet Franc or Merlot.

Quiche

Anything made with eggs has a numbing effect on the taste of wine. Don't bother with fine wines, just choose something brisk and red with a little acidity, or a full medium-dry white. My preference is for Italian or Spanish reds, and for whites such as Portuguese, Northern Italian, New Zealand Chenin Blanc. Quiches can have just about anything in them, as well as eggs; so bear the ingredients in mind too.

Vegetarian dishes

Where vegetables form the basis, a light fresh red wine, or a rosé, can work well. Much depends, as ever, on the recipe; wine does not work happily with salad dressings made with vinegar, but goes with ratatouille and other such dishes where the vegetables are stewed in oil. Here the wine usefully counteracts the richness. Dishes using cheese need a stronger, richer red wine. For those based on pasta or beans, see the comments above.

PUDDINGS AND DESSERTS

Sweet wines go with puddings, but not all sweet wines go with all puddings. Chocolate, for a start, fights with wine. Richy creamy things overwhelm most wines. The best desserts from a wine point of view are fruit pies and tarts, light creamy concoctions and fresh fruit.

Pies and Tarts

Pastry-based sweets go well with a rich, powerful white such as a Muscat. Puddings using eggs or cream and pastry also taste even better with a powerful sweet wine. But don't make the obvious jump to a sweet German white; these wines are too delicate to go with rich food. Austrian and East European sweet whites, being higher in alcohol, are a better bet. Really sweet puddings can be partnered by a fortified wine such as Malmsey Madeira, or Italian *vin santo,* a *vin doux naturel* from southern France, or an Australian liqueur muscat.

Cheese

Cheese and wine are linked too readily. Some cheeses are just too powerful, or too salty, for wine. Take care in composing a cheese selection to end a meal; it's pleasant to finish off a good bottle of red wine with some cheese, but be sure it is relatively mild cheese. The French find that strong salty cheeses go well with sweet wines such as Sauternes, and there is a compelling sweet-and-sour logic about their choice. Fortified wines, such as port, fight back briskly against strong-tasting English cheese. Keep the very best vintage ports away from cheese — they go better with a bowl of nuts. Only a few English cheeses work properly with fine wines; Wensleydale and Caerphilly can be good with fairly powerful reds such as Châteauneuf or robust New World wines. Try medium sherries as well as ports with cheese, and choose young, assertive reds (especially Italian) or solid, slightly sweet whites rather than fine Claret or Burgundy.

Fruit

Save your best, most delicate German wines and the good Sauternes for plain, fresh soft fruits. Citrus fruits do not work well with wine, and hard fruits such as apples and pears are often too acid. Peaches, apricots, strawberries, raspberries and tropical fruits can be partnered with very cold Ausleses and other German or Germanic wines, or with Sauternes. More robust stewed or otherwise cooked fruits, or desserts based on fruits, ask for lesser but still sweet wines. The sweetness needs to be matched with acidity for pleasure, so avoid cheap sweet whites.

Sorbets and other light desserts

Sorbets are a fashionable punctuation for modern meals. They bring the drinking of wine to an uneasy end, for little seems to go with them, or with ice-cream. Sweet champagne can be fun, but the expense is hardly justified. Best treat a sorbet as a rest from any kind of wine.

Light, creamy desserts based on yoghurts, cream and perhaps fruit go pleasantly with soft sweet wines such as Monbazillac, Loire sweet whites or late-harvest Rieslings (though not the "serious" ones). Don't overwhelm these delicate dishes with powerful Muscats or Sauternes.

PARTIES AND CELEBRATIONS

Lunch

Lunch can be anything from an informal meal with the family to a major social occasion (in which case it seems to become 'luncheon'). Easy-going lunches should take their wine cue from the main dish, with a bias towards light white wines: no-one wants to feel heavy-headed all afternoon due to the sledgehammer blows of a Barolo or Châteauneuf. Suitable wines are light Loires such as Sancerre or Muscadet, Californian Fumé Blancs, New Zealand Chenin Blancs, German QbA wines – there are many others. Lighter reds such as Gamay or young clarets have their place at lunch. More formal affairs might start with a champagne or dry white wine apéritif, following with a medium-weight white such as a Mâcon or white Graves and a lightish red: claret, Pinot Noir, the more elegant Cabernets all qualify. Avoid fortified wines and over-alcoholic Chardonnays and Cabernets. Formal or otherwise, a cold bottle of mineral water is a welcome addition to a lunch table – and a dash of the fizzy variety in the wine can aid the afternoon's work, too.

Dinner parties

If there's a perfect place for elegance and a degree of formality, it's at dinner. The day is over, it is time to relax and enjoy civilized pleasures. A carefully planned sequence of wines can make all the difference to the occasion. Not, I must quickly add, that you have to have more than one wine for the meal itself; a sherry or sparkling wine apéritif can lead into a good red wine which can go right through the meal. But it is fun to combine some of the suggestions on the previous pages – and by now you'll have ideas of your own – and orchestrate a sequence of wines. Consider quantities: one bottle gives a generous glass each to six people, a moderate glass for eight. Allow a bottle a head (keeping some of the bottles in reserve) and you'll have plenty. It is good manners, and good sense, to provide each guest with a water glass, and to put plenty of iced or mineral water on the table. Fortified wines round off a meal to perfection: just put the bottles, or decanters, on the table and let people pass them round. If you want to go with tradition, keep the port moving clockwise.

Outdoor parties and barbecues

Many a host has discovered (gratefully) that simple food, cooked outdoors, somehow tastes better. The same goes for the wine served with it. The main thing asked of outdoor wine is that it be refreshing: whites and rosés should be well chilled, and kept cold (see chapter 4), and reds should be light, fruity and easy to drink. A brisk, definite flavour is needed to counteract spicy barbecue food and well-dressed salads: Sauvignons, Pinot Blancs and Italian whites such as Soave and Orvieto will do, as will vinho verde, California blended whites, young white Riojas and East European Chardonnays. Relevant reds include Gamays, Vins de Pays, everyday Australian and California blends and most Italians. For picnics, the same advice applies, but consider the magic of sparkling wine, which in the right location can do wonders for a little cold chicken and some fresh bread.

Informal parties

At parties, the wine needs to be enjoyable both on its own and with food, and a lot of different tastes must be catered for. Sparkling wines, especially softer ones such as Saumur, German Sekt, the drier North Italian *Spumantes* and a wide range of New World bottlings all give good service. Mixed with orange juice, they become Buck's Fizz: a fine all-purpose drink for summer parties. Avoid over-dry whites, choosing rather wines such as Mâcon Blanc, South of the Bay California Chardonnays, Gewürztraminers from North Italy or Eastern Europe, good Moselles. If food is served, give a choice of one of these whites and a soft, light red such as Beaujolais, young Zinfandel or Barbaresco, perhaps served chilled. And keep a bottle or two of middle-of-the-road German wine – a Rheinhessen, perhaps – for those who must have their wine medium sweet. For winter parties, nothing is nicer on a cold evening than a welcoming glass of mulled red wine.

WAYS WITH A WINE LIST

If we don't like what the local wine shop has on offer, we walk out and down the street to the next one. Once seated at a restaurant table, napkin on knee, meal ordered and wine list in hand, the diner realises that half the choosing is already done — by the person who wrote the wine list.

It is easy to become despondent about human nature when faced with restaurant wine lists. So many make so little effort. In most places, what small imagination is around has gone into the food, or the decor, or choosing the colour of the waiters' shirts. The wine gets left to the wholesaler, who puts in a job lot of his steady sellers and prints the list for the restaurateur. The wholesaler has a captive customer. The restaurateur has one too: you, the diner. Neither you nor the restaurant can argue much with the wholesaler's choice.

What is wrong with restaurant lists? First of all, wines are often "safe" ones: the well-known names like Nuits St-Georges and St-Emilion. In order to get these names onto bottles and thus onto wine lists, the wine business buys up boring wines, blends them to make them more tedious still, and spends some solid money on a gold-leafed, gothic-printed label. The quirky, unusual, good-value wines never get a look-in. Restaurants reason that no-one has heard of them, so they won't sell, so they don't list them, so no-one hears of them.

Boring wines is fault number one. Bad description is the second sin. It's often hard to be sure which vintage you're buying until you see the bottle: restaurants go on selling the '84 until it runs out, then wheel out the '85, without bothering to reprint the list . . .

What to do? House wine is one answer. It won't be special, but increasingly hotels and restaurants realise that a good house wine is an advertisement for the rest of the list. If it is good, be more adventurous next time. If it isn't, at least it will be cheap.

Prices in restaurants are usually at least double the retail level, which is a scandal on its own. So think hard before ordering expensive, rare wines.

There are benefits to dining out. Restaurants are sometimes good places to try out "off" vintages of classic wines. The list-writers know many clients want the reassurance of famous names, but don't want to pay top prices for '82 Bordeaux or '74 Napa Cabernet. So they list the '77s, the '80s, the '84s. Many will be passable, some unexpectedly good, and the prices will be lower than the fashionable years. I use restaurants to keep up with the development of vintages, to buy or consume accordingly.

There is one further hurdle before you can enjoy your bottle: the staff. Few restaurants find it worth their while to hire waiters trained in wine service. So you see bottles of old burgundy swung around, with inevitable muddying of the sediment. You find white wines served far too cold, numbed by hours in ice-buckets, or reds far too warm. Yet more reasons for drinking good wines at home, where you control the conditions.

The tasting ritual annoys some people and scares others. It is tempting to wave the waiter away, telling him to get on with it and fill the glasses. Yet it pays to check out the wine. Tasting is the last stage in this process. The most important thing is the look at the bottle the waiter should give you before opening it. Try to remember what you ordered (yes it can be tough!) and check the name of the wine, the vintage and any other information the list cares to divulge. You will frequently find the vintage different: complain. Sometimes the wine is just not what the list says: a European blend instead of a German, or table wine rather than AoC French. This may be carelessness, or it may be a more fundamental fault in that the manager doesn't understand what wines he's got in his cellar. In that instance send the wine back and drink beer, or mineral water.

When you come to taste, give the wine a good sniff. Anything badly wrong will be obvious. Don't worry about the odd bit of cork floating in the glass. Cork doesn't really taste much. There's confusion in some people's minds about the term "corked". A corked wine is one where a faulty cork has let air in, and the wine has in effect rotted. The first smell will tell you. If it smells peculiar, swirl it around a bit in the glass to get some air into it. If it still smells and tastes off, send it back. A wine with floating cork fragments is merely the sign of a clumsy waiter using an ill-designed corkscrew.

Send the wine back if it is corked, or if it is very much flatter and more tired than its age would suggest, or if it smells or tastes tainted. Merely indifferent wine, or wine you don't like the taste of, is your problem. Just don't eat there again.

Wines that need decanting pose a puzzle in restaurants. There are a few places I trust to decant a wine properly, quite a few more where I do not. It is best, really, to play safe and stick to relatively young wines unless you have confidence in the wine-waiter or proprietor. But some young wines also benefit from being poured into a carafe or jug, and this is an operation any ham-fisted waiter can manage. So ask them to do it, tell them to pour the red wine into something. I find it pays to avoid the word "decant", which can put them into a panic. "Pour it out" is clearer. Make sure you see it being done to ensure you get the wine you pay for. Rarely will you be defrauded, it's just that the level of wine knowledge is so low that an honest mistake may well give you Valpolicella instead of Volnay — unless you see the label on the bottle first.

Some restaurants affect to serve wine in a basket or cradle. This is done at places where they should know better as well as those where the basket is just a piece of theatre. It may not be good practice, but is harmless enough — except when the wine has a deposit. If you use a cradle for serving such a wine, instead of only to help with the decanting, the repeated tipping forward and back will mix the sediment in with the wine — which is just what everyone is trying to avoid.

Assuming that your confidence in the restaurant's competence is established, what do you choose to drink? The guidelines are no different from eating at home, except that in a restaurant you are likely to come across some rather more exotic or adventurous dishes, unless you are a keen amateur chef. This poses few problems with simple or even "classic" cuisine, but when ethnic

and "nouvelle" dishes appear, the matching becomes more fraught.

Nouvelle cuisine – the term is now much derided but you'll recognize what I mean — has added some taste sensations to the menu that the food-and-wine textbooks do not recognize. It's common, for instance, to have dishes which combine sweet and sour flavours, or fish and meat. Ingredients such as ginger, raspberry vinegar, exotic fungi and even more exotically coloured peppercorns occur, and often unexpectedly. It's no good settling back on claret with lamb (it always goes so well) if the lamb is served with a vinegary, peppery sauce which dominates anything Bordeaux can throw at it. Similarly, "white with fish" means nothing when the fish is raw. Rice wine might suit, but little else. The truth is that the apostles of nouvelle cuisine are not very excited about wine. It is a beverage, not a partner to the food.

This is perhaps a pessimistic picture: most restaurateurs know that overdoing the novelty is bad for both their bookings and our digestions. But we are in an era of stronger flavours and, when dining fashionably, the wine must match. Luckily, the New World has been called into existence to balance the menus of the old. California and Australian wines, to say nothing of New Zealand and South African ones, have the depth of ripeness and the positive flavours to quell the nouvelle. The New World white wines, such as Chardonnays, are a blessing. They have the roundness, depth and sheer tastiness of French burgundies three times their price, and they go so well with assertive tastes. So do the Cabernets and Shirazes and Zinfandels — solid, flavoursome reds which are not knocked out of joint by unconventional combinations on a dinner plate.

Europe's equivalents are the underrated wines of Alsace, reds from Tuscany and Rioja, the vibrant Austrian and Northern Italian dry whites and the better Eastern Europeans. In France, look to the Rhône or further south. German Spätleses suit sweet-and-sour combinations well.

Ethnic food — that catch-all for anything non-European — has already been touched upon in the section on matching wine and food. Sadly, ethnic restaurants offer even less chance of a decent bottle than do European ones. Short of taking your own wine (ask the restaurant: they may be happy to let you, providing you pay corkage) it may be best to stick to beer. Or iced water.

Above: *a good restaurant ought to know about wine. Not all do: the tell-tale signs include serving wine from decanting baskets, though the couple in the foreground seem happy enough all the same.*

WHEN THE WINE COMES FIRST

Most bottles play supporting roles: they partner food, or lubricate a party of some kind. Some get star billing because they are especially good, or rare, or because we want for once to pay the wine particular attention.

Wine is an entertainment in itself. You can taste it, talk about it, enjoy it while finding out more about it. There's a solid tradition of wine tasting, based on the wine trade's buying technique, which we go into in a page or two. But without adopting the role of wine judges we can put wine first with pleasure.

If you have treated yourself to a special bottle, it will give of its best if the staging is right. Good wine decides the food rather than the other way around. A classic red wine, such as a mature claret or burgundy, needs to be drunk with food. The choice will be plain, high-quality fare: a rib of roast beef rather than a spicy stew, grilled cutlets rather than curry. Keep the flavours clean, classic and definite, and let the wine take the spotlight.

It's often alleged that good wine goes with cheese, but this is a dangerous generalisation. Mild cheese — farmhouse Cheddar, say — partners red wines well. Many cheeses are just too pungent or salty for any fine red wine: dry whites are best, or strong sweet ones.

Good white wines are harder to match. Dry ones — burgundy, quality Chardonnays from elsewhere — go wonderfully with fish, but be careful about what is *done* to the fish. Strong sauces are bad news, though really good Chardonnays have an amazing power to cut through powerful food tastes. Sweeter wines — anything Germanic of any quality, Sauternes and so on — deserve to come first and to get a solo spot. A bowl of fruit (not citrus) is all they need, and the leisure and the company to sip and think and talk about and around them.

Star-quality wines *demand* attention. Sometimes it's also worth giving an audience to lesser bottles. Make a point, perhaps, of trying something unusual like a good north Italian white, or a Washington State Pinot Noir, or an English wine, and then match the food and the occasion to them, rather than the other way round.

Regional wine and food partnerships are another area to explore. The taste of cassoulet with Côtes de Fronton, or good pasta with Chianti, or fresh simple seafood with Muscadet — all are established traditions. Do they work, or are non-local alternatives more effective partners? Some traditional matches are based on trade rather than locality. The nineteenth-century English, who imported most of their wine from Bordeaux and Portugal, found that claret went with roast lamb and port with Stilton cheese: try them to see if you agree.

One entertaining variation on a dinner or supper party is to serve several wines and let people choose the one that they like most, and which best matches the food. Informal buffets or lunch parties are enlivened if everyone brings a different wine. Such "tastings" get livelier still if the bottles are covered so no-one knows which wine is which.

Another kind of "wine first" occasion is the meal designed around a succession of wines. This can be most rewarding if carefully planned. The first principle is to involve only guests who will enjoy themselves. Everyone enjoys wine, not everyone appreciates being put through a sort of vinous Olympiad with glass following glass and long discussions about their merits. The true wine fans would reckon good bottles wasted on these people. I'd say it's bad manners to subject your guests to three or four hours of uncertainty, embarrassment and boredom.

Having picked the people, then comes the delicious process of working out the menu and the wine list, a job some hosts seem to enjoy more than they do the actual meal. We've been through the fundamentals of matching, but it is worth saying that the order of wines makes a big contribution to the pleasure. Dry before sweet, red before white is basic. Also put young wines before old, unless the old wine is such a rare, ethereal faded old bottle that it would be overwhelmed.

A more subtle approach is to put light wines before heavy ones, so a ten-year-old mature claret would, naturally, come before a Rhône wine of twenty years, which would be in the same relative state of maturity. But equally an immature young Rhône, still dark and earthy, could come after a mature claret.

How do you cope with two bottles from the same vineyard but different vintages? Young before old is traditional, for it highlights the changes produced by age. But it may not be the best for enjoyment, especially if the older vintage was a light one, which the younger wine would overwhelm.

Dry white wines are easily placed, at the beginning of the meal; but some (burgundies, for example) are so powerful that they can flatten subsequent reds on the "follow *that*" principle. Here you can borrow an idea from the chef and insert a soft, light, perhaps slightly sweet wine as a liquid "sorbet" to punctuate the menu.

Sweeter whites are notoriously hard to place. Some daring can make good matches. It is notorious that the French use Sauternes to go with all sorts of dishes that other nations would say call for dry white, or red. But the point is in the weight rather than the dryness. Some very strong-flavoured foods work well with sweet wines, as long as they are solid, French-style sweets rather than light German ones.

I've never found much to enjoy in the German attempts to partner strong-flavoured game dishes with their succulent but light sweet wines. Serve German sweet wines at the end of the meal with something soft, sweet and comforting. But don't be surprised if your guests are too overwhelmed by them to appreciate the treat. A better use for German wines is as an aperitif: a good Auslese tastes delicious before a meal. Don't serve peanuts with it, though, and keep consumption to a couple of glasses each at most or it will cloy.

It is said of sparkling wines that they go with everything, and this is just about true. But one unexpected lesson I've learnt is that there can be too much of a good thing, even champagne. When visiting Champagne I was given a succession of lovely meals, all partnered by superb champagnes — and nothing else. After three days I was gasping for a glass of red wine. The moral is that variety is as crucial as quality. Plan your wines to be different, both from each other and from the normal choices, and your guests will want to come again. Not every choice works, but that's where the fun lies. Consistency in quality is more important: there's no pleasure in slotting a minor country wine, however good of its kind, in among a regal succession of Grand Crus. It will not enjoy the exposure, and neither will you.

Taking wine seriously has led some people to take wine and food partnerships seriously too. There exist groups dedicated to finding the best match for every dish there is, and every bottle. They debate the exact wine to drink with ham, or lobster, or whatever. Sadly for them there are no absolute answers. Anyway, your tastes and your enjoyment are the only real judges of pleasure or aptness. While it can be fun trying two or three wines with the same dish, to see which one works best, don't be concerned if everyone around the table has a different favourite. Be thankful, rather, that wine is a matter of personal enjoyment not official prescription. And if there's doubt, open another bottle . . .

Château Latour is always going to hold centre stage; it is too powerful, too deep in flavour — and too expensive — to be a mere drink. Beef falls into place around it.

WINE TASTING

Wine tasting is a risible activity. The mere thought of grown men sniffing, sipping and slurping good wine – and then spitting it out! — brings a smile. And to then write down such comments as tasters are alleged to commit to their notebooks, well . . .

Behind most things we eat or drink is a taster. I was once introduced to a man whose job it was to sniff every churn of milk as it was delivered to a dairy. One shake of his head and a churn was out. His job was vital, for one bad churn could contaminate a whole tank-full of milk. Other tasters assess tea (they spit it out, too), whisky (they just sniff), cheese, sugar and any other commodity whose quality can vary. Wine tasting is no different. People who work for wine merchants judge samples to see what is worth buying, and whether a given batch is as good as its predecessor.

Wine is special in that the amateur, the consumer, has also taken to tasting. But that again is not much different from the tea-lover who is finicky about his or her favourite blend, or the cheese connoisseur who (in, regrettably, few shops) is offered morsels to taste and choose.

Most wine tasting can be safely left to the professional. They get to be able to judge which of a hundred samples of raw, young port will be delicious in twenty five years time, and which will never make the grade. These trade tasters buy and sell on a very large scale on the basis of their judgement, and they are very good at it. The only time we amateurs face the professional's problems is when we buy young wine in the expectation it will improve with time.

Most consumer tasting involves choosing among different brands, or châteaux, tasting wines already mature, or nearly so. There may be just a couple of wines to judge, or a dozen or so put up for tasting by a wine store, or at an exhibition or public tasting.

Another sort of tasting, far more a hobby (or intellectual game) than a piece of consumer judgement, is the assessment of a single wine. It may be served to you in a restaurant or a friend's table, or you may have bought it yourself. The game is to see whether it meets up to expectations: even, in some extreme cases (among the really infatuated) to guess what it is.

Whoever is doing the tasting, and whatever the wine in the glass, certain techniques apply. The taster uses three senses: sight, smell and taste. Memory is the key, thought — sheer hard brainpower — the lock it fits. Some tasters seem to have an uncanny ability to spot a wine — they'll tell you the château and the vintage after a quick sniff and a spot of thought. They are not superhuman, nor do they have "superb palates" — the usual explanation. They are just people who work hard at both tasting and memorising, and who think hard about what they remember. This party-trick tasting depends upon a process of elimination. The taster analyses the wine, eliminates a lot of possibilities by a logical process of checking, then homes in on the probables. His choice among three or four "probables" will most likely be an inspired guess, based on the host's known preferences and sources of supply.

Star tasters and novices alike use the same techniques. First, sight. The colour of a wine can be most eloquent. So can the degree of clarity or opacity, and the way the liquid clings to the side of the glass — the relative "thickness" of the wine. Smell comes next. The idea of a wine having a "bouquet" attracts much ribaldry: call it smell and perhaps we can take it more seriously. A wine tells a lot about itself in its smell. Seasoned tasters make most of their decisions on smell; those hardened souls who taste brandy or whisky for a living rely on their noses alone. The reason is that smells get straight from the nose into the memory, via a complicated human micro-circuit that neurosurgeons understand and I don't. Shorn of the technicalities, the truth is that smells bypass the thinking process. If you've smelt something before, it will be stored away in the memory and a repeat sniff will bring it to mind — instantly. That applies to the smell of a given vintage of burgundy or of wines from a certain slope in Lake County as well as woodsmoke or a girl's perfume. Trust smells: thinking too hard about them is usually a mistake.

Taste comes last, both in natural sequence and because it's the least subtle of the senses. As I've said, there are only four recognized basic taste sensations. Scientists seem to differ as to whether or not a lot of the subtler "tastes" are actually smells — sensations picked up by the upper part of the nose through our head's inner connections.

How to deploy the three senses? Little equipment is needed, compared to most leisure pursuits. Start with a clean glass. Cleanliness is less easy to achieve than you may think. Detergents leave their taint on glasses unless they are well rinsed. All kinds of smells, from garlic to cardboard, seem to attach themselves to glasses. Choose a wineglass with an inturned rim, a sort of globe shape with the top cut off. This shape helps guide the smell to your nose, where it can do most good. The only other kit needed is a good clear light — daylight for preference, and a white surface, such as a sheet of paper, as background to the wine.

Which wines to taste? If you are keen to try the technique, select four to start with: two red, two white. Let them be of different ages, vineyards and (perhaps) grape varieties. Later can come subtler comparison, where you assess different years from the same château, or various wines from the same grape. For starters, stick to widely varying wines. Don't overchill the whites, it makes them harder to taste. Just get the corks out of all the bottles and pour a little of one of the whites into a glass. Not too much, just a swallow. Look at it, preferably against the white background. Conjure up your memories of white wines. Is it light or dark? Is there much in the way of colour at all (some whites are virtually clear)? Are there hints of green or strong yellow? Store away your thoughts. Better still, write them down.

Next, pick up the glass and sniff at it. Don't be surprised if there's nothing much to smell. Some wines smell a lot, some very little. Some develop scents as they get older, some lose them. A lot need a little air to tease the smell out. With practice, you'll learn a little flick of the wrist that swirls the wine around the glass, letting air in and wetting the entire glass surface, thus enabling the wine to evaporate. Slop it around (you'll spill it at first, everyone does) then sniff again. What's there? Let the memory have a clear run. Does it remind you of grass, or cats, or apricots? Fair enough: write it down. Is there a smell of fruit of any sort, whether grapes (and how few wines actually smell of grapes!), or strawberries, or what? Does it bring back memories of food, or wet leaves, or lemon sherbet? Oddly, all the good smells, the ones that hold out the promise of a happy mouthful, are organic, natural ones. Start to smell chemicals, or other hard, man-made sensations, and there's likely to be trouble.

Now taste. Take a good mouthful — but don't swallow straight away. Hold it in your mouth and concentrate on it. Once again, trust instinct and memory to lead you to a useful tasting note. Serious tasters spit the wine out, the better to taste the next one. The rest of us will happily swallow. Swallowing is not pure pleasure. It's noticeable that the last taste as you swallow is the most eloquent one, the sensation that tells you the most about the wine. Finally, notice how long the taste lingers. Intensity is a key quality in wine.

What should you look for? Cleanliness, pleasure and interest, in that order. A wine that is not clean, pure and untainted is to be rejected straight away. Luckily for us today, the wine business is rigorous in spotting bad wines and few reach the shops. Next: pleasure. You've paid for it; if you don't like it, it is poor wine. Some subtleties may take time to appreciate, but too much is made of "acquired taste". I've noticed in talking to people about wine that if a wine is good of its type, and drunk in the right circumstances, it will usually be enjoyed. When tasting under analytical conditions, you may have to make allowances for a wine. It is harder to appreciate sweet wines at eleven in the morning than at the end of a meal, and warm, southern reds can seem out of kilter with a cold, raw northern day.

After cleanliness and pleasure, look for interest. Has the wine got anything about it? Does it surprise you by its fruitiness, or its brisk acidity? Is it softer than you'd expect for its age, better than you'd bargained for at the price? Interest is the key, but beware the obvious. Some wines always score points at the tastings because they serve up sledgehammer blows. They may be overwhelmingly perfumed, or full of fruit, or aggressively tannic. These wines will bore you quickly — subtlety linked with interest is the goal, one hardest to find in the competitive atmosphere of a tasting.

Compare and contrast

The point of tasting is comparison. Is wine A more fun, or better value, than B or C? This is straightforward enough when all the wines are on the same table, but harder when you taste at different times. Keeping notes is one way round the problem. If you do, beware duplicity. Many note-takers, including some professionals, delude themselves by writing what they think they ought to write rather than what instinct and intellect dictates. If a wine taste of nothing at all (some do), or smells of old socks, write it down. You may be the one who sees through the emperor's new clothes, who spots behind the prestige label the one bad bottle the other tasters have missed.

Except when tasting "blind", you'll know what the wine is from reading the label. This is your chance to memorize what a Gewürztraminer, or a '76 Bordeaux, tastes like. But by knowing the wine's name you'll also have a *preconception* of what it tastes like, which is something to beware of when making your judgement.

Tasting can become a ritual, full of meaningless phrases and rites. It can also grow into an absorbing pursuit, leading to membership of wine clubs and the reverent sharing of Grand Cru bottles between twenty acolytes. At its most balanced, it is a refreshing mental and sensual exercise which also helps you judge what wine is best, and best value, and best for the use you have in mind.

But whatever your motives as a

taster, there's one key tool, as vital for success as a corkscrew: it's personal honesty. Dishonest notes delude no-one but the note-taker.

Tasting is about concentrating and communicating — either writing out your notes or passing on the taste sensation to someone else.

. . . taste

Taste is the hardest thing to describe: we have a poor vocabulary for it, and unlike sight no-one's found a way to write it down or paint it. Here, though, are some of the main sensations and their hows and whys.

Tannin
A roughness on the tongue, astringency on the gums, also found in strong tea. Symptom of an immature red wine: a sign (usually) of good things to come.

Acidity
Sharpness, sourness: an essential part of a white wine — without acidity no wine is refreshing. The *balance* of acidity with sweetness is important.

Sweetness
Un-matched by acidity, sweetness in wine can cloy. The sugar should be linked with something, too — it should taste like sweet fruit, or something more subtle, rather than plain sugar.

Fruit
Some wine tastes as if it is made of fruit, some not. Neither is better: fruit is an attractive flavour, but there are other more complex ones.

Wood
Wine tastes of wood? Some wines are stored in oak casks to mature, and oak (or chestnut, or acacia) can add a taste, which at its most extreme is like drinking the smell from a joinery works.

Spice
White wines can evoke the spice cupboard: a sign of richness, quality and interest.

Yeast
New wines can smell distinctly of their fermentation. A good fresh yeasty smell is attractive, but beware the unclean smells caused by uncontrolled second fermentations.

Grass, leaves
Young, acidic white wine sometimes show a grassy smell and taste, indicating that the grapes were under-ripe. This can be a good sign, especially in hot country wines, or it may reveal an under-ripe vintage and tardy wines.

Burnt
Southern wines can smell and taste hot and burnt, which can be pleasant but is often tedious. It's a sign of what it says: hot sun, over-ripe grapes.

Chapter Two

THE WORLD OF WINE

WHY PLACE MATTERS

It takes a person of some nerve to interrogate the shopkeeper about which farm the turnips, or the corn, came from. The average fruit or vegetable is an orphan: its home field is of no concern to the consumer. Grapes, at least wine grapes, are different. People pay ten times as much for the fermented juice of grapes from one vineyard as from the next. Laws are passed, labels printed, reputations made or lost on the strength of their legitimacy.

Why does the grape's home matter? Ask any gardener, or any farmer. Some plants just grow better on one side of the street, or one end of the field, than the other. All the subtle factors that make up the natural environment conspire together to decide a plant's degree of health and success. The way the wind blows, the depth and density of the soil, the tip of the slope towards or away from the sun, all affect the plant's vigour and change the taste of the fruit — and the resultant wine.

It takes more than nature to make wine, of course. Man has a hand in it. But until very recently man may have proposed, but nature invariably disposed. Man was a mere cog in the environmental machine of soil, wind and weather: an essential cog, but not a big factor in the final shape of the product. That was why place was paramount, why every wine that had any pretensions had the name of its home field on its label.

Today the balance is different. Man has caught up with nature and now has a bigger say in the process of making wine. Modern techniques turn grapes into wine predictably. But is it still true that wine from a given field is better, intrinsically better?

The answer is still "yes, it can be" — which will come as a relief to the romantics, and to anyone who reckons that nature is still a little subtler than humans. What has changed is that while *great* wine still comes only from a few most favoured vineyards, *good* wine is made in a lot more places than it used to be. Pioneers as far apart as California, Bulgaria and England have proved this. They have studied the lessons of the classic vineyards of France and Germany. They have chosen their plot of ground with care,

planted the right sort of vines, applied the best and latest methods – and made good wine.

Thus were the die-hards confounded who said that only the traditional places could ever make quality wine. Fierce debate rages among connoisseurs about whether any of these "new" wines are, or ever will be, great. Let them dispute. For the rest of us, the news is unreservedly cheerful: there's more good wine, made in more places, at relatively cheaper prices, than ever before.

And there is more good news still. The key triumph of today's winemakers is to make passable wine possible just about anywhere. Good farming, and hygienic picking and pressing of the resulting grapes, are new ideas in most places where grapes were traditionally grown. Apply these practices and the taste of the wine will improve immeasurably. Rough "plonk" becomes acceptable everyday wine. It may never be good, it is hardly interesting, but it is a blessing for consumers today that more and more places are making this ordinary wine tolerably well.

But passable wine is just a commodity, like those fresh turnips or tinned corn. Buy it, enjoy it, but don't worry about it. Good wine is something else again. It has roots and where they are matters. The rest of this chapter tours the world's good, and great, vineyards. But first: the factors which make wines great, good – or ordinary.

Left: *The fearsomely steep hill behind the church at Bernkastel is the most celebrated vineyard in Germany, the Doctor. It makes, by common consent, the best wine in the entire Mosel valley. Why? Because it is steep, with perfect drainage; its soil is pure slate, which the Riesling vines love for its drainage and heat retention; the angle and direction of the slope catch every ray of the sun. And because it is famous: the three great estates who own the Doctor treasure their plots, nurture their vines and their wines — and go on making great wine.*

Below: *High-tech in California — man takes control.*

THE VITAL FACTORS

Frontiers sometimes have un uncanny effect. In Germany's far south, the Rhine forms the border with France. One side of a river valley is rarely far different from another, and here both countries have wooded hills rising from a wide plain.

But the border seems to change the atmosphere. The German side is neater, more arranged. The geraniums in the window-boxes are tended with care. Inns, with varnished-wood furniture, outnumber cafés. France is more profligate with its billboards and less organized about its (equally abundant) flowers. There are cafés, with metal tables on the pavement and official decrees about public drunkenness. And the wine tastes different.

Alsace – French – wine is drier, stronger and sturdier than Baden — German — wine, which tends towards sweetness, floweriness and elegance. Like breeding animals to bring out particular characteristics, the aims of the growers on either bank affect the natural product; reflecting, in this instance, the French desire for wine to partner food, the German love of drinking it alone.

Place, origin, is the key to wine quality but it is not the only thing that matters. One of the satisfying things about wine — which we soon discern when we look beyond the bottle to see who put the wine in it — is this influence of tradition. It is one of the major influences on the finished taste.

Another big factor is the choice of the variety of grape-vine; the particular site the grapes are grown on is a vital influence, as is the weather of the year the grapes are grown in. Finally, central but still subject to all the other forces, is the maker, the human being who intervenes in the workings of tradition, weather and the rest.

All these factors are neatly summed up on a wine label. An everyday, ordinary wine has a trade-name, a brand, like a pair of jeans or a type of soap. The brand name is prominent on the label and the origin of the wine is shown, if at all, in a very modest way.

A wine with more serious claims on our attention tells us a lot more about itself. There will be a place-name, a vintage year, the name of the maker and quite possibly the name of the type of grape it was made from. All the key factors are clearly spelled out – only tradition is lacking. Yet that is there too, implicit in the quality regulations local officials impose on the wine and which the label lists, and in the very style and taste of the wine itself.

So the usefulness of the vintage date on the label is as a reminder about the weather of that year. The place name suggests a certain kind of wine, the name of the maker is a subtler indication still. The label, taken as a whole, is the birth certificate of the wine.

Tradition

Tradition, among the key factors, is underrated because it's an influence less susceptible than the others to analysis.

A map and a clutch of climate figures will show that conditions in Alsace are not far different from those a few miles across the Rhine in South Germany. The French side may be a little drier, a little sunnier, sheltered as it is by the Vosges mountains. But there are sunny, dry corners across the river in Baden too. Yet the wines made in those two places are distinctly different.

Look more closely at the crucial factors, and you will find that many growers in Baden and in Alsace grow the same grape: the Riesling. And Alsace Riesling still tastes different from Baden Riesling. The reason why lies in tradition. German winemakers strive for a certain taste in their wine: a balance of natural sweetness and brisk acidity, linked to the freshness of grapey fruit. In Alsace they look for dryness, for backbone, for more strength than a German would find ideal.

A lot of the difference has to do with when, traditionally, each culture drinks its wine. The Germans drink it on its own, sitting round a table or on the verandah. The French open their bottles to wash down large Alsace meals of duck and pâté. Whatever the subtleties, the resulting wines are the products of different traditions — and they taste that way.

In today's world of science, where ideas are international, tradition can be transplanted. California winegrowers can, and do, deliberately aim at a certain Old World tradition and style — and achieve it. Science has come to their aid with a battery of tests, controls and methods. Thus there are Rieslings from the West Coast that taste very like Rhine wines, because they have been consciously made in the German tradition.

It is argued, with some force, that local traditions reflect adaptation to local conditions. It is certainly true that attempts to ignore them can lead to unexpected failure: the reasons why a certain grape is not grown in a certain place are often good ones — someone tried once, and it didn't work.

Many traditions, however, are accidents. Local grape varieties dominate because that was all the locals had to choose from. Importing a vine from elsewhere may boost quality: growers in the South of France are producing much-improved wines these days thanks in part to the introduction of vines from elsewhere in France. And white wines from Spain have improved dramatically since the abandonment of one tradition. It was customery to let the grapes ripen completely in the hot sun before they were picked. Pressure from northern European wine buyers prodded the Spanish winemakers into picking the grapes earlier, when they were less ripe and had more of their natural acidity. The resulting wine is crisper and fresher. Elderly Spaniards probably find it sharp, thin and, well, untraditional. But the English and the Swedes love it.

In central Italy it was, and still is, the custom to keep red wines hanging about in enormous old casks until someone wanted to buy them, whereupon they were bottled. Once again, commercial forces have prompted the makers into modifying their ways. In order to keep their wines fresher, the way the buyers like them, they now bottle sooner.

Grapes

The choice of a grape type is very much tied up with tradition. In some places,

notably in the great vineyards of France, the traditional choice has the force of law. In Burgundy, great red wines are made from the Pinot Noir and nothing else; similarly Chardonnay is the one grape allowed in Chablis. It is probable that Riesling would do very well in Chablis, but it is never going to be put to the test. The law would not allow the resulting wine to be sold as anything other than plain *vin de table*, and so the experiment is not worth anyone's trouble.

Most wine laws in Europe lay down a "recipe" of grapes. In Italy, for instance, the DOC regulations for each of the 400-odd zones list the vines that are allowed (mostly those traditionally grown there). Any wine made with other grapes doesn't get the DOC tag.

In France, the new Vins de Pays regulations are more subtle. The rules list the traditional local grapes, but in many cases also add superior varieties, stipulating that the wine must contain a percentage of them. This is deliberate encouragement to growers: plant better vines and you can use the local Vin de Pays name, giving your wine an identity, setting it apart from the vin ordinaire and allowing a higher price to be set.

Outside the classic vineyards of

western Europe, the choice of a grape rests entirely with the grower. Thus when Bulgaria decided that making wine on a big scale was a worthwhile investment, its wide modern vineyards were planted with French and German varieties as well as local ones.

In America and Australia, growers choose those vines best suited both to the conditions and to the wines they aim to make. This has led to the faintly absurd spectacle of the pursuit of Pinot Noir. In Burgundy, it makes perhaps the subtlest, most rewarding red wine in the world. But the vine stubbornly refuses to produce recognizable "burgundy" outside its home province. California, Oregon, New Zealand, Hungary, England have failed to duplicate the taste despite planting the vine. Nature, so far, is ahead.

Cabernet Sauvignon, the chief grape of red Bordeaux, has travelled more readily. It makes good wine in Eastern Europe, California, New Zealand, Israel — name a place and it has done well there. None of the wines taste quite like Bordeaux, but good wines they are and all are recognizably from the same family. It seems that Cabernet has a more adaptable and dominant personality than the Pinot, which depends for a lot of its taste on the peculiar local factors of Burgundy.

Climate

One of the things that stopped Pinot Noir in its tracks in California was the climate. It was too hot. Climate is crucial to the vine, and indeed is one of the keys to the choice of a place to grow grapes. Weather — what happens every year within the broad framework climate supplies — is central to the success or failure of a given vintage. Even in places with a notoriously consistent climate — California's Central Valley, or the Lebanon, or Sicily — a rogue year can wreck the crop of grapes. The grower has to face hazards at every season, from frost in April to storms in October.

Increasingly, he can fight back: sprays can ward off rot or pests which damp weather brings, oil stoves can combat early frost, picking machines speed up the harvest, lessening autumn storm damage. But the weather still has surprises, and every year the mixture it conjures up is different and so is the resulting wine. This is what makes the vintage date one of the most interesting pieces of information on the label.

Site

Inconstancy is weather's hallmark. As if to compensate for this, there is the stability of the site. Any given piece of land has an enduring underlying structure of rock, overlaid by soil, modified by wind and rain. Its exact position, the way it is sheltered or exposed, high or low, dictates how much wind and rain and warmth it will get, whether it's Baron Philippe's most prized patch or your back garden. This pattern is constant enough to override mere weather and be accorded the status of climate — a microclimate.

The first of the two tasks is pure agriculture. Fruit growers anywhere, whatever their crop, would be at home in a vineyard. The grower has to stop the vines from being wrecked by pests, the grapes from being eaten by birds. He has to prune, train, plough, fertilize and pick. His decision on when and how to do all these things matters to the quality and the quantity of the crop.

Broadly, he can grow a lot of grapes and make indifferent wine, or a few and make better wine. There is an unbreakable, irritating and universal relationship between quantity and quality. Up goes one, down comes the other. The grower has to decide whether his vineyard has the inherent potential to make very good wine. If it has, he can make small amounts of it and sell for a high price. But if the site has no reputation, small crops will only mean fewer bottles to be sold at the same low price as his generously-cropping neighbours. A name can be built in time — but it takes courage and money to try

Timing is as ticklish as the decision on quantity. The grapes must be picked when they are ripe — easy to write, but hard to judge, despite today's tests for ripeness and acidity in the grape. Once the fruit is picked, there are a hundred things to do and decide — but that's another chapter.

The geology beneath is as central as the climate above. French experts long ago decided that soil was the key factor in wine quality. Americans disagreed, pointing to the excellence of their own California wines grown on just about every kind of soil there is. The verdict lies between the two. Soil and subsoil matter, but more because they influence drainage and the root-run of the vines than because of the special nutrients or minerals they may contain. Thus the predeliction of vines for hillsides: the drainage is better there, and the one thing that assuredly kills a wine is damp. ("I, myself, would also not be happy with cold, wet feet," as one grower sympathetically pointed out.) On a subtler level, the very best vineyards of the Médoc in Bordeaux correspond to the slight gravel mounds that dot the riverside plain. The gravel drains better: it's that straightforward.

Man

Fighting against, and working with, nature's wayward behaviour is man. Man chose the vineyard site in the first place so it is his fault if nothing grows there. But by now, in the old world at least, the good places have been sorted out from the bad. It is what man does with the site that matters. He has two tasks: to cultivate the vines and to make the wine. Actually that sentence must be qualified in two ways. First, not every grower makes wine and not every winemakers grows grapes. The two tasks are distinct but linked, and in some parts of the world tradition separates them while in others the whole activity of making wine is, in commercial parlance, vertically integrated. And second, by no means every winemaker or grower is a man. When two women run Château Margaux it is high time chauvinists admitted defeat.

SOME FAMOUS VINEYARDS

Some places make great wine because all the factors combine in the right way. They are the ones everyone has heard of: the great châteaux of Bordeaux like Lafite and Latour, fabled plots in Burgundy such as Chambertin and Montrachet, steep German hillsides like the Doctor vineyard above the Mosel. Why are they better than their neighbours? One way to get some clues is to look at places in detail to see why the great vineyards stand out from the merely good.

Chablis

Chablis is a large village in a cool, green part of Central France. There is a little river, and meadows, and wooded hills interspersed with fields. Most of these fields are vineyards these days, and it is their wine that has made the quiet village a household name.

Everyone has heard of Chablis. Most people who appreciate wine at all have drunk and enjoyed it. Fewer realise how dramatically the wines carrying this famous name can vary, in price and in taste, depending on whereabouts in the district they come from.

It's here we see the quality factors in action: position on the slopes, exposure to the sun, underlying soil: it is these that determine the variations in the taste of Chablis. Canny merchants have long proved this by paying more for the wines of the most favoured sites. The authorities today recognize this by grouping the vineyards together in grades according to their suitability for growing and ripening the Chardonnay grape.

Ripeness is a key word here, far to the north of most of the French vineyards. Winter can be long, spring late and summer tardy with its warmth. A south-facing slope makes all the difference to the amount of sun the vines receive. So the Grand Cru vineyards, the highest in status, sit in a row on a south-west facing hill, tipped to the sun and sheltered from the east winds. The slope allows the cold air of frosty spring nights to drain away, saving the tender new vine shoots from destruction. The vineyards on the hills behind the Grand Cru slope are far less favoured. They face west, or northwest, or east. They are higher and thus colder. And so the authorities decree that their wine shall be mere "Petit" Chablis.

There are two other grades, "simple" Chablis and Chablis Premier Cru. The latter are the second division, plots with sunny slopes and good frost protection, but not as good as the Grand Crus.

It is noticeable that there are no vineyards at all, of whatever grade, on the flat land of the valley floor. Here the soil is too heavy, and thus cold and damp, and the risk of spring frosts too great.

The price of the four grades of Chablis varies by as much as 300 per cent – and the main deciding factor in this is the site of the vineyard.

Deidesheim

In wine-growing Germany, the vines may draw the eye but the forest, the great, dark Central European forest, is never far away. It looms over Deidesheim, a little wine town in the Rheinpfalz district west of the Rhine.

Deidesheim is one of a string of villages and towns which shelter below a great belt of wooded hills called the Haardt. The villages puncture a band of vineyards, open plains for sugarbeet and grain and sunflowers down the slope to the east, rocky uncultivatable forest above to the west. The gentle slope leading up to the forest's edge is

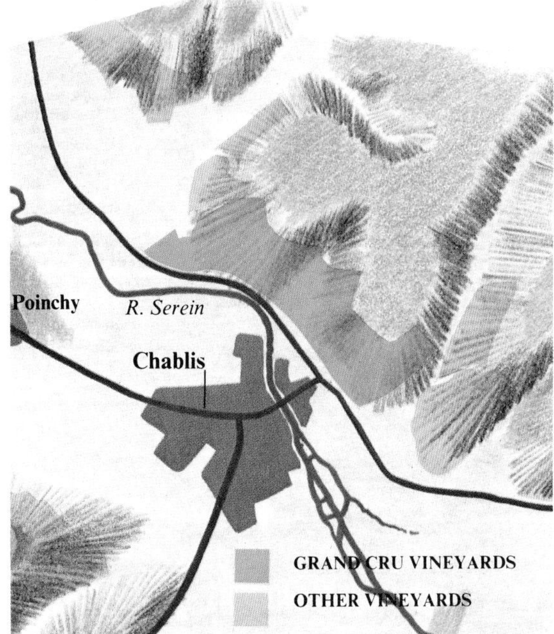

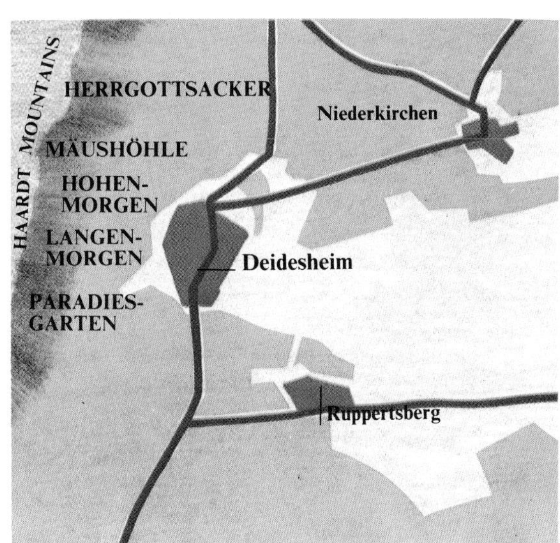

Far left: *the picture shows the Grand Cru vineyards of Chablis. All the Grand Cru sites are spread out along one slope, facing southwest over the town. There are no vineyards on the flat land beside the river, nor on the hilltop. The flat land would be too wet and prone to frost, and the hilltop too rocky and exposed. The hardy woods that do cap the hills, however, protect the Grands Crus from the east and north winds, adding shelter to the other favourable factors of the famous slope.*

Top left: *the map of Chablis puts the vineyards in perspective and shows how the less prestigous curve away around the hill, where the exposure to the sun is less advantageous. Chablis is a long way north, and every bit of sun helps to ripen the grapes.*

Below left: *Deidesheim in the Rheinpfalz area of Germany has a similarly sheltered position, though here the best vineyards face south and east. The town is tucked into a protected niche on the long slopes behind the Haardt mountains, guarded from the rain-bearing west winds. The grapes grow between the plain to the east and the rocky, forested hills to the west.*

where the vines are to be found, a succession of prized plots each with their traditional names, tags which tell much about their reputation. Above Deidesheim, in a shallow amphitheatre of vines, are Herrgottsäcker – the Lord God's portion; Paradiesgarten – self-explanatory – and Jesuitengarten: the Church always values the best.

The wines from these slopes are some of Germany's most sought-after. Why? Situation is the key. The wooded hills keep the west wind, and the rain, from the vineyards, ensuring more sun than elsewhere. Especially, and crucially, in autumn. A warm October gives the slow-ripening Riesling grapes their chance: they concentrate the sunlight and warmth into astonishing reserves of natural sugar, which the German winemakers skilfully balance with the grape's inherent tartness. The site has more to contribute: the soil is light, well-drained and, due to its origins as the eroded debris of the ancient volcanic Haardt hills, rich in elements that the vine roots take up to add to the taste of the wine.

What is perhaps most central is a tradition and a decision: the growing, and continued growing, of the Riesling. Other vines yield more grapes, and ripen earlier and more predictably. But none bears fruit with the magic balance of sugar and acidity that Riesling offers. Dedicated growers with a long view go on growing it, and Deidesheim goes on making great wine.

The Salinas Valley

The vinegrowers and winemakers of Europe have 20 centuries of example to call on. Their grandfathers and *their* grandfathers, like as not, made wine on the same bit of land. The knowledge of what will grow and what won't, what trick in the making of wine is worth trying, is almost instinctive. In California most of today's vineyards were sheep pasture, or wilderness, until within living memory. There is no folk wisdom to call on. Science tries to fill the gap, but does not always succeed.

In the late 1960s researchers noted

that the Salinas Valley, close to the ocean south of San Francisco, had a seemingly excellent grape-growing climate. In went the vines, to the tune of ten thousand acres, where vegetables had been the staple crop. At the time the search was on for cooler growing conditions than were offered by the traditional vineyards of California, in the Central Valley. The Salinas Valley, open to the Pacific, was suitably cool. But it proved to be too cool, and the ocean fog reduced the amount of sunlight. The grapes ripened slowly, if at all. Salinas wines began to be known for a "vegetable" character (there was a degree of journalistic licence here stemming from the valley's earlier career). Fashion turned against them.

Today the balance is being redressed by concentration on hillside rather than flat-land planting: the soil on the slopes warms quicker, the sunlight there is more concentrated, the fogs less frequent. The vinegrowers getting real quality from Salinas are those who picked their sites with care. Smith & Hook, for instance, tested dozens of plots before planting seven vineyards totalling 225 acres. As winemaker Duane DeBoer comments "there's a danger of falling into doing things the way they do in Bordeaux or Napa. In a new wine area like this, you'd better learn to do things in *your* area, or you won't get the optimum advantage from your product. It was like re-inventing the wheel."

Many of the Salinas vineyards have been grubbed up and the land is back to lettuces and beans. But the best sites, discovered by experiment (some call it trial and error), are making good wines, setting down their marker as California's Deidesheims and Chablis.

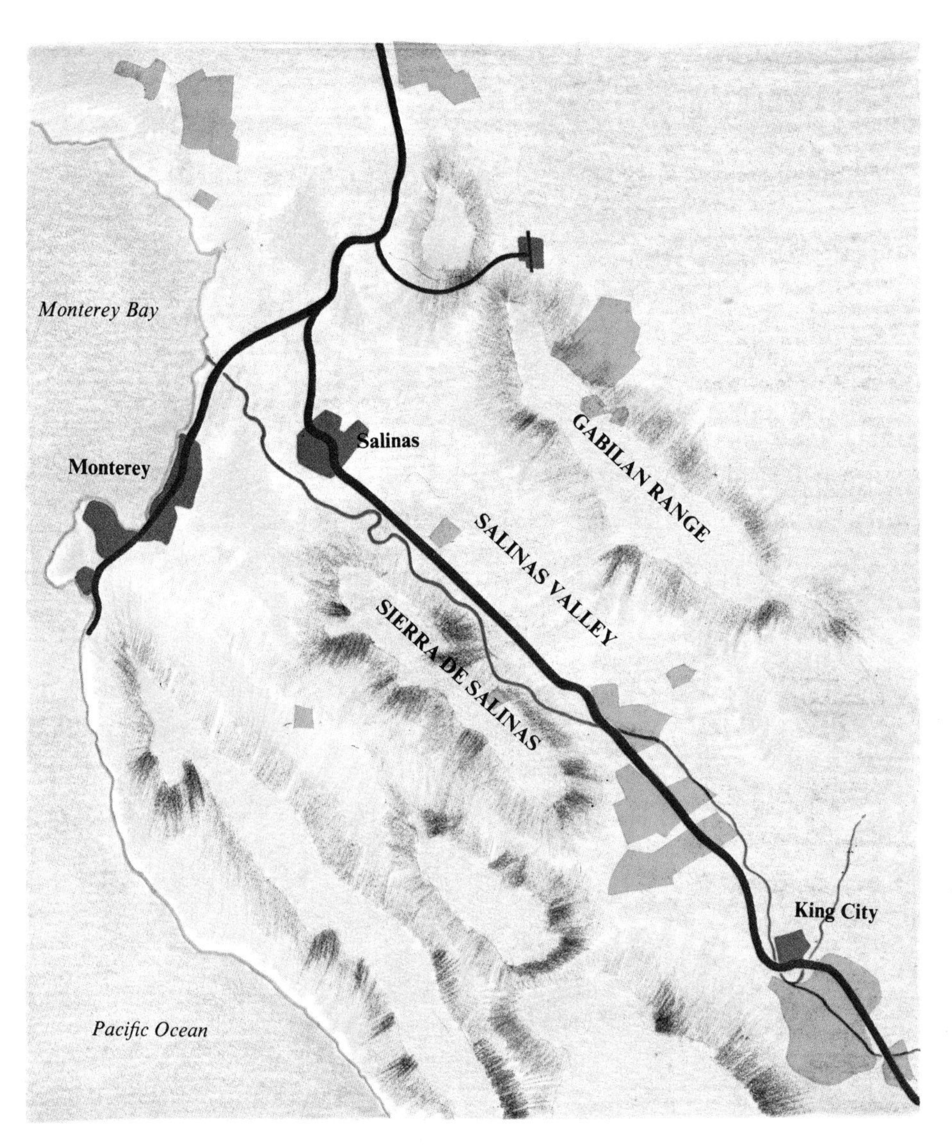

St-Emilion

Many noted vineyards have a heart and a wide surrounding zone that shares the name, but not all the qualities, of the centre. St-Emilion, for instance, gives its name to a wide band of Bordeaux vineyards. Yet it is generally accepted that the best wine comes from the heartland of the region, close about the little town. The landscape here forms a plateau, edged with a steep if not very high escarpment. The scarp curls round the edge of the plateau, facing south and southeast at its steepest and then trending round to the west, becoming gentler as it does so. The underlying structure of the rocks, and the soils that the rocks have formed are the key factor in the taste of St-Emilion wine — the rock, and, of course, the Merlot grape that does so well here.

As so often in great vineyards, limestone plays a part in the geology of St-Emilion. The limestone occurs in a great slab, which forms the bedrock of the plateau and is exposed on the steep slopes of its edge. On the top, the limestone is covered by a layer of gravelly earth, while the soil of the slope consists of lime and clay. What limestone and gravel offer is good drainage, leading to a dry soil which warms quickly. Such well-drained ground forces the vine roots to delve deep for water. The result is a hardier plant bearing tastier grapes: deep-rooted vines tap minerals and nutrients from the sub-soil, and have the stamina to live through droughts or severe frosts.

The majority of the top dozen châteaux are huddled along the edge of the plateau, or near its edge. Only Cheval Blanc and Figeac are away from the scarp: they are on a patch of extra-thick gravel and sand over clay — the limestone is deeply covered here. The scarp slopes — in French the côtes — are littered with famous names: Pavie, Ausone, Belair. The topography as well as the soil helps: the drainage on the slopes is extra good, the exposure to the sun perfect. And the slopes avoid much of the risk from frost. Just like water, cold air drains downhill, forming ponds in hollows or over flat, open land.

The taster finding his way among the multiplicity of St-Emilion wines has two main factors to consider. First, the relative proportion of Merlot to Cabernet grapes. Merlot gives softer, fleshy, wine; Cabernet more toughness, austerity and structure. The percentage of each grape grown by a château is worth knowing. Then comes the site of the vineyard bearing in mind the plateau and the slope. Plateau wine tends to be more solid and meaty, the côtes châteaux make finer, more perfumed, less long-lived ones. There are, of course, hundreds of little estates where the conditions, and the qualities, are not so clear-cut. But the twin factors are always there, and in the great wines they come through with real intensity.

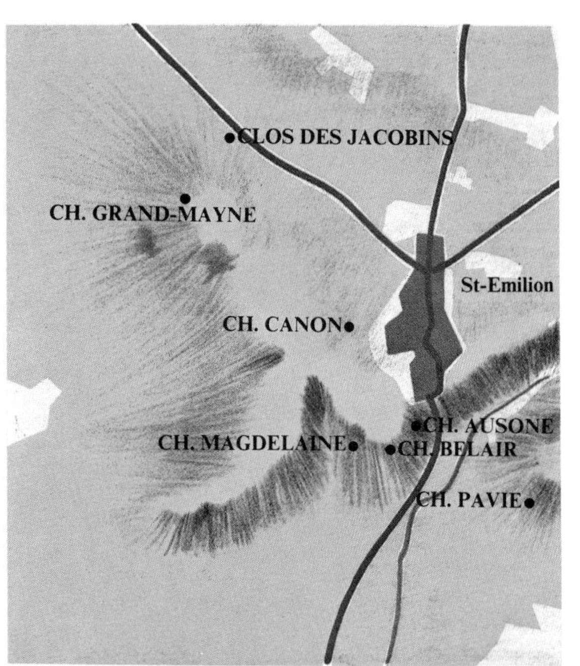

Map, far left: *the Salinas Valley in California is typical of the new vineyard districts around the world: a place of experiment, even trial and error, where pioneer growers find out where grapes thrive and where they don't. The contours of the land are what matter here. The wide Salinas valley opens out into the bay of Monterey; the Pacific air moderates and cools the microclimate.*

Map, left: *St-Emilion, by contrast, has been a vineyard since Roman times. The best sites have long been known.*

Below: *The estate of Clos des Jacobins is on the plateau, in the north of the map area. It has gravelly soil over limestone bedrock.*

THE GEOGRAPHY OF WINE

A generation ago, this chapter would have dealt with the wines of France, of Germany, perhaps Italy, doubtfully Spain and in patronising, passing fashion with a few outlandish places like Australia. The farthest-flung "serious" wine worth consideration was port.

This chauvinism was logical enough. Northern Europe and North America, the main consumers of good wine, drew their supplies from the classic vineyards of France and Germany. Everything else was of local interest only, consigned by the books to be drunk by locals. After all, it was confidently put about, such wines "didn't travel".

France had such a stranglehold on the world of wine that the cognoscenti in New York sneered at their native Napa Valley reds, and connoisseurs of Sydney wouldn't touch wines from their own back yard, the Hunter Valley.

Today there are about 30 wine-making countries in the world, and just about every one of them makes at least a few wines worthy to be ranked with Europe's best. This was brought home to the French in a traumatic way in a series of "blind" tastings. These somewhat artificial events became the fashion in Paris and New York in the early 1970s. Unlabelled bottles were offered to the supposedly expert tasters, who were asked to rank them: one notorious such event was even called a "wine Olympiad". Time after time, bottles from obscure places like Spain, Australia and California "beat" the revered French classics.

There are a lot of ifs and buts about wine judging, and it was not always clear at these circuses that like was being compared with like. But the shock was severe and the effect permanant. French wine is no longer beyond doubt the world's best. Life is tougher (if more exhilarating) for the French, for the drinker faced with a bewildering choice — and for the writer.

This burgeoning of the vine has meant more good wine and cheaper good wine. It also offers us a range of styles and tastes — and endless opportunities to confuse our friends at dinner parties with oddball bottles.

If a pattern can be imposed, let first the wine world be divided into Old and New. The "new" is not just Columbus's. It includes the Americas, Australasia, South Africa and places like Japan, China and the Middle East where growing grapes is very old but the actual wine industry is very new. The "new world" also takes in eastern Europe and England, where the wine tradition suffered a break in continuity requiring a fresh start today.

The "old" world of wine is the vinous heart of Europe, from France and Germany down through Austria and Switzerland to Italy and Greece, and across to Spain and Portugal. Here wine has been part of landscape and life since Roman times (a classicist might justly divide the modern wine world into Roman and non-Roman).

A glance at a good merchant's list will show the commercial balance between old and new. We'll choose a London merchant, because London is in many ways the centre of the wine world, the headquarters of buying and selling, of judgement and connoisseurship. France leads the list in sheer number of wines, then comes Germany, followed by Italy and Spain. Then there are the "new" countries, with wines from Australia, New Zealand, Chile and the Lebanon as well as the obscurer corners of Europe.

What is reassuring to the French, and to the more old-fashioned kind of wine drinker reared on French superiority, is how often the new world tries to imitate the old. Napa Valley Cabernets are matched against Bordeaux first growths: the Californians want to make Château Lafite, only better. The search for the Burgundian Holy Grail through the growing of Pinot Noir has already been touched upon. Australians are working to make wines that resemble white burgundy — and succeeding.

It is also reassuring to see how the prices of European wines compete with the produce of the New World's efficient high-tech vineyards. There is thankfully no parallel with the indus-

*The old world and the new. Dramatic straight-line plantings clothe the plains of Western Australia, and (**far right**) the ancient vineyards of the Rhine slope down to Nierstein. The Australian picture shows the Swan Valley, north of Perth, an area where a string of modern, go-ahead wineries make excitingly flavoursome wines in a variety of styles. The climate is hot and dry, and irrigation is essential. Nierstein is the centre of a wide zone making white wines, the most ordinary bearing the name "Niersteiner Gutes Domthal". But the vineyards in the picture — Ölberg in the foreground, Hölle on the hill beyond the town, and Hipping away to the left — make much finer, luscious wines.*

trial race between new countries and old, no Japanese (or Australian) takeover of the claret market. Indeed, thanks partly to currency fluctuations, French wines undercut Californian ones in their home State at one point in the mid-Eighties, leading to anguished demands from American winegrowers for Federal protection.

As well as the distinction between old wine lands and new, there is also the difference between mass-production and craftsman-made. Winemaking on a really big scale is new, made possible only in the last two decades by a series of technical leaps. A really advanced large winery, like those erected by growers' co-operatives in Europe and big business in the USA, is totally automated. Grapes come in by truck at one end, are moved to the crusher by computer-controlled cranes or pumps, and wine comes out the other end via an automated bottling line. Such an operation makes predictable, palatable wine and, depending on the skill and judgement of those in charge, may well make very good ones. But they'll never be able to offer what the small-scale maker can: individuality. Many drinkers today search for identity in their wines. They like to drink the produce of a person and a place. Big wineries obliterate both by their very scale.

There are two kinds of small-scale wine operation: the self-conscious and the simple. The latter takes in everyone in Europe who farms the lands his ancestors farmed, makes his wine in a fairly straightforward way and puts his name on the label. Over in the New World, growers have deliberately imitated this approach as a reaction against mass-production. They apply far more science and calculation than their European cousins, but the aim is the same: wine of identity and personality.

THE POLITICS OF WINE

Once each year Carlos Falcó, the Marqués de Griñon, pulls out his chequebook and writes out a cheque for 170,000 pesetas to the local court. It's a fine, one the Marqués pays philosophically if not happily. He is a wine grower, and he has planted a vineyard on a hilltop in his hot, dry corner of Spain so the grapes can benefit from cooling breezes. The hilltop site has no natural water, and it rarely rains, so he irrigates. And that's against the law; thus the annual ritual of the fine.

It's an off-putting thought, but politicians, judges and officials have as much to do with the wine we drink as do winemakers. Wine is a major industry, and as it contains alcohol — an intoxicant — legislators try to ensure that wine is not harmful to the consumer, is made wholesomely, and is what it purports to be. They go further: by regulating the ways grapes are grown and wine made, they attempt to raise the standard of wine. They try to stop over-production, paradoxically the curse of many countries in spite of wine's growing popularity.

Thus the Marqués and his annual fine. Irrigation is banned because ignorant or unscrupulous growers use it to boost the size of the grape crop, and Spain like every other wine country aims at fewer, better-quality grapes. Quantity is not the Marqués's motive, of course, but the law is a blunt instrument . . .

The busy hand of the official has a part in most of the wines we drink. Nearly always that's to the good. Take the rough reds of southern France. Once, they were the staple of the French diet — some people drank four litres a day. But that was a generation ago, when France was in many ways still a peasant country. France has changed. While the French still drink a lot of wine by anyone's standards, they drink less than they did, and quantity is giving place to quality.

This has meant that much of the wine of the South — the tasteless wine of the plains that sold purely on its alcohol content — was without buyers. But thanks to the politics of the Common Market, which exists partly to protect European farmers, the wine went on being made — and diverted straight into the notorious Wine Lake.

Even the bureaucrats of Brussels realised something had to be done. They had to cut the amount of wine being made, and make the wine that was produced better. With subsidies they encouraged farmers to retire, or to try crops other than grapes. They backed the efforts of Paris in introducing the Vins de Pays regulations, which offer anonymous bulk wines individual status in return for imposing quality controls. Everyday French wine is improving fast as a result, and wines with personality, which people will pay for, are surfacing from the lake.

Laws brought in with the best of intentions can be too rigid. Indeed, the experience of the wine world tends to bear out that weary old adage about every political measure having an effect opposite to the intentions of its promoters. Examples are the Italian and Spanish wine regulations. The Italian DOC laws basically fix as official whatever the local growers happen to be doing when the rules are written down. If they grow indifferent grapes and age the wine too little or (more often) too long, that's what gets into the rules. Getting the law changed, once the President has signed the decree (which can take years — there's a queue) is hard work, and it tends not to happen.

Quite a few growers have decided to ignore the DOC regulations and make wine their own way. This means their wines have to be labelled as *vino da tavola* – table wine — rather than quality wine. Some of these "rebel" tavola wines are among the best in Italy, made by skilled growers with an urge to excel. They use non-Italian grapes such as Cabernet and Chardonnay, age their wines differently, and produce stunning bottles. Yet they have no place in the official system.

Spain set up its wine regulations with aims equally as worthy as those of the Italians. But the consequences can be just as silly. Classic French grape varieties are often excluded from local lists of approved ones. They are not exactly banned (though there may well be laws against importing plants to combat disease), they are just not on the list.

For instance the Marqués de Griñon — he of the irrigation fines — has felt obliged to break the rules with both the red and white wines of his estates. The white should, the local regulations say, spend a year ageing in barrels if it is to carry the local name Rueda on its label. The Marqués, influenced by modern French practice, decided not to age his wine at all — it went straight into the bottles. It was so good that the officials were persuaded to change the rules for Rueda to accommodate his successful experiment.

For his red wines, the energetic Marqués was determined to use French grapes such as Merlot and Cabernet as well as the traditional Spanish Tinto Fino. He smuggled vine cuttings from Bordeaux hidden in a batch of fruit trees. They thrived. He decided they needed irrigation on their dry, hot hilltop — but this is where we came in. The Marqués reckons the fine worth paying because his hilltop vineyard produces wine lower in alcohol and higher in acidity than the vineyards of the plains. By breaking the rules, he is making a wine more in tune with modern taste than Spanish tradition allows. And it is a wine which, unlike many others from hot central Spain, is readily exportable.

Nodding approvingly about mould-breaking experimental noblemen is one thing, but wine rules exist to stop the unscrupulous from poisoning the public. There are two ways of breaking the law, one of which can sometimes be smiled at, the other not. The latter consists of actually adulterating the wine and is thankfully rare, but it does happen. Every country worth its name on the label carries out strict tests on its wines before they are allowed to be sold. Every importing country runs tests too. So the chances of trouble are slim. When it does occur there's a real scandal and people get put in prison.

The other crime is passing off — selling a wine as something it is not. This is far more common than adulteration and far harder to spot. There are rules about moving wine about to make sure that tanker loads of cheap stuff do not find their way into the Grand Crus, but it does go on. Colourful tales sometimes surface about secret pipelines across lonely frontiers, by which means cheap Spanish red became pricey French, or about Sicilian wine which crosses the Alps to become German. There are dark stories about the wagons to be found in the railway yards of Burgundy with Rhône waybills attached to them. Wine is a complex world, and the only rule is *caveat emptor* — let the buyer beware. Take your business to a merchant of integrity — one with a name to lose — and you'll drink what you pay for.

INTRODUCTION TO FRANCE

There are not many places in southern and central France where the vine does not grow. The journey south from the Channel soon takes one from apple orchards into vineyards. The Loire wine country runs in a band across northern France, and from there to the Mediterranean, only mountains and forests interrupt the steady succession of vines. Of course, some areas specialize in wine: Burgundy and Bordeaux, Champagne and Alsace. In others the odd field of grapes tucks in among the wheat, the corn, the beets and the fruit.

It is the ubiquity of French wine which gives it fame. For 2,000 years the French have been making wine, discovering every nuance of the soil, landscape and climate and breeding grape varieties to complement them. Thus French wine at its best is a marvellous marriage between natural conditions and man's skill, the perfect working out of a complex equation. No country takes wine more seriously than France. It is a major national industry and a source of great pride. Consequently there are elaborate rules to ensure quality and authenticity.

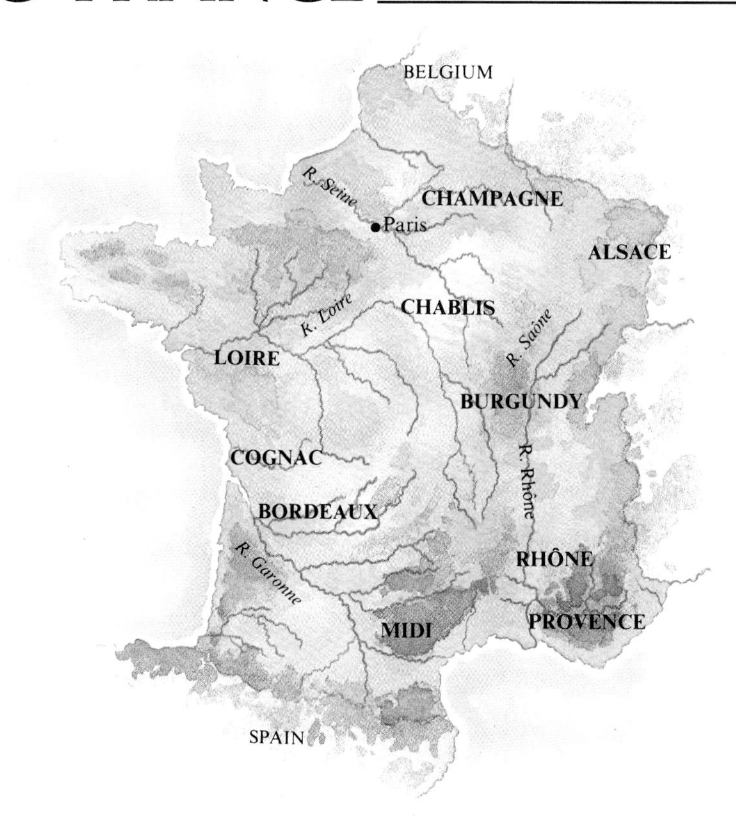

France rates geography as the key to excellence. The hierarchy of wine ascends from bottles which have no defined home, but are just *vins de table,* to the produce of individual fields, the wines which have an *Appellation d'origine Contrôlée* (AoC) — an official "birth certificate". AoCs vary in size, and often there are concentric circles of appellations ranging from the general — covering a whole region — up through grades of detail to the most specific — a single field. The AoC rules control a lot more than mere origin. Grape varieties, methods of cultivation, the size of the harvest, are all controlled, and laboratory testing and tasting by experts are obligatory.

Once, the AoCs were top of a 3-tier system, with a second rank, VDQS (Vin Délimité de Qualité Supérieure), below and basic *vin de table* at the bottom. This system is changing with the growth of interest in the *Vins de Pays,* the "country" wines. They have been a great success, and it has been decided to phase out the VDQS category to give the Vins de Pays greater status and narrow the gap between them and the AoCs. VDQS wines will still be around for a while yet, but their fate is sealed. The wines that now carry the title will become AoC, and no more VDQS decrees will be issued.

No regulation can guarantee good wine, though you can be sure that AoC and Vin de Pays wines are what they say they are, that they come from where they claim, and that they meet minimum standards. Everything else is up to the producer.

Although the lowest in rank among the legally defined wines, the Vins de Pays come first in any modern account of France, this is not because they are the best, but because the concept makes them the wines of most use to most of us. The great wines of France are the greatest in the world. Her good, and merely modest, wines are also, potentially, as good as anyone's. France is such a large producer of wine of all grades that its success or failure is vital to everyone who likes wine. If France succeeds in making good everyday wines at keen prices, we'll all drink well.

The Vins de Pays system is a new one, only dating back to the 1970s. This is a short life in wine terms, for vineyards take time to grow to maturity. We are just beginning to drink the fruits of the Vins de Pays revolution.

Most of these wines come from the South, not the South of France coastline of millionaires and casinos but the hinterland of stony hills and wide plains which stretch, under the sun, from Spain round to Italy. Here the heat is so constant and strong that care must be taken to avoid flabby, over-ripe wines.

The words "Vin de Pays" appear on labels with a local name, as in "Vin de Pays de l'Hérault". The name can be that of a widespread area – a département (county), or even a whole region. Or it can be a district as small as a valley or a group of villages. With over 100 of these Vins de Pays areas it's hard to remember which is which, but few will let you down (bearing in mind the very low prices they charge). Look out for particular grape varieties on the label, especially the "classics" like Cabernet Sauvignon or Syrah. They can signal a Vin de Pays with more than usual flavour and interest. On the whole, red wines do better than white in the hot South. For white wine of interest look a rung or two further up the ladder, at VDQS and AoC wines. But remember too that France has far greater wines than these country charmers. Which takes us to Bordeaux . . .

Vineyards in the heart of France, at Bissy-la-Mâconnaise in Burgundy.

BORDEAUX

In a successful attempt to confuse, the wine trade call red Bordeaux wines "claret" and white ones Sauternes, Graves, Sauvignon — anything but White Bordeaux. This obfuscation conceals somewhat the fact that Bordeaux is the most important of the French wine regions. It's important because it is the biggest, the most varied, the most interesting and the best. Grand claims all, but they stand up. To the ordinary winelover, the size and variety of Bordeaux are its most alluring attractions. It takes a fairly major meteorological disaster to stem the huge annual flow of wine from there. Year in, year out come 40 million bottles of red wine (rather less white). Much of the red is ordinary, but a surprisingly large proportion is better than that. It is the varied, individual, absorbingly interesting produce of literally thousands of small farms, most dignified by the name "château". It is this profusion which makes Bordeaux such a happy field for research: there's always another "petit château" waiting to be discovered.

These minor wines live in illustrious company. They are neighbours of a top few dozen châteaux which are the world's best, and biggest, sources of fine red wines. These, and their near-equals, are the classed growths (*crus classés*). They uphold, vintage after vintage, Bordeaux's claim to excellence. And it is their example which spurs on the minor properties, who share the same weather, the same grape varieties, similar soil . . . and perhaps one day similar prices.

Among white wines, standards are in the main lower. The great Bordeaux whites come from Sauternes and Graves. The first, when top-class, is illustrious sweet wine. But the world's taste for expensive sweet wine is limited, and Sauternes costs a fortune to make properly. White Graves is full and dry, at its best a match for great white burgundy. But the Graves châteaux make greater reputations and profits from red wines than white these days. Both white styles are hard for a small grower to emulate, requiring money for sophisticated equipment and the readiness to write off a crop if conditions don't turn out correctly. This is the real reason why red vines in Bordeaux are more popular than white, the world's love-affair with dry white wine notwithstanding.

Bordeaux in perspective

If size and variety are the keys to Bordeaux's dominance, so too are they snags for the wine buyer. Even the trade has trouble disentangling the names of the literally thousands of minor châteaux. The only route to true mastery of the subject is a lifetime's study — and there are worse life sentences. Luckily for the rest of us, however, a quick background sketch of the area's geography gives a good key to its delicious abundance of wines.

It is a big region, a whole slice of western France between the Atlantic and the inland hills. Two great rivers flow down from these hills, the Dordogne and the Garonne. They join to form a broad estuary, the Gironde. Vinous Bordeaux is divided by these waterways into three: the left (southwest) bank between the Garonne and the Gironde and the sea, the triangular tract between the two rivers, and the right (northeast) bank of the Dordogne and Gironde. Helpfully, the red wines are mostly grown on the left and right banks, and the whites in the middle bit (the Entre-Deux-Mers: between two waters). Like all broad-brush descriptions this one has its dubious patches, but it will do for now.

The left and right-bank reds are clearly and usefully distinct in taste. On the left, closest to the sea, are the Médoc and the Graves, making dry, even austere, wines of style, delicacy and charm. On the right bank, Pomerols and St-Emilions show — again, generally speaking — more earthiness, muscle, fruit and vibrancy. It is clear after tasting a range of Red Bordeaux that the left-right distinction has its uses. Wines from minor corners will fit into either the Médoc or St-Emilion styles, 20 Médocs will have a common "feel" when compared with 20 Pomerols.

Soil and grape type are the keys to quality and taste in Bordeaux. The left bank soil is largely gravel ("Graves" means just that) which drains well and forces the vine-roots to delve deep for sustenance. The major grape is the austere, tough-skinned Cabernet Sauvignon. Across the rivers, the subsoil is clay and limestone, and the dominant vine is the Merlot, producing grapes fuller and fruitier than the Cabernet.

Position plays a part, too. The Médoc vineyards are closest to the sea and its warm, damp winds, while those of St-Emilion are more exposed to the cold mountain air from the east. Tradition and custom are much the same across the region, with winemaking techniques varying little.

Once the broad geographical distinctions are established, the next great determinant of the taste of a bottle of red Bordeaux is status. Annoyingly, the most famous is the most expensive and the best. There are few, if any, hidden masterpieces in Bordeaux. The area has been raked over by wine merchants as intensively as Florence is overfished by art experts, and the chances of a backwoods château making the next rival to Lafite are about as great as an unknown Giotto turning up in a palazzo's back bedroom.

The great château have been first on the price-lists for three hundred years. They occupy the prime sites, the best-drained gravel banks in the Médoc or the plateau slopes in St-Emilion. It is possible to argue that even great châteaux have their off-years, or off-decades, usually when the owners are not up to the task, in resources or commitment. Then the place changes hands, improvements are made and the château in question comes back on form.

The hierarchy of greatness is rigid in Bordeaux. There is an official classification, or rather several classification lists. The words "cru classé" on a label mean a property is on one of them. These lists bear study, despite the arcane arguments among the trade and their acolytes about whether Château X or Y is better or worse than its classification. Frequent bouts of re-classification fever sweep the tasting rooms and offices of Bordeaux. It will never happen, short of a revolution: the present-day chosen ones have too much to lose. The one place where the system is less than useful is in St-Emilion, where a sort of communism of greatness rules: innumerable tiny châteaux

In Bordeaux, the château is the key. The word means both the building (rarely as grand as this one, Château Cantemerle) and the wine estate of which it is the headquarters. The reputations of châteaux rise and fall, depending on who owns them, but the fundamental quality of the land remains the same. Most châteaux handle the whole wine-making process themselves, from growing the grapes to bottling the wine. Behind the elegant château is an extensive range of buildings, plus cottages for the estate workers. The whole complex is really a large, specialized farm.

are entitled to be "grand crus".

Few can afford to drink classed-growth wines very often. If you are among the lucky, refer yourself to one or more of the excellent books on Bordeaux's great wines. The rest of us will search out the best among the *crus bourgeois* — the next rank down, and including some very good wines indeed — and the 2,000 or so *petits châteaux*. When exploring, pay close heed to the small print on the label. It will tell you the commune, or district, where the wine was made, either in the appellation or, if the wine uses a more general AoC such as plain Bordeaux Supérieur, in the château's address. (A postal code directory for Bordeaux is essential equipment for the true claret fanatic.)

The great thing about these minor clarets is that they are cheap. I make a practice of buying a bottle of every one I see. They cost little more than basic jug or carafe wines, and many a happy discovery awaits. Most wine merchants have their own brand of claret, which will be as good as the wine merchant. But for surprises (most of them pleasant), individuality and interest, search out the unknown châteaux.

These little places will never make classed growth wine. They aren't in the best spots, and they cannot afford the rigorous winemaking techniques — careful selection, new oak casks, long ageing — that the top properties indulge in. But here and there you will find a grower who tries harder, who owns a well-placed vineyard which he tends carefully and which yields wine worthy of the skill and effort he puts in. Buy his wine: you will enjoy it and he will be encouraged to greater things.

The gentle landscape of St-Emilion — one of the main Bordeaux wine districts. In contrast to the Médoc, the estates here are usually small and the "châteaux" frequently no more than farmhouses. Much good red wine is made here, the problem for the buyer is sorting out which château is which. The tangle is worsened by the St-Emilion habit of calling hundreds of wines "Grand Cru" The top dozen estates have the rank Premiere Grand Cru Classé. Next come 60 or so Grands Cru Classés, finally some 170 "mere" Grand Crus. The good news is that the St-Emilion classification is one of the most rigorous in France: any château with Grand Cru or above on its label can be relied upon. And because there are so many, the prices they charge are not outrageously high.

White Bordeaux varies more in taste than red. Much of it is sweet, including the best. Some is dry, including some great wines. Much, sadly, is neither, but a sort of bland off-dry liquid which finds little favour outside those restaurants which feel they have to list a white Bordeaux because they have a red one. It is harder to be sure of one's ground with white Bordeaux, to be certain what order of taste the cork conceals.

Sweet white wine has a bad name, conferred in large part by the dire Spanish "sauternes" of the student parties of two decades ago. Every wine writer and merchant decries this as a pity. They would, wouldn't they. But efforts to spread the gospel of luscious taste (and to sell more bottles) conceal the truth that sweet wine is far harder to fit into our lives than dry. That's why it doesn't sell.

Bordeaux's historic emphasis on sweet rather than dry whites has led to hard times for many growers. Only now is the balance settling down. Much dry wine is made under the names Entre-Deux-Mers and straight Bordeaux. Some, an increasing amount, is fairly good. Less of the ordinary sweet wine is being made, which is encouraging for it was never up to much. And there are signs of renewed interest in the serious sweet wines of Sauternes and Barsac and the good dry ones of Graves.

To make a living by making Sauternes is less sensible than professional gambling. Sauternes is the end product of an unlikely chain of chances, and three years out of four the chances do not come up. First, the gambler must grow the Sémillon grape, soft, juicy and rather bland. Then must come a warm, damp autumn, encouraging mists among the vines. This weather is bliss to a little micro-organism, the botrytis mould, which given warmth and damp will grow on the grape skins. Grapes so infected are thrown away with disgust in most vineyards. In Sauternes they are treasured, for the mould pierces the skins, letting the water out of the grapes and thus concentrating the juice inside. The owners of the Sauternes vineyards watch their grapes daily through a botrytis autumn, picking only those fruit perfectly infested by the mould. As many as a dozen circuits of the vineyard, over a period of weeks, are necessary to bring in the grapes. This costs a fortune in pickers' wages, never mind the strain on the nerves — one rainstorm, or a cold spell, will ruin the whole gamble. And each grape will make far less wine than a normal one, so a Sauternes château makes far fewer bottles per acre than a red-wine outfit.

Drinking Sauternes is an act of conservation: protection of two endangered species, the wine itself and the small band of people who make it.

Dry white Bordeaux is a more sensible proposition, but it is a drink without a clearcut image and thus unfashionable. My advice is to buck the trend: you'll drink very good wine at half the price of white Burgundy. The crus classés of Graves make the outstanding dry whites, with individual properties emerging in the Premières Côtes and Entre-Deux-Mers. Some Bordeaux dry white has suffered from the fad for Sauvignon, a grape which this far south tends to the flabby rather than thrilling. But if well made, and especially in a cool year, Bordeaux Sauvignon is good drinking. The more expensive Graves wines have a dash of Sémillon in with the Sauvignon, and are aged either in oak or steel vats (fanatics argue fiercely over which is best). They will often repay keeping for two years.

Vintages in Bordeaux

If you see a newspaper report about the vintage of the century or disaster for winegrowers (the only two wine stories most news editors recognize) the odds are it will refer to Bordeaux. This is not just because the Bordeaux trade is effortlessly good at self-publicity. It is because the vintage on a bottle of Bordeaux really matters.

The weather will determine the size of the crop, which can vary by a factor of two. It will determine whether that year's wine is one for keeping 20 years or for drinking within three. It will, most vitally, make a difference to the price the châteaux can charge.

A "vintage of the century" is announced about one year in five and actually occurs about one year in 25. That matters a lot at classed-growth level and only a little at the bottom of the quality pyramid. Take serious note of the vintage when buying fine wine to keep, or when ordering a special bottle in a restaurant. But these days, with modern techniques, really bad wine is rarely made in Bordeaux despite the weather, so the *petits châteaux* will almost always be drinkable.

Vintages differ from each other, and wines also change. The '61 tastes different (better) now than it did in '71. It will taste different again in '91. So it is hard to give vintage recommendations. The table lists the last few, with remarks on their qualities. Only Bordeaux gets this treatment. Vintages do matter elsewhere in France, but are not so clear-cut in their qualities.

Bordeaux Vintages

1985	*Top-class wines, possibly up to 1983 standards.*
1984	*A disaster in St-Emilion; average to good, if austere, wines elsewhere. Unfashionable: drink it but don't invest in it.*
1983	*A great year, with lots of stylish wine for long keeping. Good whites, sweet and dry.*
1982	*A hot summer, very ripe wines, highly rated early in their life and very fashionable. Time will tell if it or '83 is the truly great vintage. Good dry whites, poor sweet.*
1981	*Fine red wines, overshadowed by successor vintages and thus good value.*
1980	*Average, short-lived reds, some bargains to be had, some to be avoided. Sweet whites were better.*
1979	*Good quality vintage of useful wines, red and white.*
1978	*Red wines at classed-growth level are for long ageing.*
1977	*On the whole poor, though there are exceptions.*
1976	*A puzzle: very hot weather; red wines seemed good early on, but some doubts now. Drink before '75s. Good sweet whites.*
1975	*Sturdy, long-lived red wines, some over-tannic and harsh.*

Other good years: 1970, 1966, 1961.

Backstage at a Bordeaux château. The farm buildings of a wine estate have a dignity of their own, especially inside, with the massed ranks of barrels contributing to the sight, and the maturing wine to the smell. The large casks on either side are less typical of Bordeaux than the small ones — called barriques *— in the centre. (The wine making process is illustrated on pages 110–115.) This cellar is technically a* chais *— an above-ground storage place.*

LOIRE

Wine has a habit of taking its names from rivers. Vineyards, it's true, seem to grow especially well overlooking water, but the connection is still tenuous. Perhaps it stems from trade routes in the days before roads were more than mud-pits, and riverboats carried the cumbersome casks of wine. Perhaps it is just an easy way for rule-framers, and writers, to give a shape to the world's sprawl of vineyards.

The Loire crosses more countryside than any other in France. Unlike the Rhône, which is essentially Mediterranean in flavour as soon as it breaks out from the Alps, the Loire is a northern stream. It is a river of gravelly shallows, willow trees, watermeadows and rapids. It is also an unruly one, with a habit of breaking its ill-defined banks and flooding the entire valley. For this good reason it's unusual to find vines on the river's banks, but they are there, within five, ten or 20 miles of the water, everywhere from the headwaters in the forested Auvergne down to the Atlantic.

How can the wines made along such a river have any other than a forced, spurious unity? Taste them and see. From Muscadet, made within sniffing distance of the ocean, to the lost, rustic wines of St Pourçain high in the hills, Loire wines have a family tie of taste, a lightness, a coolness — an absence, if you like, of the assertiveness found in wines made further south. For the river has little to do with this unity: it is latitude which counts. Here is a countryside where apples rather than olives grow among the vines, where rich cow pastures and cool beech woods alternate with the vineyards which claim the south-facing warm corners.

Mention the Loire and most of the wines which come to mind are white or rosé. Reds are made, but the cool northern climate ripens their grapes less readily than it does white ones. In quality, most Loire wine is "good ordinary"—well-made wines with some character. Some is distinctly good, very few are great. Apart from a few specialities, nowhere does the Loire approach the stature of Bordeaux or Burgundy.

The first step towards enjoying Loire wines is working out which ones come from there. The contrary French do not aid our task by printing "Loire" on every label. There's a list of nearly 70 different wine names attached to the Loire (it is a long river), never mind the thousands of individual makers. To look at the main wines, it's easiest to split the river into three, as in an old-fashioned geography book: the upper, middle and lower reaches.

The lower Loire, the *Pays nantaise* or countryside of the seaport city of Nantes, is the simplest. Here, a generation ago, thousands of small farmers grew their patches of vines and made a sharp, appetizing local white wine called Muscadet. Today, the farmers are still at work, the plots are typically still small but the wine travels the world. Muscadet is always dry but varies, from vintage to vintage and maker to maker, in its degree of fullness and taste. The weather, here within an hour's drive of the Bay of Biscay, plays a major part. A cool, cloudy year brings mean, tart wine, a bit more sun and the true Muscadet taste emerges, too much heat and the wine is flat and bland. For this reason the vintage date on a bottle of Muscadet is worth a second glance. Don't drink a wine that is too old: it's a rare Muscadet that gets better in bottle after more than a year or so.

Some producers take extra care with their wines and make a drink that can develop complexity and interest in bottle. But that's almost to miss the point of Muscadet: it is a clean, straightforward wine, marvellous with food, especially fish.

A little red wine is made near Nantes under the name Coteaux d'Ancenis, and there is also Gros Plant, a white wine (even) sharper than Muscadet.

Moving east, up the river, we come to the first (and some say only) part of

Far left: *Château de la Cassemichère makes top-quality Muscadet in the heart of the Sèvre-et-Maine region at Vallet. Sèvre-et-Maine Muscadet is generally reckoned to be the best.*

Left: *harvesting in Touraine.*

Below: *red grapes are in the minority in the Loire, though in years when they ripen well, as here, splendid wines can be made.*

the Loire where great wine is made. In a sheltered side-valley a few small estates make superb white wines from Chenin Blanc grapes under the name Coteaux du Layon. The aim here is sweetness, but the balanced honey-and-lemon sweetness of a great German wine. These are true individuals, and not expensive for their quality: wines to sip and appreciate on their own.

The mass-market, meal-time wines from the central Loire are Anjou Rosé, red Saumur and sparkling Saumur. This last is the best, a serious contender to be the best fizz in France after champagne. Its home is the chalk labyrinths (*caves* really are caves, here) cut in the riverside cliffs near the town of Saumur, the method used that of Champagne. Still red Saumur, especially Saumur Champigny, can be excellent in a warm year. The rosé is mostly bland.

The heart of red wine-making in the Loire is around Chinon, but that district makes more of its living these days from Vouvray, a white wine, and increasingly from Touraine Sauvignon. Vouvray is a puzzle: like white Bordeaux, the name is no clue to the taste. Much as pretty average wine, not quite dry, not truly sweet: wine for people who don't like wine very much. In some years Vouvray becomes more interesting: gently sweet yet with a lot of taste and nicely balanced. The trouble is no-one, even the maker, is sure how Vouvray is going to turn out. Sauvignon from Touraine undercuts upper-Loire Sauvignons on price, and can be good value in a year when the weather is neither too hot nor too wet.

Well inland, where the Loire runs north-south rather than east-west and where the influence of the Atlantic is small, are found the upper vineyards of Pouilly and Sancerre. Both specialize in Sauvignon and have ridden a boom as the flavour of this grape has become fashionable world-wide. To taste good wines from these two villages is to realize that there's more to good Sauvignion than just the grape. The soil is special here – chalk – and there are some splendidly-placed sunny slopes.

That leaves the other 60 or so Loire districts . . . . As a general rule, any Loire wine above the basic price level is worth a try. With the cheap ones — ordinary Muscadet, Anjou Rosé and the rest – you'll get what you pay for: everyday wine. But there is a host of local traditions, microclimates and peculiarities strung along the great river. Their wines, the ones you pay perhaps half as much again for, can be splendid value.

THE RHÔNE AND THE SOUTH

The valley of the Rhône is the gate to the South, that slice of France where the buildings, the trees, the feel of the sun, the very pattern of life, are distinctly other. To the eternal surprise of northern travellers, there's a point somewhere south of Lyon where things are *different*.

The wine changes too, and "southern" is a common term in the tasting notes of wine trade people trying to sum up a Rhône. That's especially true of the whites. Different grapes, hotter sun, different traditions call forth a heavier, flatter flavour. The absence of acidity is the biggest difference between southern French whites and their northern counterparts. Tradition is the strongest force in the taste equation here. It is not impossible to make good, characterful white wines in hot places, as Californians and Australians prove.

Left: the ancient town of Châteaneuf-du-Pape nurtures a wine tradition dating back to the days when Popes lived at Avignon.

Top left: the vines are planted in ground entirely covered by large, flat stones. The stone store the sun's heat, further ripening the grapes.

Above: pickers in a Rhône vineyard load the grapes into bright-coloured plastic crates. The long-legged tractor is designed to straddle the rows of vines.

But the focus in France's South has always been on reds. They are the best wines, and the commonest. The Rhône is the source of Châteauneuf-du-Pape, of Hermitage, and of many another name more familiar from restaurant wine lists than from experience. It also produces countless bottles (or more often, plastic tanks) of Côtes-du-Rhône, an innocuous red with little of the weight and character of its classier neighbours.

This division between classic and everyday is more use to the drinker of Rhône wines than the traditional split into northern and southern ends of the valley. Look to the classics for very good, even great, wines at prices far lower than Bordeaux or Burgundy. Wines like Côte Rotie, Hermitage (and Crozes-Hermitages, its lesser understudy), St-Joseph (cheaper and more variable) and Châteauneuf (variable too) are serious stuff, needing age in bottle to bring out their best. Ordinary Côtes-du-Rhône is really a commodity wine, to be bought on price and enjoyed without fuss.

Between the two groups are a few wines in the process of rising from the mass to the elite. Look for Côtes-du-Rhône-Villages, the wine from 17 communes scattered across the southern plain. Here the appellation laws are stricter, the wines sturdier and tastier, but the prices hardly higher than for ordinary Rhône. Gigondas and Rasteau, once just "Villages", have been further promoted and can now use their own names. Among the "Villages", Vacqueyras is the best. Ventoux and Tricastin are wider areas with more variable wine, but they're nearly always better than ordinary Côtes-du-Rhône.

Down here in the South, the best wines are those made by single-minded and modern-thinking growers. Look for individual domaines or châteaux rather than negociants' blends. Only a few of the Rhône negociants, sadly, have aspirations to sell wine of character. They are happier dealing in the bland and the blended. Some of the growers' cooperatives are showing them the way.

The rest of the South, the country between Mediterranean and mountains from Italy round to Spain, obeys the Rhône rules. Many of the most interesting wines are the newer ones made under Vin de Pays regulations. Provence has an AoC for its reds, whites and rosés, most overpriced and underflavoured, though recently some estates have been making good, tasty wines. The Provence rosé is best met in its homeland, where sun, old stones and good food provide a charming frame for an insipid picture.

Further west, in the hills above the Midi plains, the wines get more interesting. The Minervois area is newly promoted to Appellation Contrôlée status, and is proving the point by turning out some sturdy, individual wines. All the wine here is red, and most meet the test of unassuming tastiness and a certain southern spice. An increasing number of estates are also making reds which show something more. The pairing of the Minervois AoC and an individual estate name is worth a trial. To the south, the wines from the limestone hills of the Corbières are as yet merely of VDQS status. This will soon change. They, like their southern neighbours in Roussillon up against the Pyrenees, will be AoC. Both places make reliable ordinary wines and occasional good ones. Whites are less successful here in the Midi: the exception is Blanquette de Limoux, a sparkling wine from the inland hills, which is well up to the status of Saumur.

Vintages matter in the south, paradoxically. Despite the steady heat, good Rhône reds vary quite a lot in their ability to age. Good years (like 1978 or 1983) are darker, more interesting, longer-lived. Even ordinary Rhône wines vary quite a lot. The canny drinker sums up the previous year's Côtes-du-Rhône and balances taste against value, using Vins de Pays as his benchmark. The latter tend to win.

BURGUNDY

Burgundy! What magic in a name, what images of priceless bottles, ancient cellars, cherished traditions! It is a region which in many ways is the heart of France, certainly the heart of its sensuous pleasures. It makes the best dry white wine the world can produce, and a red wine of only slightly more debatable excellence. Yet its complexities and subtleties are such that they distract many a wine drinker from real enjoyment of burgundy wine.

It had better be said at the start that it is a good thing burgundy is complex because it is also scarce. Leaving aside Beaujolais and Mâcon, which though geographically in Burgundy are not quite the same thing, Bordeaux produces seven times as much red wine as Burgundy. Great white burgundies are scarcer still. There are, on average, just 325,000 bottles of Grand Cru and Premier Cru wines made each year. The demand for these wines is worldwide and growing. Compare the sales of champagne, a wine of much the same price and status as good white burgundy: the world pops over 200 million bottles of champagne a year.

So those who develop a taste for burgundy had better develop the bank balance to pay for it. Sadly (for the bank balance) the wine is worth its price. The best wine, that is. Ordinary burgundy is rarely everyday in price, but frequently so in taste. Do not expect much from it unless you get pleasure from drinking the name not the wine.

The heart of Burgundy is the Côte d'Or, the golden slope, a range of low hills crowned with forests and facing, as do so many of Europe's great vineyards, east and a little south (compare Alsace and the Rheinpfalz). The sheltered hollows and slopes of these hills provide superb sites for the Chardonnay and Pinot Noir grapes, sites where long hours of sunshine are combined with good drainage and protection from frost. This hillside has been famous for so long that every tiny patch has a name and a reputation, and each name is enshrined in laws which place the plots in one of four ranks. At the top are the 30 fields called Grand Cru. Then come more than 100 vineyards entitled to be called Premiers Crus. Third come the "village" or "commune" appellations granted to each village for land outside the Grand and Premier categories. Lowest come the "general" appellations, land considered too poor for a village rating, or outside the heart of the district.

Burgundy labels bear study. If they have a village name (Beaune, Nuits St-Georges and so on) without additional names (or with a vineyard name added but in smaller type), the bottle will contain wine from that commune, though not from a Premier, still less a Grand Cru, vineyard. If another name (Beaune Greves, for instance) is added to the village name in the same size type the wine is from a Premier Cru vineyard. If the label carries a vineyard name alone, it will be a Grand Cru. They alone can dispense with the village name.

Lesser wines will carry AoCs such as Bourgogne. They may have grand labels, bearing famous merchants' names, but they will still be in theory lower in quality than those with more specific origins. There used to be a lot of good-value wine around carrying the Bourgogne tag or village names, often the surplus production of grander vineyards, but with the ever-growing demand for burgundy this sort of wine seems to have mysteriously vanished.

Each of the two dozen Côte d'Or villages, and the named vineyards within them, have their own reputations. And running across this ranking order is the status of the man or woman who owns the vineyard. Initial study of Côte d'Or land ownership sends many a wine merchant (and drinker) back to Bordeaux in despair. Not here the limpid pattern of a list of châteaux each with its vineyard and its reputation. Instead a vineyard can be owned by dozens — scores — of growers, each with a tiny plot, even a row, of vines. The growers each own bits and parcels in several vineyards, and one grower may make several distinct wines. Thus there is no such thing as Corton; there is Bouchard's Corton, and Drouhin's, and Faiveley's, and that of a long list of others. It need not be said that each is different . . .

Why is burgundy so sought after? The question is easier to answer for white wine than red. In a good vintage, from a good site and a good winemaker, white burgundy is peerless. The noble Chardonnay grapes ripen to perfection, developing nuances of taste that are fine-tuned by the oak barrels used for fermentation and the process of ageing in the cool stone cellars. Wine tasters search for adjectives — butter, nuts, flowers and spices are often spoken of – but great white burgundy strikes them dumb. It is powerful, round, full and long. It tastes like nothing else on earth and while drinking it the palate's messages totally overcome those of the brain, which is anxiously computing the cost of every sip.

Red burgundy used to be a by-word for a rich, solid wine. In the old days it was reckoned that claret was refined and subtle, burgundy powerful and robust. There is very little of that sort of red burgundy around now. The knowing attribute this to a tightening-up of the rules, pointing to a decline in the amount of Rhône (or even Algerian) wine arriving in Burgundy. More optimistic souls say fashions have changed among the growers and lighter, shorter-lived wines are now in vogue. Whatever the cause, the prevailing style of red burgundy is light, clean, and at its best tasting of the Pinot Noir grapes yet more so. Good mature red burgundy is subtle, long-lived and soft to the tongue, yet with an unsurpassed depth and range of flavours. The one thing it is not is sweet or over-strong. Bad red burgundies (and sadly there are more bad than good at the moment as scarcity drives on greed) often betray the sugar that is (legally and universally) added to them. This comes through in a burnt-sugar taste and an over-alcoholic headiness. A great red burgundy has a flavour blended from farmyard earthiness and ethereal perfume that make it truly worth 20 times an ordinary bottle of wine. But if all burgundy is scarce, the great, the truly great, is as rare as liquid gold.

Luckily for Burgundy's export statistics, it includes within its borders two great wells of wine: Beaujolais and Mâcon. Beaujolais is a triumph of image-building. It is, at its best, a delightful wine: bluey-red, vibrant in taste and smell, filling the mouth with simple, cheerful pleasure. Sadly, little Beaujolais lives up to its image, though the proportion is growing. Nouveau, or new, Beaujolais is a fashion that has become an institution: the new wine, only weeks old, released in November each year. It is the first chance to assess the new vintage, to see if the delicate balance of rain and sun in Burgundy has settled on the right side. If the Nouveau is good — strong and heady rather than flabby and soft — it will keep well beyond the Christmas deadline (it used to be Easter) that greedy merchants say mark the end of its life. I have enjoyed Nouveau at eleven months old, well into its dotage by conventional standards.

Beaujolais comes in several grades, with the Villages level perhaps the best value: better than ordinary, cheaper than the produce of the nine "named" villages of the area. These village wines, or *crus*, are good in ripe vintages, and when not overpriced: pay no more than twice what Villages Beaujolais costs.

North of the Beaujolais hills, in an equally alluring wooded countryside, is the Mâconnais. From here comes Pouilly Fuissé, one of the best marketing ploys every played upon the American public. The white wine from there is made from Chardonnay grapes, and is clean, scented and characterful. Yet familiarity with its name has driven its price up to twice the level of its neighbours. For value rather than reputation, try the wines of Pouilly-Vinzelles, Pouilly-Loché or St-Veran.

Between Mâcon and the Côte d'Or come the hills of the Chalonnais, with the villages of Givry, Mercurey, Rully, Montagny and Buxy making red and white wines which taste like "real" burgundy at a fraction of the price. The names of any of these five villages are a welcome sight on a restaurant wine list.

It is fashionable to be cynical about Burgundy. But it makes wines which taste unlike anything else, which despite frantic efforts no-one else in the world has managed to match. Burgundy, like diamonds or Rolls Royce automobiles, is impossible to imitate. Like those superlatives, (love them or loathe them) it's unique.

Left: *the Côte d'Or is an east-facing slope of vines crowned with sheltering woods. One of its monuments is the château at the centre of the Clos de Vougeot. This 125-acre field is surrounded by an ancient wall built by the monks who once owned this superb vineyard. Today it is split between dozens of owners.*

Above: *glossy black Pinot Noir grapes are brought in from the vineyards in traditionally-shaped baskets. The machine in the background is a mill which partially crushes the grapes and tears off the stalks.*

ALSACE

Alsace is where France meets Central Europe. Not just Germany, which it faces across the Rhine, but the whole landscape and culture which takes in Austria, Bohemia, even Hungary, the endless stretch of forest and clearing, farm and woodstack, that reaches to the Carpathians. Grand generalisations, but the wines bear them out.

Alsace wine is white, it comes in tall green bottles, and it is made from grapes like Riesling and Gewürztraminer. These clues mislead many into expecting a German taste. It's not there. German wine is sweeter, softer, more luscious, Alsace is stronger, drier, more solid. But taste an Alsace Riesling alongside an Austrian one, or one of Hungary's better, old-fashioned whites, and the link is plain. Compare Alsace with Burgundy, or, still more, Loire whites and it's hard to find a point of contact. Alsace spells fullness, a lip-smacking earthiness of taste, dryness. It lacks the acidity, the elegance of other good French whites.

This crisis of identity makes Alsace wines harder to sell than other French wines of the same quality. Good news for those prepared to try them: they'll

soon find a niche in your wine repertoire as splendid "food" wines, characterful enough to cope with powerful tastes (Alsace takes meal-times seriously). The Rieslings are the best, and the most subtle. Gewürztraminer is the ideal wine-bar bottle: everyone likes it and it goes with anything. But it is a little obvious in taste and it palls: I ration myself to about six bottles a year. Sylvaner and Pinot Blanc are lighter and "easier", Muscat heady and scented. Pinot Gris is hefty and robust.

It's hard to find bad Alsace wine – the growers are competent and the local rules strict – but some are better than others. Individual growers are less important than the merchant houses, most of which own vineyards as well as buy in grapes grown by other people. The merchants make various grades of wine: their "reserve personelle" or some such name denotes a serious bottle, "grand cru" wines come from a couple of dozen named vineyards, on the east-facing slopes of the Vosges mountains. Here, the sun ripens grapes consistently and well, leading, in very warm years, to sugar levels which in Germany would make Ausleses and the like. Alsace makes them too (*Vendage Tardive*) but the wines are not really sweet: strength and dryness still show.

Far left: *the little town of Husseren-les-Château typifies Alsace. The steep forested hills form a barrier against the west winds, the vineyards slope gently south and east to catch the sun. The three towers on the skyline are a reminder that Alsace was, and is, a frontier province.*

Above: *the wine villages are characterful places of old buildings and flowers.*

Left: *the tradition in Alsace is to store wine in very old casks, often with elaborately carved end panels.*

CHAMPAGNE

In Champagne they have two unique skills. They can make superb sparkling wine. And they can sell it. It is not cynicism to say that the marketing skills of the Champenois have been as crucial as their winemaking abilities in raising their local drink to its present status. No other wine name has built around itself such a wonderful aura of excellence. It is a name synonymous with celebration. It starts ships and marriages off down the slipway. It inaugurates, celebrates and commiserates everywhere money is made and spent.

Another weapon in Champagne's armoury is its ability to protect the famous name. Plenty of sparkling wine is made around the world, much of it by the champagne method. But only if the grapes are grown and the wine made in the Champagne district of northern France can it be "champagne". In Europe it is illegal to so label anything else. The New World is less impressed with the French claim to exclusivity, but even there "French champagne" is recognized as the real thing.

Despite their impressive business track record, the Champenois would not have got far without decent raw materials. The wine of their cool, windswept chalky hills and valleys is the real basis of champagne's quality, as other districts prove when they apply the same techniques to their own grapes. The major vines of Champagne are Chardonnay (as in white Burgundy) and Pinot Noir (as in red). The black Pinot grapes are pressed in such a way that they yield white wine — the red colour in any wine comes of course from the grape skins, not the juice. Both grape varieties tolerate the cold winters of the district, producing wines of distinction and backbone. It is possible to make sparkling wine with any grapes. It helps considerably to start with the best.

***Far left:** The big presses traditional in Champagne demand careful handling if they are not to over-crush the grapes, adding unwanted "stalkiness" to the taste of the wine. The same presses are used to extract the (white) juice from red grapes: then care is more vital still if the wine is to stay white, not tinted rosé by the skins. The presses have slatted sides to allow the juice to run out as the great disc descends under pressure. The men (**below**) are breaking up the pile of grapes in the press to prepare for a second pressing.*

***Left:** the monotonous but meticulous task of remuage; turning the bottles each day to shake the sediment into the neck. Remueurs are the highest-paid of the cellar workers: the technique takes years to master, but a skilled remueur can turn 100,000 bottles in a day.*

The great wines of the world are those made from a single year's output from a single property; the exception is champagne. Champagne is a blended wine, from different vineyards and usually from different vintages. In many places this would spell indifferent quality, but the champagne-makers use the variations of year and place to ensure consistent high standards.

The sparkle in champagne is a 17th century addition. A whole cycle of legends clusters around the discovery of the bubbles. Simply put, the wine is made in the normal way, but then encouraged to ferment a second time — in the (securely corked) bottle. This is done by adding a small amount of sugar, which is fermented by the yeasts in the wine. The products of the fermentation are carbon dioxide the bubbles – and a residue which has to be ejected from the bottle without losing the sparkle. Champagne is thus born upside down: the bottles are tilted downwards and gently turned each day to encourage the residue to settle in the neck, where it can be removed. The turning — called *remuage* — used to be done entirely by hand; the argument as to whether the increasingly-used machines are as skilled still rages.

Time has a crucial role in the taste of champagne. The second fermentation is slow, and the disgorging of the residual deposit must be followed by rest if the flavours are to develop as they should.

The wine from most years is blended with others for the non-vintage (NV) wines. After particularly good harvests — about one in four — the makers keep some of the crop aside to bottle as a single-vintage champagne. It is by definition the best of a good crop, so will taste richer and more "weighty" than NV champagne. Pink champagne, which comes in NV and vintage forms, traditionally is made in the same way as other rosé wines, though increasingly it is produced by adding some (local) red wine to straightforward white. Luxury champagnes — Dom Perignon is perhaps the best-known — are made from the top wines a firm has available.

Even with the latest automated techniques, the making of champagne is complicated and expensive in work and time. It can never be cheap. But, at its best, it is unsurpassed.

It is rare, but possible, to buy "single-vineyard" champagne, much as one buys a Grand Cru burgundy or a château's claret. One of the most expensive champagnes is made by the firm of Krug from a superb small vineyard they own. And many a small farmer today makes his own wine and sells it from the cellar door to Parisians who drive down at weekends. But since most champagne is blended, big concerns dominate the business. They alone have the cash to buy grapes from all round the district and to hold large stocks of wine for blending. About a dozen call themselves *Grandes Marques*, but there are perhaps 20 others big enough to operate in the same way. These concerns export champagne all around the world.

Many growers sell their grapes to the big houses, but quite a few belong to cooperatives which make the wine for them. These places — large, efficient and modern — are often the source of "own-brand" champagnes sold in supermarkets and restaurants.

Between the big houses and the individual growers in size are the several hundred small firms.

In good times, when harvests are large, the small houses and the individual producers can make interesting, good-value wine. But when times are hard, the "maisons" alone have the buying power to get the best grapes, the capital to blend and age their wines properly. And they can keep up the consistent quality that is the reason for the high price of champagne.

THE REST OF FRANCE

France has so many odd corners where wine is made that it is impossible to write about them all. A great thick book which has just landed on my desk contains notes on 5,000 of them, and it still misses some of my favourites. Finding out about French wines can be a lifetime's pursuit: I can think of few nicer lifetimes.

There are a couple of areas missing from the round-up so far which clamour to be included. They are the country wines of the South-West, and Cognac, where they make brandy, not wine, but where the grape is still the starting-point.

The South-West

The vine crops up in patches all the way from the mountains of the centre of France across to the Pyrenees. Names of hitherto obscure appellations like Bergerac, Cahors and Gaillac occur with increasing regularity on wine lists as buyers search them out as alternatives to the classic names. In such places the growers are frequently organized into cooperatives, which these days can afford the latest equipment and university-trained technicians. This spells good everyday wine, pleasant dry (and sometimes sweet) whites and a range of reds increasingly worthy of respect. The co-ops are not the only places where wine is made: as the reputations of these areas grow, small châteaux are gaining the confidence to make quality wine, as they used to do in centuries past.

As well as the three names above, look for the Côtes du Duras, the splendidly-named Côtes du Buzet, Jurançon, and Madiran, the last being especially known for good, solid reds.

Many of these South-West districts grow the familiar grapes of Bordeaux: the Cabernets and Sauvignon Blanc. Few have the keeping qualities of serious claret, but overall standards are high and the wines of this part of France offer a rewarding field for bargain-hunting.

Cognac

The other thing you can do with wine besides drink it is distil it. Brandy is made all over France (the South-West offers a fine example in Armagnac). The senior brandy of France, in most people's estimation, is Cognac. It is made in the Charente, the coastal province north of Bordeaux, where the wines are white, acidic and are nearly all distilled. Cognac, the town, is devoted to the production of Cognac, the brandy, and great warehouses full of barrels line the quiet streets of the place. The big companies, many of which seem for some reason to have been founded by Irishmen, buy up the wines of the Charente, distil them and age the spirit in wood. It's the casks which give it the characteristic colour: new cognac, like any spirit, is clear.

Like Scotch whisky with its single malts, Cognac has its connoisseurs' specials in the form of single-property brandies and especially old blends.

Cognac of a single vintage is, unaccountably, against the regulations these days. The most expensive blends of Cognac include brandies going back a hundred years. If you visit the great "houses" (they are very hospitable) they'll show you the *Paradis*—the locked cellar where the really old brandies are kept, stored in great glass demijohns.

Ordinary Cognac is a good, straightforward drink, but a fine blend of old Cognac is worthy of respect in the same way as a rare wine. It does not, however, age in bottle, only in wood.

***Far left:** the making, or rather the maturing, of Cognac is endlessly photogenic. The distilled wine is first put into oak casks for a minimum of three years, and, in fact, the brandy will age and improve in cask for up to 50 years or more. The cask pictured is well on its way, as the chalked date proclaims.*

***Left:** when the brandy is judged to be at its peak, it is transferred to wicker-bound glass jars. These very old cognacs are not sold on their own: each firm jealously keeps a supply to add to younger brandies in the making of their top blends. The oldest and most valuable Cognacs are stored behind locked gates in the "Paradis".*

(The makers take it out of barrels and put it into glass jars when it is mature enough.) So don't bother to lay it down unless you suspect, as I do, that the really fine Cognacs will become rare as demand for the everyday stuff increases.

Other French Wines

The far east, the Jura, makes wine, as does Savoie in the Alps. Both places provide good ordinary wines and some rarities worthy of the attention of the curious. These wines are perhaps something to store up for one's second decade or so of wine exploration, when the mainstream areas have begun to pall.

The future for French country wines seems to be a progression from obscurity to *Vin de Pays* status and then, if all goes well, promotion to full Appellation Controlleé. This organized system will bring wines at present obscure out into the open, so there's plenty of discovering to be done yet. Modern techniques are doing a great deal to make country wines worthy of comparison with their better-known neighbours.

It is notable too how the lesser appellations within the classic districts are improving. Côte du Rhône Villages and Croze Hermitage, the Haut Côtes in Burgundy, the Premières Côtes in Bordeaux; all have raised their standards as the top wines of the area have increased in price. The buyer has to be on the alert for these changes in status and not be hide-bound by the out-of-date lists of good wines presented in books and (still more, sadly) wine merchants' lists. There is more good wine in France than has yet come out of it.

ITALY

Italy is joyously awash with wine. It is a staple of daily life like bread, or olive oil, or politics. The Italians make more wine than any other country, and drink more of it per head than anyone else. Consequently it is treated with the amiable indifference granted to, say, the water supply or any other such basic commodity. We, to whom wine is something a little more special, take the opposite view. This contrast in the attitudes of seller and buyer comes out clearly when an export deal is done. The British, or the Americans, want to buy some wine? Sure. They want Chianti? Sure, they can have Chianti. The vats are tapped, the tankers filled, a few million Lire change hands. Enquiries about exactly where the wine comes from, or how (or when) it was made, or whether it is strictly entitled to be called what the label proclaims — all such quibbles are put down to strange foreign fastidiousness.

This worked well when all the outside world asked of Italy was a copious flow of cheap drink. The trouble is that we've woken up to the fact that Italy makes some very fine wine. A trickle has always been exported, but the vast majority of these splendid bottles have traditionally been drunk at home. Now the well-intentioned but hard-to-grasp Italian wine regulations are being scrutinized by people accustomed to French and German methods. It is becoming clear that the 400-odd officially defined quality wines include some very doubtful characters, and that not every grower in the wine zones is playing strictly by the rules. This is not to say that Italy is more fraud-ridden than anywhere else — just that the complexity, and unfamiliarity, of the wine scene there make the quirks more noticeable.

There are good Italian wines, and there are everyday Italian wines. There are even some good everyday wines. But the majority of bottles bearing familiar names are to be treated, sadly, with caution. Names like Soave, Orvieto, Chianti and Lambrusco have been devalued, having been applied to indifferent mass-produced drinks whose only claim to a local identity is being produced in a giant factory in or close to the named region. Individual estates, and some larger concerns, do produce good Soave or Valpolicella, but their efforts are undermined by the mass-marketeers. These big firms are merely responding to the world-wide demand for very cheap wine bearing familiar Italian names. Interestingly, much of this demand comes from the owners of Italian restaurants abroad, who should know that their homeland is capable of better things. But for them, as for most Italians, wine is a commodity . . .

For value and enjoyment in everyday wine, look beyond the known names. Try the unusual, trusting especially in wines from Italy's northeast: the

***Left:** a good harvest in Piedmont, and a chance to relax. The wooded hills of this northwestern region shelter some superbly-placed vineyards. The range of wines is wide, with rich solid reds and delicate sparkling whites.*

***Far left:** at the far end of Italy, the Apulian vineyards with their strange conical buildings have a Greek air. Wine has been made here since pre-Roman times. Today, most of the wine goes for blending, but there is a small and growing number of estates making good wines, including a notable rosé.*

Veneto, Friuli and Trentino provinces. Most of the these will carry a "DOC" tag on their label (or the full mouthful: *Denominazione di Origine Controllata*). This indicates that the wine meets local regulations: DOC is no guarantee of excellence, but these letters attached to a wine show it is well above the basic.

A little searching through the wine lists will soon unearth local specialities from all corners of the country: robust red Rosso Cònero from the Marches, silky-sweet Moscato from Sardinia, a whole range of light, lively red Barberas from Piedmont. There are hundreds of these wines, thousands if you count variations on local themes composed by determinedly individualistic producers. These wines are best approached through the study of regional styles — though Italian wine varies from valley to valley, never mind about the changes from the Alps to Sicily.

The hilly vineyards of the northwest, on the fringes of the plain on which stand Milan and Turin, make perhaps the best red wines (Barolo is the top name, one of Europe's classics) and some classy sparklers. If Italy's wine scene is a kaleidoscope, these vineyards of Piedmont are its most complex pattern. There are dozens of grapes and hundreds of named wines. The key red grape is Nebbiolo, the raw material of Barolo, Barbaresco and a score of lighter-weight wines. Most Nebbiolo wines benefit from ageing, though the Italian DOC rules see to it that they get quite a time in cask or bottle before being released for sale. Barolo certainly needs cellaring: ten years old is reckoned the right age. Other Piedmont reds vary in character from quaffable at 12 months to inpenetrable at 12 years. The various Barberas come round sooner than the Nebbiolo-based wines, but much depends on the maker's idea of what makes good red. As so often with Italy, a little research is essential for full enjoyment. If you take to the Italian style, buy the wines from a knowledgeable specialist — there are an increasing number around — and read up on the rules and regulations, the quirks and the people. It's an absorbing hobby . . .

After Piedmont, the rest of Italy seems a little simpler. East, in Lombardy, they make fine sparkling wines from Pinot Bianco grapes, good reds

from Nebbiolo (in the Alpine valley of Valtellina) and a range of everyday whites and reds. The northeast corner is the most bustling, go-ahead Italian wine zone, with mass incursions by foreign grapes like Merlot and Welch Riesling. The staples here are Soave and Valpolicella and Bardolino; as discussed above, they *can* be good, but the lesser-known names provide better value. Among these are Grave del Friuli, which comes in a range of colours and tastes; and Collio, the wines from the hills on the Yugoslav frontier. The white wines from these vineyards are especially good value (Pinot Blanc — or Bianco — and Tocai are the best grapes).

The northern valley of the Adige river, which forms the ancient route across the Brenner Pass to Austria, the North, has made a name for itself with its expert winemaking and attractive wines. The fame of the Alto Adige (or Südtirol as its German-speaking natives call it) perhaps owes as much to the relief felt by foreign wine merchants at finding there a degree of un-Italian orderliness. Grape names are the norm on labels, with familiar (to Northeners) varieties like Riesling, Gewürztraminer, Chardonnay. The white wines are, in a good year, characterful, crisp and easy to enjoy. The reds are more Italian and can be good, but only exceptional summers make wines to age.

Beware of the sweet reds made in quantity here for the German taste.

Central Italy is the home of Chianti in all its various guises. Chianti's image is damaged by its sheer diversity; the name applies equally to a soft, new café wine and a venerable, perfumed pensioner worthy of comparison with classed-growth claret. The confusion has been compounded by the new DOCG law; Chianti is now elevated to the top rank of Italian wines; not just *controlled* but *guaranteed* too. How anyone can authenticate such a vast and varied amount of wine is open to question. The Chianti growers have for many years responded to the official confusion by stressing their own, voluntary, codes of conduct. The more quality-conscious estates are grouped into *Consorzi* — Chianti Classico is the best-known, with its members' bottles branded with a black rooster.

This being Italy, there are excellent wines made outside the rules. It is almost a fashion in Tuscany to make a wine which *cannot* claim a DOC. Such wines use foreign grapes (Cabernet Sauvignon is the favourite) or are aged differently, often using small oak casks in the Bordeaux fashion. The best are very good indeed, and play a valuable rôle in showing Italy that there is much to learn from other traditions; if Italian wine law has one central fault it is the enshrinement of local habit (probably born solely of necessity in days gone by) as unalterable tradition. To confuse a lover of French or California wine, slip in an unannounced bottle of Sassi-

cai, or Tavernelle, or Sammarco, or Carmignano (this last a DOC, but one which allows a dash of Cabernet).

Chianti is not the only Tuscan red; Montalcino and Montepulciano, further south, make some splendid wines. There is white wine too in abundance, but nothing with a well-known name. For that, travel further south to the hinterland of Rome, whence comes Frascati, which can be better than its reputation (though most is ordinary if pleasant). For individuality it's best to look east to the Adriatic seaboard, where reds from the districts Cònero and Piceno, and from the grapes Sangiovese and Montepulciano, show promise.

Italy's south, and the islands of Sardinia and Sicily, are almost uncharted as far as serious wine goes. The good wines are there (and have been since Classical times), but little is exported. What does get abroad is a vast amount of pallid red and insipid white, bound for blending vats in France and Germany, and a growing quantity of "good ordinary" wine of the sort made under the Corvo name in Sicily. Among the unknowns are the sumptuous sweet Moscatos — well worth sampling.

It's too easy to make rude jokes about Italian wine. There is so much of it, and so many names, that hardly anyone, native or foreign, can encompass it all. As a field for personal study, no other wine country offers as many hidden delights once the bland and the brand-named bottles are shouldered aside.

Left: *at the heart of Italy's wine world is Tuscany. From these cypress-shaded vineyards near Siena comes Chianti, the most famous of Italian red wines.*

Far left: *the sub-Alpine vineyards of the Alto Adige are being hailed as some of Italy's most remarkable. The district is German-speaking and northern grape varieties such as Gewürztraminer and Rhine Riesling are successfully grown. The red grapes being harvested in the picture are destined for Kalterer See (in Italian: Lagi di Caldaro) wines.*

GERMANY

Making wine in Germany is such a tough proposition that one is tempted to conclude that no-one but the Germans would be stubborn enough to bother. A glance at a map of Europe shows that the German vineyards are a tier further north than even the most northern of those of France: only Champagne and Alsace are on the same latitude. The Loire, to a Frenchman a dangerously brisk and cold place, is on a line with the southernmost German vineyards, where the locals reckon the climate is virtually sub-tropical. Germany is further away from the sea than any other European wine area, with consequently colder winters. The landscape is one of forests and hills, with the vines appearing in sheltered patches.

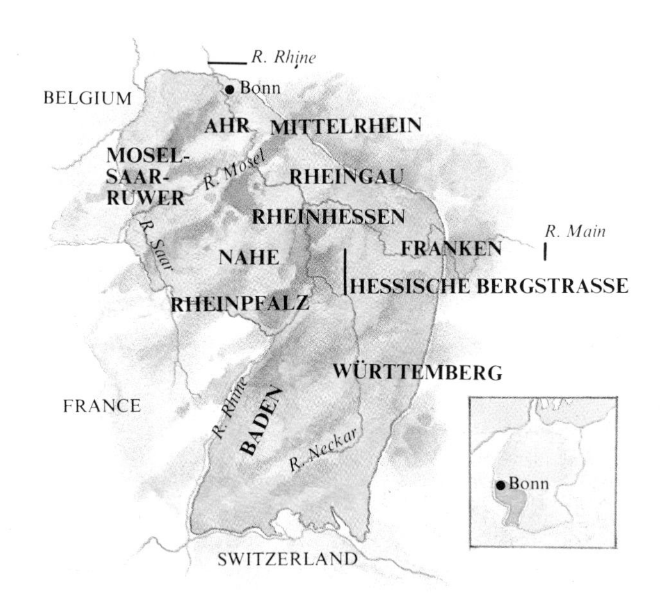

Below left: *most of Germany's best vineyards are on hillsides, there the drainage is best and the sun warmest. Traditionally, the slopes were split up into little terraces to conserve the soil.*

Left: *recently a government-sponsored scheme has carved the fragmented hillsides into orderly shelves and benches, as in the background of this picture. The growers' small scattered plots of land have been re-grouped into larger units and new roads and drainage put in. But the biggest gain of this massive landscaping programme is that tractors can now be used in the vineyards.*

Why *do* the Germans bother? Partly because of tradition: before the wine moved about freely (and pre-unification Germany had a customs post every few miles) you either grew it yourself, locally, or drank water. And partly because the results are so good. Due to the stressful climate and meagre soil, Germany's white wines can, at their best, be among the most sublime made anywhere. They avoid the blowsy blandness of wines made from vines that have an easy life.

German winemakers have a different set of priorities from their colleagues in France, or indeed anywhere else. In Germany, there is no tradition of dry wines. Some are made today, in a rather self-conscious attempt to match the French. But the almost instinctive aim of a German winemaker is sweetness. He hopes for a warm summer, and above all a warm autumn, so that the grapes go on ripening for month after month, building up the natural sugar within them. He picks as late in the year as he dares, then makes his wine in such a way as to preserve that natural sweetness.

This quest for sweetness can result in some superbly balanced wines, for the classic Riesling grape (and some others) also contributes refreshing acidity to the final taste. The tension between sweet and sour, allied to the intensity of flavour which the Germans coax from their stony fields, is absorbing and unique.

That, however, is true of the best of German wine, and only the best. Germany's winemakers have two key skills. They can conjure beauty out of their stubborn combination of soils, latitudes and climates. And they can produce, and market at a low price, blended wines which find favour worldwide. This latter skill owes as much to the chemist and the market researcher as it does to the winemaker. Faced with implacable conditions, the Germans have learnt how to control fermentation, how to "back-blend" with sweet concentrated grape juice to add weight to thin wines, how to pitch the resulting taste to the palate of Britain, Scandinavia and America.

Thus German wine has a schizophrenic character. There are the wonderful bottles of fine wine. And there are the tanker-loads of Liebfraumilch and other basic blends.

It's necessary to recognize the split personality in order to understand and enjoy German wine. Both sorts are valuable additions to our range of choices. The ordinary wines are, when representative, pleasantly medium-sweet, low in alcohol and fruity. They appeal to most tastes and offend no-one (except the occasional wine snob). The quality wines are subtle, complicated, intense: a pleasure both sensual and cerebral, drinks for contemplative moments. The problem is to sort out which is which.

I called the second group "quality" wines, which is clear enough English, but it doesn't help. I have beside me a report from Germany on the latest harvest. It was a good one: 99 per cent of the wine will be of Quality status. That's right – 99 per cent. It's rare for the Quality wine to be less than 90 per cent of all wine made.

What does this Alice in Wonderland statistic mean? Are the Germans so good at winemaking that nine bottles in ten are "good"? Or have they set the Quality rules to make it appear so? The cynical might be forgiven for thinking so. The key to all this is buried in the small print of the wine laws. There are two kinds of "quality" wine in Germany: QbA and QmP (see p 174 for their full names). The latter is the real thing. It has to be *naturally* sweet: its sugar coming from sunshine and grapes. QbA wine can be sweetened with *Süssreserve:* sweet grape juice. QmP wines, the top ones, are further divided into grades according to the level of sugar their grapes produced.

Before I get banned from Germany forever I must stress that there's nothing wrong with (most) QbA wine. The trouble is that ignorant foreigners, unversed in the subtleties of the most complicated wine laws in the world, keep on missing the point. Think of QmP wine as the serious stuff, and QbA as the everyday, and you won't go far wrong (I find it helps to see the "A" in QbA as standing for "Average").

That's enough legalities. What

different kinds of German wines are there? The first point is that all the worthwhile stuff is white. There are red wines made, but it is hard to see why: being so far north, the grapes struggle to ripen and the wines are light in colour and taste.

Germany's vineyards are grouped in 11 regions, and within the regions there are *Bereichs,* broad sub-regions; *Grosslages,* smaller regions; and finally, the smallest unit, individual vineyards or *Einzellages.* It's up to the grower whether to sell his wine under a label bearing the name of its vineyard of origin, or one of the larger units. It depends, often, on what the customer is most likely to have heard of. This (after the quality wine conundrum) is the second big trap for the buyer. There's no way of knowing, short of looking it up, whether the name on the label represents a little vineyard or a great swathe of countryside. The best wines come from the individual sites, corners of hillside where the sun shines longest and the drainage is best. Grosslage wines will nearly always be less fine.

This stress on vineyards is most crucial in the northernmost region, the Mosel (or Moselle in the English spelling). A Mosel wine made from Riesling grapes is potentially among Germany's best: taut, balanced and full of fruit and flavour. Here, and in the side-valleys of the Saar and Ruwer, about one year in every two is too cold and cloudy for much QmP wine to be made. The locals make their living from the oceans of Bereich Bernkastel and similar wines they turn out: QbA wine which, from a good producer, can be pleasantly fresh and balanced but from a lesser source can be mere sugar-and-water. The Moselle's fame as a great wine river rests on the QmP wines from villages like Wehlen, Graach and Bernkastel itself (as opposed to the Bereich which has borrowed its name).

The Rhine vineyards stretch from the far north, near the Ruhr, south to Switzerland. The Rheingau, a south-facing sheltered slope, makes the best wines: rich, more solid than Moselles, and long-lived. Liebfraumilch, the great export success that the locals never drink, comes from the Rhine vineyards. It is defined as QbA wine from certain

grapes and from one of three Rhine districts. As with all everyday German wine, its virtues stem from the producer: there is, sadly, more indifferent stuff about than good.

Further south, the Rheinhessen and Rheinpfalz villages make some interesting wines with a more sturdy, earthy character than those from the Rheingau or Moselle. Here, other grape varieties jostle with Riesling in the top vineyards. The best wines are flavoursome and complex.

The southernmost Rhine vineyards, in the state of Baden, produce Germany's strongest, driest wines. They are promoted by the locals as being the best German bottles to open at mealtimes, and they are quite right: Baden wines have a depth of flavour that goes well with food.

Further east, hidden amid the endless forests, are the Franken (Franconia) vineyards. They use here a distinctive squat bottle, and they make dryish characterful wines whenever the harsh winter weather lets them. Franken wines are rare outside Germany, but worth a trial when they do appear.

The wines of Germany can provide much pleasure. Once the legal puzzles are solved, there are thousands of variations to sample: different estates, nearly 3,000 named vineyards, subtle

Far left: *the majestic sweeping curves of the Mosel, a river lined with vineyards. The best sites are those on the steepest slopes, such as those on the extreme right of the picture. Here, Reisling grapes are grown for QmP wine. Müller-Thurgau grapes are more typically grown on the flat and gently-sloping vineyards with the aim of making straightforward QbAs.*
Left and below: *the winelands of Germany are charming places to visit, with plenty of opportunities to sample the local produce.*

grades of intensity and sweetness. These can be brought to mind by looking at the length of the name: Kabinett is the driest, Trockenbeerenauslese the sweetest and most complex, with Spätlese, Auslese and Beerenauslese in between. (For definitions, see page 174.)

It is remarkable how cheap these quality wines are compared to their equivalents from elsewhere. Enjoy them before everyone finds out – but bear in mind the intentions of their perfectionist makers and drink them on their own, not with food.

THE AMERICAS

It's an oft-told tale, but still poignant; how the first settlers in Virginia found luscious grapes growing wild, but when they came to make wine from their bounty they found it virtually undrinkable; and how when they brought vines from Europe, they all withered and died.

The East Coast environment — and indeed that of much of North America — is hostile to the classic vine-plant of the Old World. Harsh winters, humid summers and indigenous pests give it no chance. Today, helped by science, some growers are finding climatic corners where the European vines can survive. But nearly all wine made east of the Rockies is from a different kind of vine, a native sort — the one the first Virginians were deluded by.

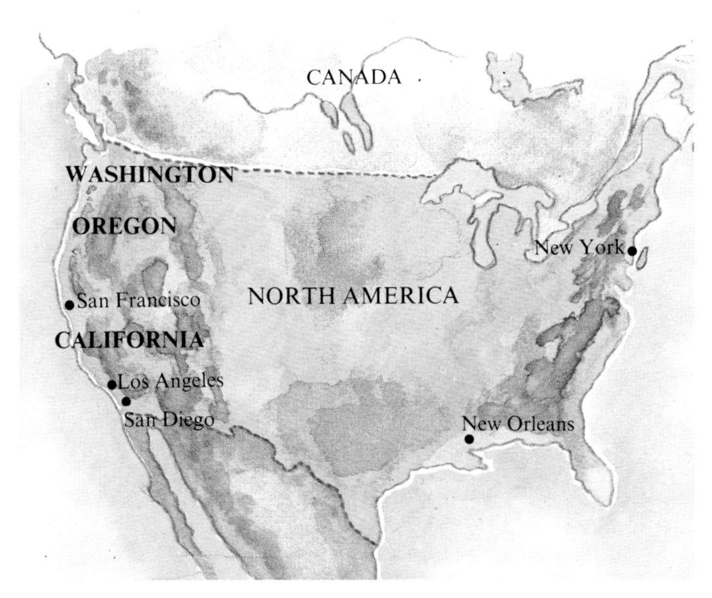

The wine made from the grapes of this native vine tastes distinctly different from "normal" wine, and its consumption is very much a local habit. Some hybrid vines have been bred which combine American hardiness with an element of European taste, but even their fruit does not compare with that of the classic Old World vine.

Over on the West Coast, nature is more benign. The first Spanish missionaries, pushing up from Mexico in the eighteenth century, found that vine cuttings thrived around their missions. And these vines were the European sort, brought by the Church from Spain to make wine for the Sacrament. Today, the West Coast is by far the biggest provider of wine in North America. California wine and increasingly that of Washington and Oregon (these two tend to get called "the Pacific Northwest") is of world class. The West is in many ways the frontier of wine, the place where new ideas are being tried, where old traditions are being examined and tested.

California wine is mostly drunk in the USA, where the wine drinking habit has been growing fast. Little is exported, partly because there is little to spare and partly because fluctuating currency exchange rates have made it seem expensive in Europe. But enough wine gets out, and enough ideas, comments and controversies too, to shake up the Old World of wine. If anything has driven winemakers in the

***Far left**: picking grapes by hand is a declining trade in California as the giant harvesting machines make their inroads.*

***Left** many vineyards are on the valley floors, flat and open, making the use of machines possible. In the constant search for yet higher quality, some growers are planting vines on the rocky hill slopes that bound the fertile valleys. These hill vineyards avoid much of the danger of late frosts, which can be a problem for valley-floor growers in some of the northern California vineyards.*

***Below**: for most growers the problem is over-abundance rather than a shortfall: vineyards like those in the Central Valley are prolific and predictable in their crops. With more and more vines being planted, some farmers have to search hard for a market for their grapes.*

classic French regions to re-examine their approach, it is California. The Americans began with unashamed imitation of the European styles. Very quickly they were turning out wines that could stand comparison with their models. Now they are making, in some cases, better ones. The imitations are also giving way to self-confident native styles of wine, true Californians rather than West Coast "claret" or "Chablis".

In California, the constant debate about the factors that make a wine's personality has taken a novel turn. Free from Europe's sometimes shackling traditions, and with no official regulations to speak of, winemakers are able to try any trick they like. There is nothing to stop them growing what grapes they want to, where they want to. They can make their wine in any way that science, or their imagination, or their bank account, allows. This has led to some bizarre goings-on: "port" made from Cabernet, red Zinfandel grapes turned into wines that range from black and sweet to dry and white, Chardonnays as strong as a sherry.

All the experimentation has yet to settle down into an accepted recipe for California's classics. It is accepted, though, that people make as much difference as nature to the taste of a wine. Fans follow the movements of fashionable winemakers from property to property, and just as a star player can revive the fortunes of a football team, so the West Coast's top technicians seem to be able to transport wine success. The style of the maker transmits itself to the style of the wine. This is aided by the California habit of separating grape growing and wine making. Some estates work on the classic European principle of a winery surrounded by its vines. But the majority of wineries buy their grapes, often from several hundred miles away. This allows the farmers to concentrate on growing the best fruit, and the winemakers to pick and choose between many suppliers of raw material.

The dominance of the human factor is not quite complete. Recently, there has been more recognition that soil and site make a difference to the quality of the grapes. It has long been recognized that some grapes grow best in cool spots while others need warm ones. The state's vineyards were divided up into zones by University of California scientists, and a list of suggested grape varieties for each zone was issued. But being California, that proved just a starting-point for experiment. Exceptions and anomalies abound in the complicated mix of weather and topography there. The next generation of winemakers — and drinkers — will probably have enough data to work out the best spots to grow different grapes and make different wines. For us, it is a question of try it and see.

California's great gift to America is very good everyday wine. The quality of the "jug" wines (as opposed to the artificial "pop" concoctions, coolers and so on) is very high. An ideal climate and clever technicians allow the making of tasty, fruity, enjoyable wines at a predictable rate and at cheap prices. The West Coast's gift to the world is an ever-growing range of interesting wines, both of bottles to try out against European classics and also some that are unlike anything else.

The best of these, so far, are the red Cabernet Sauvignon wines. The Napa Valley was the first area to emerge as a classic wine zone, in part because it is close to San Francisco with its large and discriminating population. Napa Cabernets came forward in the 1970s to challenge the best that Bordeaux could make. And in blind tasting after blind tasting, they came out on top. This is in part due to the abundant freshness and vigour which California soil and sun confer on the fruit that grows there, and thus on the wine. But the main factor was human skill, closely followed by ideal conditions. California Cabernet, today from a dozen other areas as well as the Napa, is an international star, and deservedly so.

Having got the measure of Cabernet, West Coast fashion turned to Chardonnay. The race was on to make the nearest thing to a great white Burgundy. The success rate was perhaps lower than with Cabernet, but what emerged was a new kind of white wine: the rich, powerful (sometimes overpowering) California Chardonnay. The best winemakers are now adding subtlety to muscle to make some very fine white wines indeed.

Just about every grape that is grown has been tried in California, most with success. Pinot Noir is proving hard to master, showing just what a subtle balance of factors is at work in Burgundy — and also how fickle this grape is. Riesling, Sauvignon, Gewürztraminer — all have been triumphant.

Any account of California soon starts to sound like a vine-nursery catalogue. The stress on "varietals" — wine made from one variety of grape — has been almost total. There is now, however, a welcome trend towards blending the juice of different grapes, in

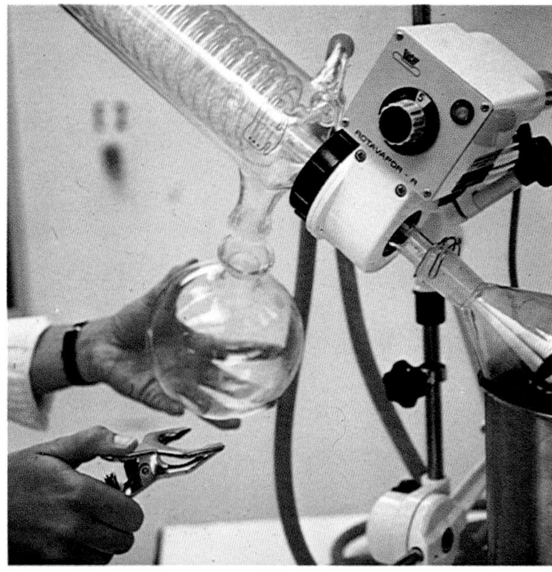

Far left*: in the Americas, technology is the keynote. Irrigation, tapping underground water supplies via pumps and storage towers, is one way to control the growth of the vines. Note also the sheer size of the vineyard and the straight, wide-set rows of vines: they're planted with mechanization in mind. Outdoor stainless steel vats are kept cool by a constant spray of water, allowing the winemaker to adjust the fermentation temperature to suit the wine he or she has "designed". At last, the variables are under man's control.*

Left*: laboratory research is another weapon in the winemaker's armoury.*

the European manner. Silkier, more perfumed red wines are emerging from blends of Cabernet and Merlot and/or other red grapes. A leading light in this trend is the Opus One partnership (see page 132). If anything has signalled that California must be taken seriously, it is this Franco-American venture.

North of California, up towards Canada, conditions are cooler — less Mediterranean, more French. Recently, fine wines have started to emerge from the valleys of Oregon and Washington. Keen young winemakers have managed minor miracles with Pinot Noir, outclassing California with the aid of the more moderate climate. White wines such as Rieslings are especially good. The Northwest's wines are complementary to California's: lighter, cooler and more relaxed. Lucky America, to have such a choice.

The enthusiasm for wine in the USA has prompted plantings of vines in places as far apart as Texas and Rhode Island. Many have done well, from a technical point of view, but there is some doubt who is going to drink all the wine when the frenzy subsides. Looking from the outside in, there is no world-class wine apart from the produce of the West Coast, though the local markets around these new vineyards will be well served. These other American areas stand rather in the position of the English vineyards: a source of pride and patriotic drinking to the locals, of no more than academic interest to the outside world.

Canada, too, makes wine, in British Columbia and in Ontario, where the lakeside climate provides a warm pocket in the middle of the continent. Good bottles are produced, but quantities are small, so the Canadians drink it all themselves.

Mexico boasts the oldest winery in the New World, with a 400-year history. Good wines (and some indifferent ones) are made in the high, cool interior of the country. They, like the wines made by the large-scale industry of Brazil, are of purely local interest.

Two South American countries have wines which the world has to take note of. They are Argentina and Chile. In both cases, unstable currencies and political upheavals have sapped the potential of their wine industries. Every time a good Chilean Cabernet is opened in London or New York, people ask why is there not more of it? The answer is that the big buyers of the wine trade have had their fingers burnt too often in South America. The buyers want safety and continuity. If a wine goes well, they want to be able to buy the next vintage at a comparable quality and a not dissimilar price. With Chile and Argentina over the last few years, that has been too much to ask.

When and if things settle down, the world will seize eagerly on the deep, rich red wines of Chile, and the varied but often excellent produce of Argentina. The vineyards are on either side of the Andes, irrigated by water from the mountains. So isolated are those of Chile that many of the vines are ungrafted — phylloxera, the 19th century vine disease, never got that far. These ungrafted vines are said to give a richer, better wine than others.

When Chilean or Argentine wine does appear on the shop shelves, it is well worth a try. The Chilean Cabernets are softer and less structured than most Northern Hemisphere wines, and should not be kept too long despite their inky colour. Argentina produces many good everyday blended wines, some of which can give European staples a shock with their robust fruit and hearty, cheerful taste.

AUSTRALIA AND NEW ZEALAND

It is technology which has rushed Australia to the forefront of the wine world. Wine has been made there since the first settlers two centuries ago, but the climate it too hot for really good wine to be made without the help that modern techniques can give: control of fermentation temperature is especially important. The mastery of temperature and the successful search for cooler microclimates have given Australian growers the chance to excel.

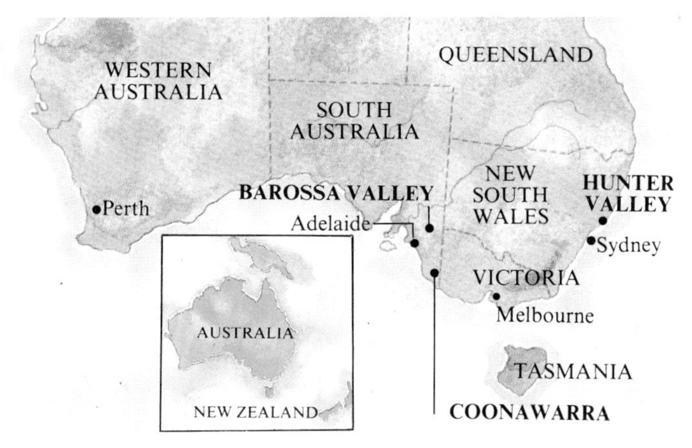

The keen domestic market, however, gives the Australians their biggest advantage. South Africa, Chile, Spain all have similar environmental conditions. But none of them (Spain is getting there) have a critical, enthusiastic, prosperous public for their wines. The nearest parallel is with California.

Australia is enormous, yet its population is small. Geographically, its grape growers and wine makers have only just started to scratch the surface. The search is on for high (and thus cool) ground, favourable soils, the right grape for each area and each site, and all the natural quirks and human manipulations that can make a great vineyard. And underpinning this search for excellence is a thriving business in everyday wine of a very good standard. Australians have taken to wine as an everyday drink: every home — well practically — has its "wine cask" in the icebox.

It used to be that very little good Australian wine reached the rest of the world. Production was too small, and exporters had got used to the protected market of the British Isles, where "empire" fortified wines were a staple. However, British tastes changed with her entry into the European Common Market, and this market died away. It was only slowly that the unfortified wines of Australia trickled out onto the world markets. Often, there was not enough of the best wines to satisfy the thirsty locals. Now winemakers are realising that export success fuels domestic demand; there's a certain understandable wish for overseas accolades to convince Australians that their own wine is world-class.

Today, Australia is lucky enough to have a whole range of wines, in just about every style. How relevant are these wines to the pampered palates of Europe or North America? They have been promoted as curiosities, but have survived to gain a status of their own. Major advances in techniques have meant that there is far more good wine about, certainly enough to make exporting a commercial, rather than just a patriotic, proposition. Australia's wines are a new and major force in the world's wine marketplace.

The geography of Australian wine is confusing, with relatively small vineyard areas dotted all across the south-eastern bulge of the country, with some more in the far southwest. Local enthusiasts delight in distinguishing regional characteristics, but for the foreign buyer it is perhaps more relevant to think in styles rather than places.

Red wines were the first to make a mark, partly because red wine making is less temperature-sensitive than white. The Shiraz (local name for Syrah) proved as at home in Australia's heat as beside its native Rhône. Shiraz or Hermitage reds are usually solid, dark and tasty, needing bottle-age to mellow and merge their strapping flavours into subtlety. Cabernet Sauvignon is the other big red grape. It is often blended with Shiraz, or increasingly with Merlot and Malbec, and is also served up true to international fashion as a "100% varietal". Australian Cabernet is perhaps a decade behind California in sophistication, but it is coming on fast, and can offer increasing complexity and

Left: *modernity and expansion are the keynotes in Australia. The new style of winery may not have the romance of an old-world château but it does have grandeur. The open-air vats in stainless steel are cooled by pouring a stream of water down their sides. The horizontal press on the left of the picture is the favourite pattern today. It is gentler on the grapes than the old vertical models. The whole set-up is floodlit to allow night working. This means that the harvesting machines can work at full capacity, bringing in the grapes exactly when they are ripe. Night harvesting also means the grapes are cooler when picked.*

Above: *Australia's vineyard area is expanding. New vine rootstocks are being planted in typical red soil.*

charm as new vineyards in well-chosen spots grow to maturity.

Pinot Noir, the grape of red burgundy, finds its best Australian conditions in the far west, where the Margaret River and Mount Barker vineyards are barely a decade old. There are experiments with this contrary grape in Tasmania, too, but Australian Pinot Noir seems likely to stay but a curiosity for a while yet.

Australia has a strong tradition of fortified wines in the style of port and sherry. To these it has added a unique dessert wine in the liqueur Muscats of the state of Victoria. These splendidly sticky, chocolate-brown drinks mingle richness and length of taste — they are unlike anything else the wine world can produce. Australian port- and sherry-type wines have less to offer drinkers with easy access to the real things, but they are honest drinks and good value locally.

White wines have burgeoned in quality and variety since cold fermentation became the norm. Semillon, used in Bordeaux to make sweet Sauternes, makes wines of all styles in Australia, where it is confusingly called "Riesling" in some places. The chance to sample an Australian Semillon should not be missed; the better ones age in bottle, developing dry yet rich flavours which the winemakers of the grape's homeland would never have guessed at. "Real" Riesling, usually labelled Rhine Riesling, does well, but makes fatter, softer wines than in Germany. Again, cold fermentation has recently made possible more acidic, brisker styles of Riesling. It is one of the styles of wine benefitting most from the search for cooler vineyards.

Chardonnay is the most fashionable white wine grape, and, to the surprise of the outside world, a most successful one in the warm Australian conditions. Chardonnay wines made in places most unlike Burgundy have been compared to good effect with their distant cousins from Meursault and Mâcon. Good Australian Chardonnay usually has some oak cask ageing, and the combination of richly ripe fruit and oak-induced austerity can be most enjoyable; a fat, round, yet fascinating wine.

These are the main styles, yet such is the confidence and keenness of Australia's wine industry that it is a certain bet that more, perhaps novel, styles will emerge. For outsiders, the real value is in the middle-priced wines. The mass-market everyday produce is very good, but cannot be shipped around the world to Europe at a price that can match French or German equivalents. The really fine wines are made in very small amounts and will always attract just the connoisseurs. It is the good, rather than great, which is the really top-class value. Mature Hunter Valley Shiraz and Chardonnay, Western Australian Cabernet, Victoria Muscat and Semillon — all these can compete with European and Californian classics.

Above: *the showplace Leeuwin Estate winery in Western Australia is an example of the self-confident expansion of this state's vineyards. Leeuwin, whose Chardonnay and other wines have been well-received world-wide, is in the Margaret River area, south of Perth. The fact that Robert Mondavi of the Napa Valley in California has been involved with the development of the estate is a reminder that the "New World" wine countries have much in common.*

New Zealand

If anywhere is going to make the Southern Hemisphere's claret, it will be New Zealand. She stands a good chance of making the South's equivalent of white Loire and Burgundy too.

New Zealand is further south than Australia, and thus cooler. The climate is also moderated by the vast expanses of ocean in which the two lonely islands sit. Even so, it has taken the technical revolution of the last two decades to really get New Zealand's wine industry going. A small and traditionally-minded population did not help — winemaking was for many years a peasant pursuit carried on only by settlers and their descendants from Mediterranean wine-drinking countries. (New Zealanders of British descent drank tea.) Then wine caught on with a more outward-looking generation of New Zealanders, and it was belatedly realised that the country is purpose-built as a quality wine region. Mountain ranges and sea coasts provide a variety of suitable sites, and the climate avoids extremes. Progress has been rapid: both wine production and wine consumption have leapt ahead since 1970.

The rest of the world has discovered in New Zealand a source of well-made white wines, and is beginning to recognize the country as a useful supplier of good, subtle red ones. As in Australia, the details of geography matter little to the foreign drinker. What is attractive is the steady flow of good-value Rieslings, Sauvignons and Chardonnays. These white wines are especially useful in those years when France and Germany suffer poor harvests and the European wine-lover is casting around for alternatives in the medium price bracket. This is not to say that New Zealand wines are not in themselves excellent: the standard is high for such a new industry. But the quantities are small and will probably remain so.

New Zealand has yet to develop its own styles of wine — the reborn industry is too new to expect that. In time, the best sites will be discovered and individual styles will start to emerge. It is already clear that red wines, especially Cabernet Sauvignon, can age in a positively French fashion.

This affinity with France will influence the wines still more once the present love affair with German-style whites wears off. This Germanic emphasis is a testimony to the influence of the wine educators of Geisenheim on the Rhine, who trained many of the New World's winemakers. But New Zealand is not as cold as the Rheingau — its climate is more akin to southwest France or Portugal.

New Zealand wines will bear watching over the next ten years. With the high standards of education and equipment, it will be hard to find a bad one.

Above*: inside the Montana winery in New Zealand. This large-scale operation pioneered the development of the South Island's vineyards. Montana makes a range of wines including a much-praised Cabernet Sauvignon.*

Left*: the Margaret River vineyards are well-placed with a cool climate and are set amid attractive countryside.*

SPAIN AND PORTUGAL

Spanish wine took 20 years to recover from its first foray into the international mass market. In the 1950s and 1960s, the cheapest bottles in every wine-store in Northern Europe were labelled "Spanish Sauternes" or "Spanish Chablis". The borrowed French names were supposed to lend respectability to a factory-made concoction. The French soon saw to it that this name-borrowing was made illegal, and as winedrinkers increasingly looked for quality as well as cheapness — and started to find it — Spanish wine fell from favour.

All the time the tanker-loads of sweet white and rotgut red were trundling across the Pyrenees, the Spanish were also making excellent wines. The trouble was that few non-Spaniards had ever heard of them.

Rioja, Sherry, Malaga and half a dozen more have traditions as old and proud as any in Europe. Travellers returning from Madrid told of hotel winelists packed with superb silky vintage Riojas. Just as the mass market turned sour, the fame of Rioja began to spread. Spain today sells less bulk wine than it did, but more bottled wine.

Sherry, of course, was always the mainstay of Spain's trade in wine, and even today is the Spanish wine most people have drunk. It is made in the deep south, in hot dusty country west of Cadiz, around the town of Jerez (hence "sherry"). Sherry is an undervalued drink. Everybody who takes the trouble to taste the stuff has been saying so for years, but sales of sherry in northern Europe have obstinately declined (a good lesson for wine pundits who think people take note of their pronouncements). At last there is sign of a change. Sherry's fortunes have been determined by social changes as much as value or taste; it is a drink associated with old ladies; with people who "don't drink, but I'll have a small sweet sherry". Quite a few winelovers didn't consider sherry a wine at all.

Sherry comes in such a range of styles and qualities that it is a study on its own. To find the interesting ones, pay about twice the price of the cheapest bottle around. This sacrifice unlocks the doors of some of the most venerable cellars in Jerez. With no other wine can you sample the very best for such a small premium.

The great virtue of sherry is consistency. Like champagne, it is made rather than grown; man's hand is the major influencing factor. All sherry is a blend, the product of a process of ageing called the solera system. The wine of each vintage is stored in casks or butts. Wine for bottling is drawn from the butt holding the oldest sherry. Only about a third of each butt is used, the rest remaining and being topped up with sherry from the next-oldest cask, and so on. The older the solera, or collection of casks, gets, the older the average age of the wine in it. There are no vintage-dated sherries, but the starting date of the solera is sometimes printed on labels. Wine from a solera started in 1900 (and many are older) will contain traces of wine from that vintage and every harvest since. This process establishes and keeps up a distinct taste; the new wine added to a solera is as close in character as possible to the sherry already in residence.

Thus the continuity of sherry; at the final blending before bottling the cellarmaster knows exactly what tastes he has to choose from. It is a sure and certain thing that one bottle of a given brand of sherry will be the same in taste and style as a bottle bought the previous year. This applies of course to the established producers and to the wines above the basic price; really cheap sherry will be a blend of whatever batches of wine could be bought at the time, and will be neither consistent nor especially appetizing.

There are other factors at work in Jerez besides the solera system. The soil, a mixture of clay and chalk in the best vineyards, adds interest to the wine by retaining moisture and allowing a slow ripening of the grapes, while the baking hot southern sun builds up sugar levels. Then comes the winemaking technique, which is ordinary in most respects apart from the use of a naturally-occurring yeast, called *flor*, which forms on the surface of the wine, protecting it from oxidation while it is maturing. It is the presence or absence of flor which decides the style of sherry each butt will contain; if it is there, the air is kept out and pale fino results, without flor a darker, more oxidized oloroso sherry will be made.

Sherry comes in styles from water-white and bone-dry through to black and stickily sweet. The drier ones make fine aperitifs and can be drunk with food – they go well with smoked fish. The sweeter sherries, especially the high-quality ones, are after-dinner drinks or perfect refreshment for odd times like mid-morning. Fino is the driest style, with oloroso the sweetest. These are the terms used in Jerez, but the wine trade has devised other names for styles of wine between very dry and very sweet. Amontillado, for instance, means a medium sherry to the consumer (and his wine merchant) but a specially aged fino in Jerez. A Jerez

Amontillado is a dry wine, but darker and more substantial in taste than the delicate fino. Cream sherries are another kind invented by the importers rather than the makers; the dark ones are olorosos further sweetened, the pale cream ones fino sherry sweetened with fortified wine. All sherry is fortified – that is, brandy or some such spirit is added to strengthen and stabilize it. More is added to export consignments, which explains why fino sherry tastes even more delicate and delicious in its homeland.

Sherry is the best, but not the only, fortified wine of southern Spain. Malaga has an equally long pedigree, and makes very good sweet wines like a more luscious sweet sherry. Montilla's wines are unfortified, but otherwise

Inside a sherry bodega, where the maturing wine rests in casks under a high, cool roof, the cellar-master uses chalk marks to comment on the contents of the barrels. The elaborate arrows on the end casks show that the casks to the left belong to the same criadera, or "nursery" for young wine.

very like a softer version of sherry.

Sherry apart, the great wine of Spain is Rioja. It is made in the high, cool northern valley of the Ebro, not far from the French frontier and close enough to the Atlantic for wet west winds to be a dominant factor in the weather. Rioja makes great red wines and very good white and rosé ones. The reds are produced in a range of styles from unaged (*sin crianza*) to vintage, *reservas* and *gran reservas*.

All the better wines must be aged in oak casks. These are the same size and shape as those of Bordeaux, one of the many similarities between the two regions. Some Riojas spend too long in oak for foreign tastes, losing colour and acquiring an austere vanilla flavour. The best wines, from good vintages, have enough fruit and body to stand oak ageing and to survive with character unblemished. Such wines are very fine value for money.

White Rioja comes in one of two styles; old or new. The tradition is to age the whites in oak until they gain a strong yellow colour and a vigorous solid taste. Such wines are still made, but increasingly white Rioja is made by cold fermentation and stored in steel tanks rather than oak casks. The result is a fresher, more subtle wine, more appealing to modern taste. New-style white Rioja may be more obviously enjoyable, but the virtues of the old stuff — vigour, ageing potential, sheer depth of taste — should not be forgotten. Rosé Rioja can be very good, too; dry, fruity and deep.

Rioja is made by large firms with big, well-equipped bodegas (wineries). Therefore it, like sherry, is of consistent standard. All Rioja (except suspiciously cheap ones) is reliable, but the mass of good wine sometimes hides the few great bottles: I have had Riojas 50 years old which are a match for any claret.

The rest of Spain has pockets of interesting wine, of which the biggest is Pénedes in Catalonia, in the northeast. Here good wines of many styles are made — look out especially for the *cava* sparklers — soft, dry, the best ones with delicious fruit. Good red wines are made in Catalonia too and there are new plantings of Cabernet Sauvignon and other classic French vines here, introduced by some of Spain's most go-ahead growers.

The remainder of the country's enormous wine production is divided between oceans of anonymous, over-strong stuff used for blending or café drinking and a small amount of quality wine made according to scattered local traditions. As Spain enters the European Community, it is likely that her winemakers will look more towards exports, and some of these local characters may find their way abroad.

Portugal is another new recruit to the EEC. Like Spain, her table wines have been overshadowed by a fortified wine — port. However Portugal has made a success of Vinho Verde, the fresh young white wine of its northern province, which exactly suits the palates of the growing wine publics of Britain and America. It also has good supplies of mature red wines from Dão and other regions — wines which sell at very reasonable prices considering their maturity. But it is rosé for which Portugal is best-known, paradoxically enough. One firm invented the style of slightly sweet, slightly fizzy Portuguese Rosé and it swept the world. There are signs that the fashion is waning, which may mean more attention for the traditional table wines, which are various and often good. Bairrada, for instance, makes red wines, which can improve in bottle for decades, and aromatic white. Setúbal makes sweet Muscat, Bucelas makes a good dry white.

Dão is, however, the best-known and the biggest table-wine region. Its products are sympathetic to bottle-age, though the red wines can be over-oaky and dried-out, suffering the same fate as some Riojas. The whites can be good too, with a solid, earthy taste about them that goes well with food.

A word to look out for on Portuguese labels is *garrafeira*, which means the wine is a merchant's specially chosen selection — by implication good stuff. It usually is, too.

Vinho Verde — the name means green wine, in the sense that green means young — comes in red or white forms. Nearly all that's exported is white, and having once tasted the red I can see why. It was a dramatic colour, more like a lipstick shade than something one expects to find in a glass. The taste combined agressive fruit-juice sweetness with searing acidity. The white vinho verde is naturally very dry, though most of the wines bottled for export are slightly sweetened, which detracts from their charm. They are, or should be, very fresh, acidic and slightly pétillant or fizzy.

Portugal has been selling port for many generations, although the fizzy pink wine now brings in more cash. Port is a fortified wine, made from the red grapes of the oven-hot and dramatically steep Douro Valley. They make the wine by allowing the fermentation to go ahead as normal until it is not quite complete. Then brandy is added, which kills the yeast and stops the fermentation with some of the grape sugar left intact. This is what makes port sweet. The brandy must have time to marry with the wine, and the harsh red wine also needs a few years to soften, so all port is at least two years old before it is bottled. The better ones are kept for longer. Aged by the makers in wooden

Left: modern terracing is bringing new land into production in the Douro Valley, birthplace of port. These elaborate new vineyards belong to Quinta do Noval, one of the most famous port shippers. The shippers both own farms, or quintas, in the valley and store and blend the wine at their lodges in Oporto and its suburbs. The land in the Douro is extremely hard to work, with hardly any soil and a severe climate.

Below: a bygone scene — the old method of transporting the wine from the quintas to the lodges. The flat-bottomed barco rabelo *boats were able to negotiate the shallow river, propelled by the current and steered by giant oars. Today the wine travels by truck; boats would be no use as dams obstruct the Douro's course.*

vats, they lose some of their colour and develop subtle tastes and aromas, becoming tawny port. Tawny is bottled after a time in wood; the ones to go for are those which promise a number of years' ageing; 10, say or 20. Good, old tawny port is reckoned by connoisseurs, and by the port trade itself, to be the best and subtlest of ports.

The finest wines, from only the outstanding vintages, are bottled after two or so years as vintage port; the product of a single harvest. Vintage port needs to age in bottle, and will take anything up to 20 years to reach its best. During this time it develops a deposit, making decanting essential. The port trade reckon buyers are shy about decanting, and this is why they have introduced ports such as "late bottled vintage", which avoid the need for messing about with funnels and filters. They also contrive to avoid the real port taste in the process. It's nice enough stuff, but good 10-year-old tawny is a better use for your money — though there is nothing in the world to compare with a mature vintage port.

Cheap port is fiery, red and sweet. Good port is red, rich rather than sweet, with a kind of fruity softness that is immensely enjoyable to sip. Like sherry, it is an underrated drink, though the price of vintage port is hardly too low.

Portugal also possesses Madeira, an unexpected island far south in the Atlantic, where they make a fine fortified wine. Not content with fortifying it, the islanders (or rather the venerable Madeira-wine companies, many, like the port concerns, of British origin) *bake* their wine. It is put into casks and heated over slow fires for six months. This gives it a particular burnt, slightly oxidized taste (so characteristic that wine people the world over speak of oxidized wines as "maderized"). Madeira also has the distinction of incredible hardiness; it can age seemingly indefinitely in cask and in bottle.

Most good Madeira is made rather like sherry on the solera principle. Occasional bottles of vintage Madeira can be found. Sadly, much Madeira is rather run-of-the-mill stuff and made by blending very ordinary wines to fit one of the four well-known styles. These are (from dry to sweet) Sercial, Verdelho, Bual and Malmsey. According to tradition, these names should apply to wines made from four different varieties of grape, but the terms have been taken over to refer to blended styles with little or none of the named wine in them. New regulations, forced on Portugal by the Common Market, mean that more of the classic grapes must be used in Madeira in the future. With time, the quality of ordinary Madeira will thus improve.

Madeira is truly unique, with a tangy, nutty taste of its own, be it sweet or dry. It is obvious, though, that it is worth spending money on a wine above the minimum standard.

EAST EUROPE & THE MEDITERRANEAN

It's the fate of wines from about a dozen countries east and south of Germany to be bundled together in this very mixed bag. The bundle conceals a fine diversity of traditions and tastes, from which two classes of wine stand out as useful contributions to the world's well-stocked cellar. First there are the mass-produced "ordinary" wines. Such names as Jugoslav Riesling and Bulgarian Cabernet, and, to earlier generations, Algerian "burgundy", have spelt cheap, flavoury, happy drinking to many. Large-scale wine-making, a modern approach and a certain amount of State control (and subsidy) guarantee continuity and value.

Far left, top: *Hungary's Lake Balaton provides a sheltered microclimate for these vineyards, where good-quality white wines are made. The names to look for are Badacsonyi or Balatoni.*

Bottom: *in Greece, winemaking takes place in the open air. The two small basket presses are modern successors to the large stone trough in the background. In many parts of rural Greece, such treading troughs are still used. The juice is then filtered through a thyme bush into a cask; winemaking technology as old as civilization and still remarkably effective. Most of the crop goes to the local cooperative, but each farmer keeps some grapes to make into wine for his own use.*

In the other class are the individual, local wines from hundreds of quiet valleys and hidden upland corners. They find their way to us only in odd parcels, and are tending to die out as mass-production gets into gear. These traditional wines include some which rival, for interest and quality, many exalted French or German names.

Not all the wines of the east and south succeed in joining these two groups. Millions of bottles of bad, sad, over-ripe and under-flavoured wine are made — and consumed — for they are ever cheap. A roll-call of the good basics would start with Yugoslavia, where the Welch Riesling grape and Germanic techniques produce a flood of clean, slightly sweet, fruity white wine. Yugoslavia has yet to repeat the trick with other styles: rather too much wine from there is still made and traded as a commodity. Yugoslavia is keen on barter as a means of trade and I once tasted some appalling red wines that had been used to pay a Western firm for a steel-mill. Yugoslavia has its proud local traditions and unpronounceable names, as summer visitors will find with pleasure, but no real personalities stand out in export markets. Given time and luck, good wines will emerge.

Bulgaria and Romania both grow western European classic grapes like Chardonnay and Cabernet with a single-minded view to export. Bulgaria, with no real tradition of wine, or of any kind of sophistication, has done better than cosmopolitan, French-influenced Romania. The Bulgarian system of appellations is admirable. They produce various grades of wine, all carrying grape and territorial names in the approved fashion, and all good value for money. Cabernet Sauvignon is perhaps their best wine, though the traditional Mavrud, a stiff, dark, red, which improves with keeping, can claim true local character and real quality. Romania's Cabernets and Rieslings show less conviction of taste. Much of their wine is designed for the German market, which demands sweeter red wines than other western countries.

Hungary has the strongest tradition of quality wine in the East. Tokay, fabled for reviving dying Tsars, is still made. It comes in varying degrees of sweetness (the more "puttonys" on the label the sweeter) up to the true imperial reviver, Essencia. Try 5-"putt" Tokay with mince pies at Christmas. Hungary's other big name in the West is a strong-flavoured red wine called Bulls Blood. The blend they send abroad is sweeter and less interesting than the one they keep for themselves, but still a tasty and enjoyable wine. Elsewhere in Hungary large amounts of Welch Riesling and other mass-produced wines are made, but without quite the success of Yugoslavia. Hungary's characters include some fine whites made around Lake Balaton, which are worth a try if you come across them. Don't bother to pronounce the names on the labels: no-one can understand the Hungarians except the Finns.

Greece, home of wine, is struggling to shake-off a peasant tradition and emerge into the modern wine world. Her traditional wines include some compelling rarities like Samos Muscat and other sweet, dark Mavro (black in Greek) wines from the islands. Retsina, white wine flavoured with resin, is enjoyed by tourists in the Aegean heat but never quite tastes the same at home. The best Greek wines are dark, earthy reds which need age in bottle to soften. These come from Crete, from Attica and other corners of the mainland. Greece, in general, is a country to watch as Common Market membership spurs her winemakers to look to export markets.

Cyprus, with much the same tradition as Greece, got into the export business earlier thanks to preferential trade terms with Britain. Her sherry-style fortified wines are better than their image suggests, and her light wines competent and fair value. The real surprise of Cyprus is Commandaria, a sweet wine in the classic Mediterranean mould which has developed into a drink of some style.

The east and south shores of the Mediterranean have marvellous climatic conditions for wine, but the pressure of religion — Mohammed's disapproval of alcohol — has stunted the vine's growth. Good wine is made in the Lebanon, competent wine in Israel, there are pockets in unlikely places like Syria and Iraq and a fair-sized industry in Turkey. North Africa made oceans of wine for the few decades of French rule, but many of the vineyards have been dug up since independence. You will still come across wines from Tunisia, Morocco and Algeria, and they can be good. But in this whole belt from Morocco to the Black Sea only Lebanon's Château Musar has emerged as an international name. If there is ever peace, quiet and toleration, there could be a dozen more as good.

Central Europe

Three countries, Switzerland, Austria and Czechoslovakia, form a sort of island in European winemaking. They do not attempt to compete with the East and South in the mass market, relying instead on individuality. The Swiss drink most of their own wine (and quite a lot of other peoples'). It is always expensive, usually good, and of interest only in Switzerland or to dedicated seekers after the esoteric. It cannot be said that Switzerland fills a gap in the world's wine repertoire. Austria is different: it makes whites of French strength and dryness and Germanic flavours, an attractive combination. The 1985 scandal involving some of her sweet wine makers quashed for a time Austria's hopes of more fame for these wines. The sweet wines were always remarkably cheap and will (sadly for their makers) now be even cheaper. The Austrian government has stamped on the fraud very firmly and brought in strict new laws, so you can try Austrian wine with confidence. Czechoslovakian wine is similar in tradition to Austrian, but little is made and less exported. It is another name to try if you see it: medium to dry whites, mostly.

Above: *a Biblical scene of vines growing precariously in an oasis in Sinai. Egypt was famous for its wines in Pharaonic and classical times, but there was a gap of 20 centuries before wine started to be made again in 1903. Today there is little of it, and what there is is indifferent in quality.*

Below: *Tunisia has a thriving wine industry. These Berber women are engaged in Spring hoeing and weeding. Algeria, Morocco, Israel and the Lebanon also prove that hot climates can produce good wine.*

Left: *Czechoslovakia has a cool Central European climate, suitable for the vine varieties of Germany. This vineyard, north of Prague, clings to a sunny hillside in the German manner. There are more vineyards in the southeast of the country, where very good white wines are made. Few Czech bottles ever appear on the world market — the locals drink them all themselves.*

THE REST OF THE WORLD

The "rest of the world's" vineyards are largely in two very different countries, South Africa and the USSR. The first is a keen exporter, the second an equally avid importer of wine. South Africa's wine trade has suffered in the last few years from politics: there were signs in the 1970s that it might become accepted in the Americas and Europe as a "New World" producer on a par with Australia and California. But boycotts both organized and spontaneous have sapped the Cape wine business's export growth. The exception is, curiously, in black Africa, where Cape wines enjoy a brisk sale, ideology notwithstanding.

The Cape

Dutch settlers started the wine business in South Africa, and their influence is still very visible in the architecture of the Cape which is unanimously described as the most beautiful wine district on earth. Stark mountains rise sheer from the vineyard valleys, their lower slopes clothed with forest and their summits bare rock, which turns a dramatic purple in the evening light. The climate is a benevolent Mediterranean. Soil, slope, the abundant and various microclimates — all are virtually ideal for growing healthy grapes. Many of the wine estates can boast a 300-year history and some have been in the same family for six or seven generations. These vineyards, far from being "new", have pedigrees longer than many in France or Spain. The wine farms are often centred around beautiful, white-painted manor houses, with the 20th century amenities of pool and terrace added to lovely old gardens.

These wonderful vineyards stayed in a condition of pleasant slumber for decade after decade. Wine, to South Africa, was unimportant, and until the 1960s, this was a country where the men drank brandy and the women watched. Thus the wine industry was denied a discerning local market, a factor crucial in the breeding of good wine. Exports, under the old, linked trading system with Britain, consisted largely of sherry and port-style fortified wines.

Things began to change in the 1970s, with a growing interest in light wines. South Africans found that the old Cape estates were capable of making world-class wines, and of providing them with a steady supply of good everyday ones. The outside world began to take an interest in the Cape's produce.

A new set of wine laws, which insist on strict standards for "estate" wines and formalise labelling regulations, was brought in in 1972. The consumer is well-served by Cape wine: it is honestly made and the labels clearly tell what is in the bottle.

Just about every kind of wine is made in the Cape. The tradition of fortified wines is still strong — the climate is far closer to that of Jerez than Burgundy. The last ten or 15 years have seen the making of serious red wines, using the methods of the Old World and paralleling the efforts of California. White wines suffer from the hot climate, but modern methods of temperature control have allowed some good ones to be made. Rather like New Zealand, the Cape has both gained and suffered from German techniques. Many winemakers and estate owners have trained at Geisenheim on the Rhine, and have a sound grasp of winemaking and an affection for Riesling and Riesling-style wines. Bearing in mind the conditions they have to work in, these young men and women would have been better off at Davis in California, or Montpelier in the South of France. The legacy of Geisenheim has been a struggle to make fresh, delicate off-dry white wines when something a little more solid and "southern" would be more appropriate to the environment.

Great white wines may be still in the future for the Cape, but good everyday bottles from Steen (the local name for Chenin Blanc) are abundant. Steen makes a flavoursome, off-dry wine with a slight "cut" which makes it refreshing. Semillon used to be quite important, but is declining. Some estates make good, sweet, late-harvest white wines from Steen and from what they call Riesling, which isn't what's grown on the Rhine but an ancient French variety. Sparkling wines are the Cape's latest fashion, as elsewhere in the world. First efforts have been entertaining rather than exciting.

It is with red wines that the Cape has established a bridgehead in the world's fine wine list. Cape reds used to be akin to Australian "burgundy": more a meal than a drink. Dedicated estate owners have, however, turned to classic grapes such as Cabernet Sauvignon in an effort to rein their reds in. Replanting in cooler corners, the use of modern techniques of winemaking and the adoption

Far left: *the elegant mansion at the heart of the Uitkyk estate in South Africa. The house, built in 1788, is typical of the large farms of the Cape wine region. The vineyards cover 400 acres of the slopes of the Simonsberg Mountain, near Stellenbosch, and a wide variety of wines is made.*

Left: *in total contrast, Indian vineyards are an unlikely thought, but in Maharashta a collaboration between French experts and an Indian company grows Chardonnay grapes for sparkling wine. The wine is made by the champagne method using French equipment. The vines are trained tall to provide shade for the grapes, thus mitigating the effects of tropical heat, and to allow air to circulate to combat rot.*

of barrel ageing have all played their part. There are still plenty of solid, robust red wines (and they can be very enjoyable) but there is also a growing list of lighter, more elegant, complex ones. The best Cape reds are now very serious wines, though there is still some doubt about their ageing potential. It is probably necessary for the vineyards to mature, and for the experimental ferment to calm down, before we can really judge these wines.

The term "estate" is used very precisely. If printed on a label, it means the wine was made at the estate, from grapes grown there. By no means all the serious wine made in the Cape is estate wine, though much of it is. The big cooperatives and commercial firms play their part, especially in the middle sector of the marketplace.

With all the attention focussed on the light wines, it is easy to forget that Cape sherry and port are as good as ever. One of the best-value dessert wines around today is the port-style wine made by the KWV, the giant cooperative, and aged for up to 30 years in giant casks.

The Cape vineyards cover only the very southwest corner of the continent of Africa, North, between them and Morocco, is a wide belt devoid of vines except for some experimental plantings in Zimbabwe, which are reputed to be doing well.

Russia

Russia is, famously, the home of vodka. The citizens of the USSR go through heroic quantities of the stuff though, as official figures have been supressed since the mid-70s, no-one is sure quite how much. The story goes that officials, feeling that the vodka habit was sapping the national will and slowing down production, looked for a way of weaning the people off it. Wine, they decided, would be a healthy alternative to vodka. So vineyards were planted — 2½ million acres since 1950. The USSR is now the third-largest wine producer in the world and its wine is made on a super-industrial scale. The citizens duly drank the wine — and went on drinking the vodka as well. In the litres-per-head league, Soviets are well ahead of Americans, Swedes, Britons and Cypriots . . . The USSR now imports vast quantities of wine as well as making it, thereby causing wild fluctuations in the Mediterranean bulk-wine markets. Cyprus, Spain and North Africa are the main sources.

All this explains why so little Soviet wine makes it to the West. What does varies from the, well, amazing to the palatable, even good. There are areas within the boundaries of the USSR with long wine traditions: Armenia and Georgia, for instance. They continue to make wines which must be distinguished from the mass-produced blends of the new vineyards. The Soviet consumers seem to have (or are deemed to have) a taste for sweet wine and much of the sparkling and even red wine is made to suit. When dry reds can be found, they are occasionally good. But the best drink to come out of Russia remains vodka. It appears in a variety of lovingly-concocted guises, flavoured with all manner of things. Pepper, wild grasses, port and brandy (in the same vodka) can all be found. These flavoured vodkas are among the undiscovered great drinks of the world. Search them out, and leave the wine — those so far exported, anyway — for the natives. You'll be doing the Kremlin a favour.

England

At the other end of Europe, in England, a wine industry has also developed at the same time as Russia's. Nothing, though, could be more different. The damp but surprisingly mild English climate allows vines to grow, much to the surprise of both visitors and, indeed, the locals. Grow they did in Roman times and right up to the Middle Ages, but a gap of centuries was only bridged when a few amateurs started to grow vines again 30 or 40 years ago. And only recently have their efforts been taken remotely seriously by their compatriots, never mind the French. But today there are some thou-

Young vines are nurtured amid the apple trees of Kent in southeast England. The English vineyards of today are new, though vine-growing in the country dates back to the Romans. Many different vine varieties, including new experimental ones from Germany, are being tried to discover which best suit the relatively cool conditions.

sand acres of vines and perhaps 100 commercially viable vineyards. Even the French have had to admit that English wine can be a proper drink.

Nearly all English wine is white, because the relatively short growing season and low temperatures suit white grapes best. But there are pioneers of red-wine making in England who insist that Pinot Noir, which thrives in cold, northerly Champagne, can survive in England. Their experiments are in the early stages, and for the moment white wines of a mid-dry, fresh, delicate style are England's trademark. Given a warm year, and especially, a warm Autumn, the wines can show depth of flavour and distinction well up to European standards. Grapes grown include Müller-Thurgau, the German standby, and various other German cross-bred varieties.

It has been fascinating to watch English wine develop. Increasing experience and (just as crucial) the increasing age of the vines brings better wine each year. It is possible to foresee the time when estates will earn reputations for particular styles of wine, and when regional variations will start to show up. So far, the location of the vineyard has depended more on where the would-be winemaker owned, or could buy, land. There is a natural correlation though between the fruit-growing districts of Kent and Sussex and the new vine districts: conditions which suit raspberries or blackcurrants usually suit grapes.

English wine still depends to a great extent on enthusiastic producers and loyal local customers. With growing production and a trend towards national distribution, buyers will now choose the wines more for value and taste than loyalty and curiosity. The scale of vineyards is growing as farmers find that vines are a useful alternative or additional crop: one Kentish grower finds that the ripening time for grapes — October — slots neatly in after his other fruits have been picked, allowing the pickers to keep working for another couple of weeks. The big investment in winemaking machinery is offset by the fact that the "crop" — bottles of wine — is easy to store and can be sold when the market is best, not straight after the harvest when gluts may occur.

China

If wine from England is surprising, what of wine from China? For years, canny French merchants have labelled bottles of very ordinary *vins de table* with oriental names and done brisk business with the Chinese restaurants. Recently, word has come from China of real wine being made there. A French company set up a joint venture and shipped a "kit" of equipment — a complete winery — from Australia to the Shandong Peninsula, south east of Beijing. The result is known as Dynasty and is a slight advance on the old French stuff with Chinese labels. More interesting wine, however, is also being made in Shandong from Chardonnay and other European grapes. It may be that the future for wine in China is primarily to be distilled into brandy. The Hong Kong Chinese show an enviable ability to consume Cognac, which they reckon has medicinal, even aphrodisiac powers. The mainland millions would drink Cognac itself dry if they were to get the chance!

Japan

Japan, too, has a wine industry. The climate is by no means ideal, but there are pockets where the summer heat and damp are not too severe. I once heard a very surprised and chastened senior wine taster tell me he had mistaken a sweet Japanese wine for a good Sauternes. The "nobly-rotten" flavour finds favour in Japan, where wine is regarded as a foreign novelty rather than an everyday drink. So far, the Japanese have shown little sign of taking to winemaking in the same way as they have adopted whisky. Considering the success of the Japanese whisky industry, the world's winemakers should be profoundly grateful.

TOMORROW'S VINEYARDS

The recent explosion in the making of good wine, both in quantity and in terms of the variety of places where it is done, has been astounding. It is likely that there will soon be a slowing, even a halt, in the rate of change. A period of absorption, of taking stock, is needed. So many new wine areas have been pioneered that the consumers need to get used to them, to find out just what is to their taste. There is also a questionmark over just how much wine the world is ready to drink. The thirst of the developed countries is not infinite, and there are other drinks competing with wine to satisfy it. Much of the current interest in wine may turn out to be mere fashion.

One thing is certain, though. The preeminence of the Old World is broken. No-one, not even a Frenchman, can now deny that good wine can be and is being made on every continent. The vineyards of the next century will be those where the basic quality equation, the balance of the vital factors discussed at the start of this chapter, works out best.

One factor, man's role, seems likely to become more and more dominant. Man has wrested control of the winemaking process from the ill-understood yeasts. He is taking over in the vineyard, too, manipulating microclimates and plant genetics to grow the grapes he wants.

Nature still has the last word, and the very best vineyards will still be those where all the factors are benign, but good wine will be more and more the product of human effort, not natural serendipity.

The grape grower of today and tomorrow has far more choice than formerly of where to plant. There is now a fair understanding of why some places are better than others, and the importance of traditional sites is being questioned. This is especially the case in the New World, where former sheep patures in Los Carneros and the Barossa valley, orchards in Oregon and Tasmania and Kent, are being turned over to vines. The reason for this is that studies have shown these areas to have favourable local climates and good soil. Scientists now have an accurate yardstick for what makes a piece of ground a possible vineyard, and an approximation of the ideal ecology of the vineyard once it is established. And they know a lot about how to influence the microclimate; the direction in which vine rows are aligned affects the sun they receive, and helps or hinders cold air drainage; the height at which vines are trained, the method of pruning used, the distance between rows – all influence both the crop the vines bear and the microclimate around the vine.

In the laboratory and the plant nursery, geneticists are tailoring the classic vine varieties to produce more and better fruit, to ripen earlier and to be resistant to pests and diseases.

Unless a slump makes winemaking totally uneconomic, the happy wine drinker has more and more good wine, from more and more places, to look forward to.

In the new vineyards, machines will be commonplace. They will plough, prune and harvest; if necessary — as here — by night. This nocturnal activity is desirable in hot countries to pick the grapes at their coolest. Here, at Rosemount in Australia's Hunter Valley, the winemaker wants the Chardonnay grapes to be as fresh and cool as possible when they arrive at the winery. Cool grapes keep their freshness and acidity, and there is less chance of them spoiling in the sun on their way in from the vineyard. Also, cool grapes mean the fermentation starts off at a low temperature, and the modern winemaker likes things in the vat to start cool and stay cool.

Chapter Three

MAKING WINE

MAN'S ROLE

Place has been the main theme of the last few pages, the rôle that soil and slope, latitude and climate have in deciding the taste of wine. Now it is the turn of people. Growing grapes is a special form of farming. Making wine is a technical skill. The fact that in so many places the two trades are carried on by the same people should not conceal this. And it is when wine-making takes over from grape-growing that Man really takes over from Nature.

The growers influence the wine before the grapes are even picked, of course. They cultivate the vines in every sense, from pruning them to keeping down the weeds and scaring away the birds that would eat the grapes. Yet it is farming – or perhaps market gardening. The same skills applied to different crops will grow fine raspberries for canning, or apples for the fruit bowl. Grapes are different because they can be turned, by a different skill, into wine.

What people do to grapes is best expressed in pictures, as the following pages illustrate. But it is worth putting into words what happens. Ripe fruit, any fruit, will ferment given warmth. The yeasts, micro-organisms only recently understood by science, are naturally present on the fruit skins. The trouble is that laissez-faire or natural fermentation rapidly spoils — vinegar, not wine, is Nature's end product. Man steps in to control things.

Grapes ferment best if they are crushed, to break the skins and release the juices. This is why until very recently (and still, in some out-of-the-way places) people physically trod the grapes. Feet are good at the job: they are not hard enough to squash the grape pips that give a bitter taste to the wine, and their warmth encourages fermentation. Today machines crush the grapes, and the juice and pulp go into a vat to ferment. If white wine is the object, the skins get left behind. For reds, the skins go in too. It is the colour in the black grape skins that gives red wine its redness: look at a grape, any grape, and you'll find the flesh pale and the juice clear.

Vines need constant care — pruning and training the shoots, weeding, ploughing and fertilizing the soil. These Riesling vines are growing in the pure-slate soil of the Mosel vineyards. The picture was taken in spring just as the first green shoots were appearing.

Fermentation is naturally uproarious. Sugar is rapidly converted into alcohol. Froth spills out of the vat, and carbon dioxide gas forms a cloud over it. The key to modern winemaking is to keep rein on the yeasts: to adjust the temperature so that they ferment, but don't get carried away. Controlled fermentation helps keep flavour, acidity and other desirable attributes in the wine. The plonk of yesterday was over-fermented, and one of the key reasons for the rapid improvement in the standards of cheap wines has been the understanding and control of fermentation.

The yeasts subside in two or three weeks, leaving a residue of solids — what's left of the skins and pulp and dead yeast cells — and alcoholic fruit juice: young wine. It will be a rather nasty fluid at this stage, still cloudy, pungent and distinctly unpromising. The winemaker moves in again to teach the wine some manners. He or she ages it, sometimes in wooden casks, sometimes in giant vats. It is filtered to remove the left-over particles of solids. It slowly settles down. The awkward, spiky flavours mingle and mature.

The winemaker will now blend various batches of wine from different vineyards or grapes to make the most of his spectrum of tastes. A common and apt comparison is with a painter, mixing from raw colours on his palette the exact shade he wants. Constant checking, tasting and even chemical analysis goes on. At a certain stage the wine is ready. It is stabilized, chemically or by cooling, and then bottled. Giant production lines carry the sterilized bottles through machines which fill, cork, label, wrap and pack them.

There are of course hundreds of variations on the straightforward process outlined and illustrated here. White winemakers put more stress on freshness and fruitiness, picking their grapes a little earlier to make sure they have all their acidity and taste and are not over-ripe. With a white wine, there is the decision on sweetness to be taken. Left alone, the fermentation will eat up all the sugar in the grapes and a dry wine results. But not every wine is best when bone dry. Some winemakers stop the fermentation so as to leave a little sugar in the wine. Others, especially in Germany, "back-blend" a little natural grape sugar to add roundness and sweetness. Sometimes the grapes are so full of sugar that the fermentation cannot cope: the alcohol level mounts until there is enough to stun the remaining yeasts. Sweet wine results.

Red wine is always allowed to ferment right out and so is naturally dry. Reds pick up astringent, tart flavours from the inclusion of the grape skins (and sometimes the stalks) in the vat. This tannin is essential to any red wine that is going to last. In the maturing process it blends with the fruit tastes and the natural acidity to give the complex, subtle flavours of mature wine. When young, such wines taste harsh and unappealing.

Oak barrels have a lot to add to red wine, though fewer wines get to see them all the talk about casks would imply. The privileged wines in wooden casks undergo a natural reaction with the oak wood, breathing through it and picking up the faintest of tastes from it. Oak, when new, has sundry natural tannins and essences — vanilla is one. They find their way into the wine, adding to its repertoire of tastes. Good white burgundies were traditionally, and still are, fermented as well as matured in small barrels.

Winemakers have to go to great lengths to purify their wines. Not because there is anything inherently harmful in them, but because there is always a certain amount of solid mixed with the liquid. Fermentation leaves behind yeast particles, and if the wine is to be clear and bright they have to be removed. One traditional way is to "fine" the wine – to add to it a natural coagulant. Blood is one such; so, luckily, is egg white.

Some old-fashioned wineries still use eggs. In Burgundy, they found that the fining was not going as well as it used to. It was a mystery until someone spotted that the eggs laid by today's well-fed hens are bigger than they were. The same number of eggs per cask were being used, but bigger eggs meant more white — too much, it turned out. One of the steadiest if tedious jobs in wine must be that held by the egg-breaker I watched at the Muga bodegas in Rioja who was steadily breaking dozen after dozen eggs, carefully pouring the yolks into one goldfish bowl and the whites into another.

Fining has been replaced in many wineries by filters. These have their detractors: some say that the micro-fine filters take the taste out of the wine along with the particles. Another way of losing the solid sediment is to "rack" the wine — to pour it from one container to another, leaving the sediment behind in the first.

Vintage wine has become a synonym for good wine, but not every time is this true. In making champagne, port, sherry and several other wines, it is the custom to blend the produce of several years to ensure a consistent taste. Most ordinary wines are "non-vintage" for the same reason: consistency is best served by blending. But in places where the use of a vintage date is the custom, such as Bordeaux and Burgundy, it is a key indicator of quality. Each year, the winemaker will have a different set of ingredients to work with. Not all the grapes from all the vineyards, or varieties, will ripen equally well. In 1984, for instance, a widespread failure of the vines to flower properly meant there was little or no Merlot in Bordeaux. The châteaux which habitually blended Merlot wine with the produce of their Cabernet vines had to make a Cabernet-only wine for the first time for many years. 1984 will therefore always be an oddity among clarets.

This brings home the truth that it's only possible to make wine once in twelve months. A winemaker cannot practice: he has one chance a year, perhaps only 30 in an adult lifetime, to make wine. That's why he or she has always relied on tradition: it worked in my father's time, therefore that's the way I'll do it. Today, research and the work of consultants has partly supplanted tradition. A consultant can be involved in the making of perhaps a dozen wines a year, and has that much more chance to build up experience. But for most winemakers, in most places, every time it's a bit of a gamble. And every decision, from when to pick the grapes to when to bottle the wine, adds its little detail to the success or failure of the vintage.

MAKING WINE

Making wine is simple. Making good wine is complicated.

Wine is the fermented juice of grapes. The process happens naturally, because the yeasts which cause fermentation are found on the skins of the ripe grapes. The most basic form of winemaking merely guides and channels the natural process. Sophisticated winemaking does this and more.

Before anyone can make wine he must have grapes. Today it is the breeding and growing of vines which is at centre stage in the efforts to make better wine. But before we delve into agriculture let's follow the ripe grapes through the steps to the making of a bottle of wine. These pictures were taken in France, in Bordeaux to be precise, but the story is the same the world over. Red, white and rosé wines demand variations on the basic process, but again the underlying story is the same. So imagine yourself in Bordeaux. The month is late September (or it might be early October). The weather is fine, the grapes ripe. Everyone in the district is busy with the vintage. It is the climax of the year . . .

Stage one is the picking of the grapes. Ever since wine began to be made, this job has been done by hand. It is hard work, involving much bending and an inevitable backache even for the hardiest picker. Secateurs and a tub or basket are the only tools. A picker must be skilled in rejecting unripe or diseased bunches of grapes.
Mechanization is replacing pickers in many vineyards, especially in the New World, though France is taking to it rapidly. The giant tractor drives along the rows of vines, shaking or slapping the bunches from the vines onto a conveyor belt. The belt dumps the grapes into a trailer.
Such contraptions have several advantages over gangs of pickers, the chief being speed and cost. A machine can strip a vineyard of its crop far more rapidly than can humans, ensuring that the grapes are picked at exactly the right time. The speed-up also evades dangers such as rain which can ruin the crop in mid-harvest. And the machine slices through the estate's wage-bill as well as its vineyard.

The pickers are supported by other workers who collect the grapes and deliver them to trailers or hoppers. The large plastic hods which have replaced the traditional baskets are heavy and unwieldy: the carriers earn their pay even more than do the pickers.
The process of treading on the grapes in the trailer is, shall we say, non-standard. Normally, the winemaker puts a premium on undamaged grapes, for grapes that are crushed begin fermentation straight away and can spoil before they reach the winery. The importance attached to this varies from region to region, depending upon the type of wine being made.
The enjoyment of the fruits of the previous year's vintage, pictured ***below right****, is, however, typical. Much wine is drunk, and many large meals eaten, at vintage time. The pickers are traditionally rewarded not just with wages, but with accommodation and free meals, which consist of the best of local food often cooked over a vine-twig fire.*

Once picked and carted to the winery, the grapes are crushed. The rather elderly contraptions pictured ***right*** *include a de-stemmer (in doorway) and vertical presses. The modern equivalents are the horizontal presses* ***below****. In some types, a giant balloon inside the slatted cylinder is blown up, crushing the grapes against the sides. In others, a plate moves along the cylinder, and in others chains revolve inside, crushing the grapes. The juice is channelled away, but the pomace — the residue of skins, pips and pulp — has to be shovelled out by hand.*

Whatever the pressing device, the job it does is to first tear the stalks off the grapes, then crush them to extract the juice. For red wine, the roughly-crushed grapes are put with their juice into a vat. For white wine, the grapes are pressed completely and the juice pumped into a vat.
*Vats are the containers where the juice or crushed grapes ferment. They used to be made of wood (****far right****) but other materials are now replacing wood. Stainless steel, shown beyond the wooden vat in the picture* ***right*** *and again* ***below right****, is the favourite. Steel is easier than wood to keep clean and hygienic, but its main advantage is that it is easier to keep cool.*

Making wine involves control. The fermentation takes place naturally — though the winemaker may add his own chosen yeast to supplant the "wild" ones on the grape skins — but it has to be guided. If the weather is warm, the temperature inside the vats will get too high and the wine loses flavour. Various techniques are used to reduce temperature; the grid affair pictured ***left*** *is a form of refrigerator through which the fermenting wine is pumped. Red wine vats contain the skins as well as the juice. These form a floating cap at the top of the vat, but the wine gains colour and taste if they are mixed back into the liquid below. So pumps are used to take wine from the base of the vat and return it to the top. The wine is passed through an open tub, pictured* ***below left****, to allow air into it.*

When the fermentation is over, the wine is pumped into containers for storing and ageing. Although technically now wine, the new liquid is not ready yet. The storage process is essential to soften and mature it. Red Bordeaux and similar wines spend their first winter in large tanks or vats similar to those used for fermentation. While thus stored the wine undergoes the secondary, or malolactic, fermentation. Then, in the spring, it is pumped into small barrels for a period of ageing. The chais *(**below**) in which the oak barrels are housed is a fine sight — and an expensive one. The Bordeaux technique demands that a large proportion, sometimes all, of the barrels be new each year. The new oak casks add to the complexity of the wine, adding subtle flavours of tannin and vanilla and allowing the wine to breathe gently through the wood. These casks are very expensive to buy, to store and to handle, and are only used for the best of wines. Indeed, lesser wines would be overwhelmed by the pungency of the oak.*

While the wine is ageing in the barrel chais, *the winemakers keep a watch on it through occasional tastings. The two methods used are to suck wine up through the bung-hole with a pipette (**far right**) or by levering back the end of the cask to drive a thin stream of wine from a special hole (**right**).*

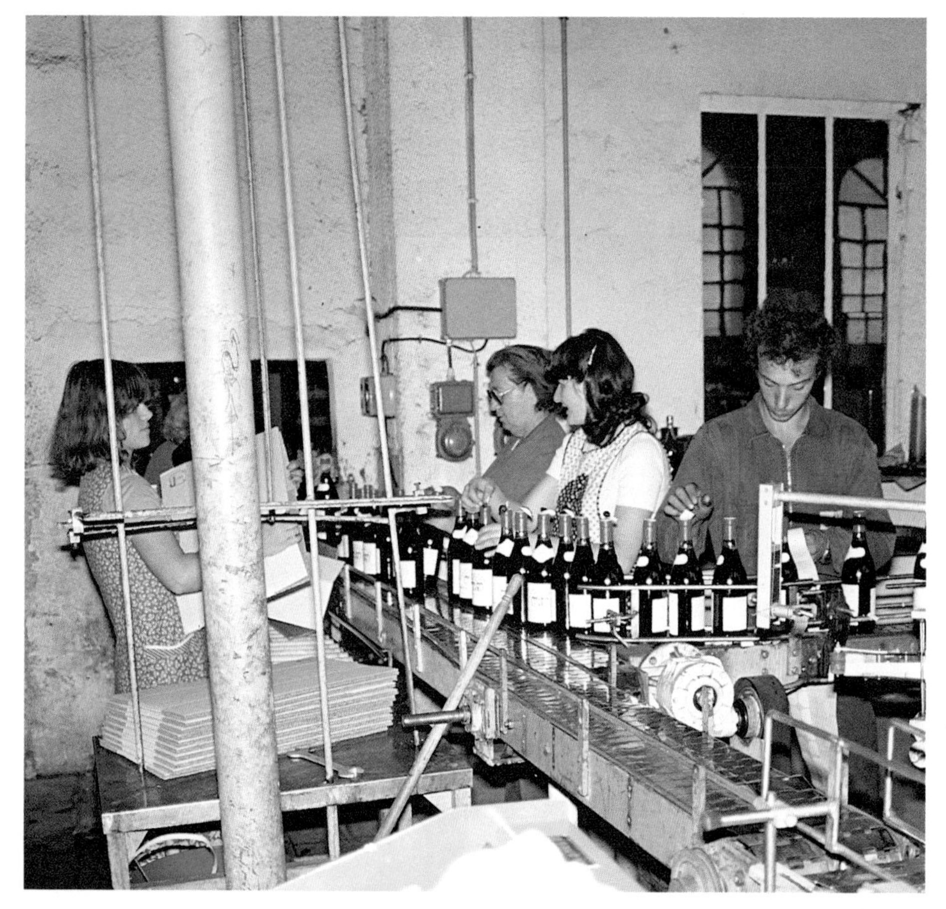

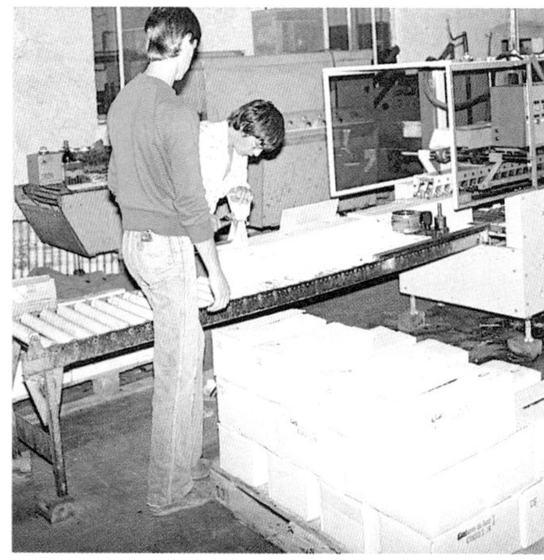

When the wine has finished its maturing process it is bottled. With some white wines, this takes place after a matter of weeks spent in a tank, just enough time to allow it to settle after fermentation. Great red wines may spend two or three years in various casks and containers. Bottling is now automated, with marvellous clanking, clinking machines to sterilize and fill the bottles, drive home the corks and stick on labels and capsules. Some even fill and seal the cartons in which the wine is despatched. The one ***above left*** *uses human hands for this process. Many wines go straight off to the merchant or other customer; some spend more time in the winery, resting after the shock of bottling. No champagne house or Bordeaux château will release its wine straight after bottling. And some Italians and Spanish red wines have a compulsory period of bottle-ageing.*

GRAPES

Grapes make wine, and different sorts of grapes make different kinds of wine. There are many varieties of grapevine, exactly as there are breeds of roses or apples. Some grapes have come to be seen as classics — such as Albertine or New Dawn are aristocrats among roses, or Cox's among apple trees. The names of these grapes are increasingly seen on wine labels. For both growers and drinkers are realising that to know what grapes the wine was made from is to get a useful early clue to the taste inside the bottle.

Grapes are not everything — all the other factors still apply, however prominent the name Chardonnay on the label — but they are the starting point. Grape flavour is an open, accessible secret. There is a lot more chance of tracing the Cabernet flavour in a clutch of different wines than of spotting from the taste that they all grew in limestone soil.

There are well over a thousand different grapes, with perhaps 50 that matter and only half a dozen that are of world stature. These key grape varieties have travelled out from their breeding grounds in France and Germany and are now found everywhere wine is made.

The great grape varieties were bred, partly by accident, hundreds of years ago. There is evidence that the French classics had already been discovered, and improved, by the time the Romans took over the Gallic vineyards. The Gauls had found the vines growing wild, or had brought them from elsewhere on their migrations, and had established most of the vineyard districts now recognized as great. The long pedigree of the European vines has given them an almost sacrosanct status in their home vineyards. All European wine regulations lay down which vines can be planted. In some areas, the choice is of one: all red burgundy is from Pinot Noir (with a very little Gamay) and all white from Chardonnay (plus a trace of Pinot Blanc and Aligoté). Other places allow a range of grapes, and the grower's choice is one of proportion; how much weight to give to this, or that, variety.

Few European wines stress the grape variety in their names. In Alsace, Riesling or Gewürztraminer or whatever is always listed. In Germany, many winemakers add the grape name to their labels, though it is not obligatory. In France outside Alsace, and in most of Spain and Italy, it was unheard of until recently. What you were told about a wine was the geography — where it was made — and the personality — who by. This began to change under the influence of the New World of wine.

Outside Europe, there were no traditions of classic grapes, no recipes that stipulated one or two varieties and banned the others. The pioneers of the Australian and Californian vineyards took cuttings of any and every European grape they could get hands on. They tried them all, and some thrived. In the last 20 years, the educated and ambitious winemakers of the new wine revolution have studied the classic European wines and aimed to emulate them. They realised that even if the soil and the climate of their vineyards were inevitably different from the Médoc or the Loire, grape varieties were one factor they could duplicate.

Soon they got more ambitious still. Disdaining to copy Europe, they launched out on the search for completely new wines. A vital part of this search is the matching of grape variety to environment. This is going to be a long process. Elaborate measurements of climate compiled by California scientists have not proved to be as good a guide to grape choice as was hoped. The "wrong" grapes have a habit of doing well in the places that are "right" for quite different ones. But the New World growers have complete freedom to choose the grapes they want to grow, and thus to decide in large part what kind of wine they want to make. They are using this freedom to slowly build up a dossier on what succeeds, and what excels, and what fails. Eventually, areas will be matched with varieties in much the same way as in Europe.

New World winemakers have given the drinker a new key to understanding wine. Variety labelling is becoming the norm on all but the established Old World classics. And despite the very wide range of growing conditions in vineyards from Zimbabwe to Brittany, grape flavour keeps coming through. Not the same, but always in the background.

There is nothing to force a winemaker to use just one grape — unless the local regulations say so. Many great European wines stem from a mix of several grapes. Châteauneuf-du-Pape, for instance, traditionally uses a dozen, and a fine claret may contain five. Some of the most exciting new wines are blends. In the South of France, growers are these days encouraged to use a small proportion of "aromatic" grapes as spice for their bland, flat wine. Thus a dash of Cabernet Sauvignon or Syrah

Cabernet Sauvignon

Merlot

Cabernet Franc

goes in with the Carignan, and the result is a wine with a new spark of interest. New World winemakers who searched for the elusive Bordeaux taste, and failed to find it in 100% Cabernet Sauvignon, are looking in more detail at the recipe. They are planting a little Merlot, a little Cabernet Franc, to add to the Cabernet Sauvignon.

A wine with a variety name will not always be a good wine. But if the winemaker starts with good raw ingredients, he has one less mistake to make.

RED

Cabernet Sauvignon

The most important of red-wine grapes, Cabernet Sauvignon has spread from Bordeaux all over the world. It is the dominant grape in Médoc claret, in a minority, with Merlot, in Pomerol and St-Emilion; it makes good, even great, wine in California, Australia, Chile, East Europe, New Zealand and South Africa; and is now being introduced to Spain and Italy, where, typically, it thrives. Cabernet Sauvignon wine tends to be hard, tannic; it needs ageing, has dark red colour and powerful smell of fruit and herbs.

Merlot

The other key grape of Bordeaux, with the Cabernets, is Merlot. It dominates Pomerol and parts of St-Emilion. Widely grown in Northeast Italy it is being introduced into Eastern Europe and to the Southern French vineyards. It adds a fruity, sweet note to claret, and when used alone is soft, fresh, tasty — a wine for relatively early drinking (though Pétrus fans would disagree).

Cabernet Franc

Cabernet Franc is grown in the same Bordeaux vineyards as Cabernet Sauvignon as an ingredient in claret, especially in the Graves district. Also grown on its own in the Loire, it makes good wines in warm years with a heady smell of fresh fruit. In cool vintages, however, the wine can be thin and tart; acidity is always higher with Franc than with "Cab Sauv".

Pinot Noir

The sole grape allowed for classic red burgundy, and also used in Champagne and Alsace, is Pinot Noir. Growers outside Europe have had less success with it than with Cabernet. At its best, in burgundy, it makes supple, subtle wine that can age and improve in bottle to considerable effect. In champagne, it is fermented without the skins to make a white wine, except in rosé champagne and the small amount of still red wine made there. It is used in Germany (as Spätburgunder: "late burgundian"), Austria and Hungary, and the best New World Pinot Noirs so far are from Washington State and New Zealand — both have cool climates.

Syrah

From the Rhône, Syrah is the only variety in Hermitage and Côte Rotie wines. It is grown too in Switzerland, and in the New World as Shiraz. Australian Shiraz can be notably good, and it does well in South Africa. Its use is spreading in Southern France as an aromatic addition to bland wines. At best, Syrah is very spicy, full and dark. Hermitage and wines of similar stature need long ageing.

Gamay

Gamay is the grape of Beaujolais, and it is also grown along the Loire, in central France and in Hungary and Austria. At its best, it makes fruity, flavoury wines. The top Beaujolais, grown on granite soil, can age in bottle, but most is made to be drunk quickly. Typically, Gamay wines have attractive grapey smell, light colour and a full slightly tart taste.

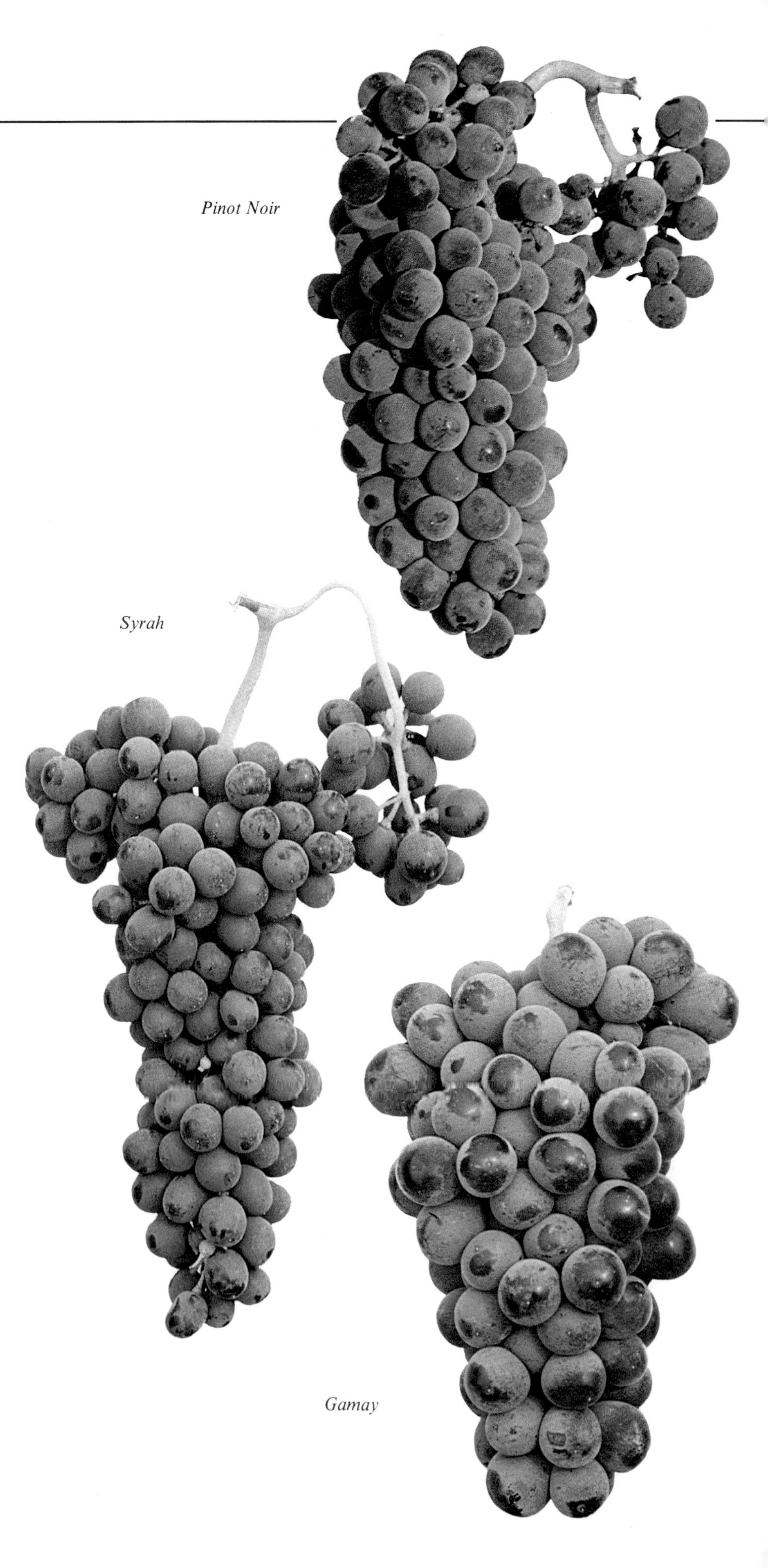

Pinot Noir

Syrah

Gamay

Zinfandel

Nebbiolo

Tempranillo

Zinfandel

A California curiosity; Zinfandel is found only there, though experimental plantings are being tried in other New World winelands. Possibly of Italian origin, brought over in the 19th century, it is versatile, and in West Coast hands makes wines from fresh, tart Beaujolais-style to heavy, sweet semi-ports. Most Zinfandel wines are fruity, the best age well in bottle and develop complex flavours.

Nebbiolo

Nebbiolo is the starting point for Italy's great red wines, Barolo and Barbaresco. In its most extreme form, Barolo, Nebbiolo wine is black, powerful and packed with scents and flavours. It needs age in bottle and air on serving. Long misty autumns in Piedmont's valleys ripen and concentrate the grapes. Not all Nebbiolo is ink-black; under the name Spanna the grape makes lighter, more elegant reds in other parts of North Italy. Like Pinot Noir, Nebbiolo has had little success outside its native place.

Tempranillo

Spain's greatest red wine, Rioja, is built upon Tempranillo. The grapes are black and thick-skinned and the wines dry and rather soft. Other varieties are blended with Tempranillo to add stiffness and strength and to help the wine age. Tempranillo is grown elsewhere in Spain under varying names, forming part of blends in Catalonia and La Mancha.

WHITE

Riesling

Riesling is the great grape of Germany, and one which makes fine wines all over the world. German scientists have spent a hundred years searching for a vine that has the taste and finesse of the Riesling without ripening so late in the autumn, when weather can wreck the harvest. They have found — or bred — vines that meet these criteria. But all have some disadvantage. Many, for instance, are less resistant to frost than Riesling. In the severe winter weather of 1985, it was the "new" vines that died, not the Riesling. Well-made Riesling wine has both acidity and natural sweetness, and can age into a rich, complex drink. It depends a lot on its site; steep, slatey hillsides suit it best. In Australia and California, fine Rieslings are made in the German and (drier) Alsace styles. Only true Riesling has these qualities; Welch or Laski Riesling is a different grape.

Sylvaner

The other quality grape of Germany, Sylvaner, makes less solid wines than Riesling, but ones with great character if grown in the right place. Acidity can be pronounced, depth and substance in the wine considerable. As with Riesling, its only great when from the best vineyards. (Ordinary Sylvaner is — ordinary.) It predominates in Franken and other southern areas, as Riesling dominates the best vineyards in the Rhine and Mosel. Sylvaner is also grown in Alsace and, patchily, in Eastern and Central Europe.

Müller-Thurgau

A century old, Müller-Thurgau is the first successful compromise between the qualities of Riesling and early ripening. A cross-bred grape, mixing Riesling and Sylvaner genes. Today it is Germany's most-planted grape, having ousted Riesling. Its virtues are a large crop and early ripening. The grapes are low in acidity and fruity, and the wine tends to flabbiness. Rarely named on labels — most Müller-Thurgau goes into blends such as Liebfraumilch.

Riesling

Sylvaner

Müller-Thurgau

Sémillon

Chardonnay

Sauvignon Blanc

Sémillon
Sémillon is a grape of markedly varying character. In Sauternes, it makes the world's best sweet wine. In Australia, it is vinified dry and is equally interesting. Sauternes exploits Sémillon's tendency to rot on the vine in a warm autumn, but to rot in such a way as to concentrate the juice, the sugar and the taste. Australian Sémillon is dry, but soft and with a solid structure. Well-made, it can age into complexity. Confusingly, some Australian Sémillon is called Hunter or Clare "Riesling".

Chardonnay
Chardonnay is the fashionable white grape, just as Cabernet Sauvignon is the red. At home in Burgundy — it's the grape of Chablis, the Côte d'Or and Mâcon — and in Champagne, it's exported around the world; Chardonnays from Australia, North America and New Zealand have been startlingly good, and the grape gains ground in Italy and Eastern Europe. It responds well to oak ageing and, if high quality to start with, to bottle age. Chardonnay wines vary from brisk, appley and early-maturing (the Chablis style) to complex, rich, deep drinks such as Montrachet. New World makers attempt both styles; some are over-rich and too alcoholic, but many are superb. This is a grape of taste, in every sense.

Sauvignon Blanc
The source of Sancerre and Pouilly Fumé from the Loire, Sauvignon Blanc is also a part of the blend in white Bordeaux. The smokey, strong-scented Loire wines are a fashionable success. New World growers — and those elsewhere in France — rarely achieve the steely astringency of the Upper Loire. These other Sauvignons are usually less emphatic — and none the worse for it. In Bordeaux, more Sauvignon is grown than formerly, adding freshness to dry wines previously rather bland. In Sauternes, Sauvignon is blended with Sémillon. New World Sauvignons are sometimes labelled "Fumé" to stress the Pouilly connection.

Gewürztraminer
Also called Traminer in some German-speaking districts. Gewürztraminer is a major grape in Alsace and is also planted in North Italy, Austria, Germany (the south) and the New World. When fully ripe, the grapes make unmistakeable heady, powerful-smelling wine. The spice and concentration varies: few wines made outside Alsace seem to match these Alsatian qualities. All Gewürztraminer wine has a certain flat, sometimes metallic, feel to it: the grape lacks acidity.

Chenin Blanc
South Africa and the Loire are the far points of Chenin's power. In the Cape, it makes large amounts of straightforward medium-dry wine. The Loire has this sort too, and at Saumur there are good sparkling wines. But Chenin can make great medium and sweet wines in odd corners like the Coteaux du Layon. It is a grape that reflects site and climate rather than any great personality and it can be over-acid.

Muscat
Perhaps the oldest grape variety, or rather family, for there are dozens of Muscats. Wine made from it smells and tastes like the luscious, scented Muscat table grapes. It is most used for sweet wines in Southern France and elsewhere in the Mediterranean, and for sparklers in Asti, Northern Italy.

Gewürztraminer

Chenin Blanc

Muscat

GROWING GRAPES

The transformation of a vine from a bare stump into a fruit-covered plant is a yearly miracle. The vines are pruned back hard every winter to stimulate new growth. The branches that will bear fruit are carefully tied in ***(top left)*** *to train the vine bush to the right shape. Different vineyard areas have different ways of training and pruning the vines: some use high trellises, others restrict the vine to a low bush shape. Tradition plays a part in these decisions, but a major influence is climate: cool places demand low-grown bushes so heat reflection from the soil can help ripen the fruit. Modern mechanical harvesters can only be used on high trained vines.*

In the spring, when the new growth begins, the vines are vulnerable to frost. In northerly areas like Chablis and Champagne, growers employ a variety of precautions against the cold. Among them are stoves ***(top right)*** *which raise the temperature a crucial degree or two. Another technique is to spray the vines with water. This freezes and paradoxically protects the shoots from very low temperatures.*

The end result is, if all goes well, ample ripe grapes. The pictures ***(left)*** *show red and white grapes in Bordeaux, ready to harvest. The white grapes are destined for Sauternes, and some of the berries in the bunch have started to rot "nobly" — an essential process in the making of Sauternes. These grapes have to be harvested individually, a costly process.*

THE WINE BUSINESS

Unless you have the good fortune to live in wine country, there will be quite a chain of people between the chateau's bottling line and your dinner table. Every one of them will have an influence on the price and the quality of the wine.

The people at one of the big champagne firms in Rheims once showed me round a part of the place normally thought uninteresting to visitors — the despatch bay. I found it fascinating. There were consignments of champagne labelled for the most unlikely places. One stack of cases was for the Ivory Coast — apparently a big buyer. Another for Venezuela — regularly in the world's top ten champagne-drinking nations. And duty-free shops as far apart at China and Scandinavia.

The sight of all those export consignments made the point that champagne is an international drink. It may come from a few square miles of France, but it's drunk everywhere (if not by everyone).

Wine is forever crossing the world: Australian Cabernet on its way to the curious and adventurous in Europe; French Bordeaux going to Australia for the status-seekers, the restaurants and the traditionally-inclined. Not all wines travel; some, though fewer and fewer, are drunk where they are made. Nearly everyone in the wine world is busy seeking export markets. This is because there is too much wine about. Consumption may by increasing in many countries, but it is dropping in others; France and Italy for instance. And modern techniques mean that more wine is being made, and that harvests are more predictable. It was only a decade or so ago that gluts of wine were accepted as an insurance against a disaster the next year. Today, with better husbandry in the vineyards and more precise controls in the winery, complete failure is rare.

Every now and again, though, something happens to remind everyone in the trading chain, including the drinker, that wine is essentially a crop. The early months of 1985 saw very severe frosts in many parts of Europe, so severe that vines were killed. The Chablis crop, among others, was small that year as a result. The 1984 harvest in central Italy was a virtual write-off because of constant rain. An off-course hurricane in early October of 1985 wrecked the prospects of some Bordeaux vineyards. The consequence of such natural calamities is a small harvest — and a price rise.

Wine, like any other traded commodity, is at the mercy of international economics. The relative rates of exchange in buyer and seller countries make a big difference. When the US Dollar was very high against the French Franc, the price of French wine in America became very low. This had interesting results. First, the amount of French wine crossing the Atlantic rose. This led to shortages of some fashionable wines — Pouilly Fuissé was one — and thus to price rises for everyone, including the disgruntled British drinkers who were innocent victims of the whole affair. Second, French wine was so cheap on the US shop shelf that California wines suffered. There were demands from growers there for a block on European imports. The same thing happened in reverse when the Dollar was very low; California wine became fashionable in London and Paris, not only because it was good and novel but because, due to exchange rates, it was very cheap.

The people buying and selling wine do so against this uncertain background of weather and economics. Therefore price rises at the corner store are usually out of the control of the merchant, and his wholesaler, and the importer too.

Luckily, there are plenty of wine countries and regions chasing the drinker's pound or dollar. New ones appear all the time, each with a million to spend on advertising and promotion. This is good news for consumers as well as ad men. It means choice; if claret gets too costly, we can switch to Australian, or Chilean, or Lebanese . . . The need to conquer foreign markets has also helped raise standards in wine making countries. Central government officials soon realise that there is no future in spending promotion money on rotten wine. Quite a few of them have tried, but a year or two of London or New York public relations budgets soon brings home the point. There is an ever-growing market — for good wine. And, in response, ordinary wine across the world is getting better.

This book is not the place for a detailed guide to the wine trade. It is a complex and fascinating business, full of quirks and with a long history. It is worth noting though that wine was one of the first things to be traded, before history, and one of the last to be abandoned when times because hazardous for shipping in the Dark Ages. The last pockets of civilization in post-Roman Britain, for instance, had the comfort of French wine as the barbarians encroached; archaeologists have found the empty winejars.

Wine stacked ready for shipping at a modern winery. The bottles are stored in large steel racks, ready for packing into cardboard cartons ***(left)****. Sometimes wine is stored for a certain time in bottle to mature before being released. But most wines are bottled and shipped as needed, with no "bottle-age."*

It is the retail end of the business that we have most to do with, and the various ways in which people sell wine are discussed in the pages on buying it. The growers, at the other end of the trading chain, work in differing ways too. The grandest estates offer their wine on the open market, knowing there will be plenty of bidders. An opening price is fixed, but it tends, if the vintage is any good, to go up quickly. The buyers are either brokers, big wine-merchant companies or smaller merchants buying on behalf of customers.

Less prestigious growers may have an exclusive deal with a merchant, who agrees to take all their wine and then offers it on the wholesale market to stores and restaurants. Many growers are members of cooperatives, which are associations formed to pool the making and marketing of wine from a district. Members deliver their grapes, or sometimes their wine, and are paid according to the quantity (and quality, ideally) of their contribution. The buyers are again merchants, though increasingly big retail concerns like supermarkets or wine store chains will buy direct.

An increasing amount of wine is sold direct to the consumer, either in bottle or at taverns or restaurants run by the growers; this last practice is especially common in Germany.

This sounds like a lot of middlemen and it's true that, unless you buy from the cellar door, there will be at least two people who handle the wine before you get at it. This is very necessary in a complicated business like wine. Merchants have two crucial jobs. One, to maintain quality. Two, to hold stocks. They keep the standards up by being able to shop around, just as we do to them. If a château or grower is slipping from the prevailing standards, or is charging too high a price, the merchants can and do go elsewhere. The best of them are very adventurous in opening up new areas to buy from, often providing advice and technical help for promising but rather backward growers, whose improved wine the merchant can buy at a good price. The stockholding function enables us, and the shops, and the restaurants, to be sure of getting a range of well-chosen wines. It used to be the practice for merchants to see to the bottling and maturing of the wine, but that is now increasingly the province of the grower. A good merchant will be able to ease the inevitable price and quality fluctuations between vintages by holding stocks.

Other people get involved in wine besides grower, merchant and drinker. Most producing countries have officials whose job it is to keep a check on the wine business. Their powers, and efficiency, vary widely. But there are few countries trading in wine where there is not some attempt to see that wine is at least what it says it is. Fewer, sadly, make any guarantees as to quality.

But the most intrusive outsider is the taxman. Wine, along with other alcholic drinks, is a favourite source of revenue for governments. The producer

countries tax it hardly at all; what French politician would dare put a centime on wine? But in Britain, and to a lesser extent the USA and other drinking rather than making countries, wine is fair game. The purchase of a basic bottle of wine in Britain is far more beneficial to its Exchequer than to grower, merchant or shopkeeper. Every bottle has a basic cost, regardless of the wine that's in it, of which the biggest fraction is customs duty — the tax. The British system means that the tax is the same on every bottle, be it Valpolicella at £2 or Château Lafite 1961 at £200. The more you pay, the smaller the share the Government gets. Which to me at any rate is a good argument in favour of the £3 as opposed to the £2 bottle: you get twice as much worth of wine.

The tax system in other countries is less arbitrary, but the American consumer has to put up with a jigsaw of State taxes and restrictions on selling, moving and dealing in wine. He or she still pays less a bottle than their British cousins, though.

The British system is unpopular in Europe, where the draining of the Wine Lake is thought a high priority and the British are looked upon as likely drainers. The European Commission has told London that it reckons the wine tax discriminates against wine — the tax on beer is quite a lot lower. This pressure meant that in 1984 wine duty actually went down for the first time in over a century. The grateful British rewarded the Government by boosting their wine consumption by 20% in a year. The quantity went up so fast that the tax coffers ended up fuller than before, despite the lower rate, which shows that a good deed is sometimes doubly rewarded.

Tax is not the only fixed cost on a bottle. The people in the trading chain have to make their profit margin, and finance their stocks. The grower has to pay for bottles, and capsules, and corks, and labels, and cases, all of which seem to increase in cost at a faster rate than the price of wine. All these can add two or three francs to the price of a basic bottle which the French consumer will expect to pay seven or eight francs for. It can be seen that, what with taxes and fixed costs, there is not much left in the middle for the wine. . .

Far left: *wine has to be transported to the shops much like any other comodity. But wine needs carefully controlled conditions: too much heat or cold in transit can cause damage.*

Above: *the selection process is a crucial part of the wine business. The pictures above show Master of Wine David Beford at work tasting wines for Victoria Wine. His assessment, and that of equally skilled and experienced colleagues, decides which wines the consumer will find on the shop shelves. Tasting at this level is no mere recreation: hard commercial decisions, and large amounts of money, depend upon the palates of the tasters. Often, the trade tasters are looking for potential rather than present enjoyment. Samples of vintage port or claret will not be ready to drink for 10 or 20 years, but they have to be judged if the firm's list is to be comprehensive in the future.*

PROFILES

Where wine is concerned, Nature and Man both throw something into the scales. A ripe grape, bursting with flavour and sugar, and with yeasts already present on its skin, comes close to turning itself into wine, of a sort, unaided. Winemakers, though, take control of nature — to a limited extent. People who make the best wine work harder and more successfully at this than others.

Those who are profiled here are all different; they work in different places, with wholly varying traditions, soils, grapes, and climates. Yet if they have anything in common it's a desire to throw more into the scales than their neighbours — to shape Nature instead of taking its buffets and blows without argument. No-one who makes wine can meet natural forces head-on, of course. And the pressures of business have to be coped with too. But the winemakers who do best seem to manage to use these forces instead of being pushed around by them.

Louis Métaireau

LOUIS MÉTAIREAU

"There are," says Louis Métaireau firmly, "no good and bad vintages. There are only good and bad *vignerons*." You listen when Métaireau speaks to you; a forceful middle-aged Frenchman, he's notable for dark glasses and gold teeth. And the sheer quality of his Muscadet adds its weight to his argument. His direct style grates on some of his more traditionally-minded neighbours, but no-one can argue with his wine.

One of Métaireau's key winemaking tools is a large easel equipped with a sheet of blank paper. It stands in the hyper-modern, glass-walled tasting room built on behind the family house in the village of St-Fiacre in the heart of the Muscadet country. Métaireau, a bustling man, is the moving force behind a unique group of nine Muscadet farmers who work together to market their wine. The easel comes in as a scoreboard for recording the blind tastings; each grower's wine is judged, blind, by all nine.

Keeping score does not make good wine, but competition does. The best wine made by the group gets the backing of an imaginative marketing programme, ensuring that it sells at a high price. And the group makes an award — 40,000 Francs — to the top wine. Naturally, each grower wants his wine to earn the accolade; it's good for both bank balance and self-esteem.

This unusual cooperation in a countryside full of individualists has done much to raise the marketing profile of Muscadet, which because of the lack of substantial estates and the dominance of big merchants has tended towards a certain blandness, both in taste and in commercial personality.

The nine who follow the Métaireau route to the market farm their own land, growing the grapes and making their own wine. When the wine is brand new, in November straight after the harvest, all the growers taste all the wines. The samples — perhaps 30 of them, as each man makes three or more "cuvées" or selections — are tasted blind to eliminate bias. The aim is to weed out faulty wines. Each sample is rated out of 20. "Fifteen," says Métaireau, "— OK. Fourteen — KO." Six or seven wines might be knocked out at this stage; a faulty fermentation by one grower eliminated two out of his three cuvées recently.

Then in January there's a second tasting; in a typical year, another two wines go. Another couple are weeded out in February. Two months later the wines are bottled. The nine employ a lawyer — a notary — to witness the bottling of each cuvée to see that the right wine gets into the right bottles. Each cuvée has a branded cork to ensure that its identity is clear. During the busy bottling period the Métaireau growers make enough work for two notaries, working in shifts.

In September, a year after the vintage, the final selection of the wines is made — again by blind tasting. The best 14 cuvées, half the original number, are selected. The top wine is given the Gold Label accolade; it is reserved for the lists of 50 top restaurants, half in France and half abroad. Next comes Cuvée LM: 50,000 specially-labelled bottles for the general market. And so on in descending order of prestige — and price.

Métaireau and six of the nine collectively own an estate, Le Grand Mouton, whose wine is sold in the same way. (The other two, Métaireau explains, kept out of the Mouton venture because they have no heirs to inherit, and thus no interest.) Le Grand Mouton is 50-odd acres of well-placed land, in one block on a plateau in the centre of the Sèvre-et-Maine country, the heart of Muscadet. It is run as a collective property — owned and farmed in common — though it's clear that Métaireau is the boss. The wines from the estate are tasted and selected, blind, along with the produce of the individuals' farms.

Tasting is at the heart of the Métaireau system, so it's natural that an interested visitor be put through the process. To taste a range of year-old Muscadets at ten in the morning is to put both palate and digestion to severe test, but Métaireau thrives on it. The easel is set up, the paper pinned on, the glasses ranked on the tables. The wines work up from a borderline case (only 15 points) to the top. It is a lesson in wine to follow the tastes and aromas through. The first cuvée is fresh, yeasty, not star-bright (which is as it should be; all Métaireau wine is bottled *sur lie* — straight from the cask, without being filtered). "Colour," observes Métaireau in his best schoolmasterly manner, "is very important. It is correct; very pale, slightly green." the wine tastes crisp and appley, but the flavour fades fast.

Next comes a wine scoring a point higher. It is brighter, yet darker in colour. *"Plus de fruit,"* comments the boss. There is more weight in the mouth, more acidity, generally more to say about the wine. The first two, Métaireau reckons, are two-year wines. Third comes the second cuvée of Grand Mouton (*"mon enfant"*). It is a slight, almondy wine, with powerful acidity. Its maker reckons it needs two years. Next up the scale comes a cuvée labelled with the initials of one of the other growers, JOL. "It's soft — it has different vinification." Métaireau comments "Mouton is to my taste; rapid fermentation, over in seven days. JOL prefers cold fermentation, three to four weeks at 16°, therefore less acidity. The original analysis of the wines was the same — but the final tastes are quite different. JOL is a wine to accompany food, for gastronomy. Grand Mouton is especially for seafood."

Last in the tasting comes the other Grand Mouton cuvée, a wine which came second in the growers' tasting. It is an austere, interesting wine, far more satisfying than a Muscadet has — according to the textbooks — any right to be.

Métaireau's next hurdle for the visitor is a blind tasting of different vintages. He has strong views: "vintages are just not that important, despite what the press say. It's not true of all Muscadets, of course; some people's wines need alcohol, and thus sun; for us it is not necessary." The aim, he stresses, "is fineness and lightness of personality; finesse." So out come the four shrouded bottles to prove his point. "No-one else in Muscadet would do this," grins Métaireau with a flash of teeth. I settle down to taste four different vintages of the same wine. Is one darker than the rest? Is there a hint of freshness there — or here? In the end my score is two out of four correct. Métaireau gets none of them right (or is he bluffing?). "It confirms what I said. It's continuity, good vignerons, that count."

There is no doubt that selection is the key to Métaireau's success. He and his colleagues are ruthless in only selling the wines that are worth it under their own name. The rest goes anonymously to a merchant for blending. This is the practice adopted by the top Bordeaux château, where vats of wine which do not meet self-imposed standards are ruthlessly eliminated from the final bottling. Métaireau's Muscadet is of course technically correct. In an area with many small, ill-equipped growers, he has the stature to invest in decent modern equipment. And he has turned another modern art, marketing, to good effect. Every detail is thought of, down to labels in a new special polymer paper from America, which doesn't tear and does not float off the bottle in an ice bucket. Métaireau makes good Muscadet, and he wants the buyers to remember whose wine they are drinking, right down to the very last glass.

BOB MONDAVI

One person who talks as fast as Métaireau is Bob Mondavi, the Californian whose showpiece Napa Valley winery epitomizes the New World. He works as hard, if not harder, in a single-minded attempt to make the best wine there can be. Not for Mondavi the good-humoured acceptance of what Nature provides; he is tireless in his efforts to do better.

The Mondavi operation is unique, even in California, in being both very big and very good. It is also unique in being totally committed to experiment. "We've travelled the world over and learnt what makes a fine wine," he told me. "Then we go back and try to learn what's best for ourselves . . ." The travels include constant visits to France, especially Bordeaux and Burgundy. Mondavi's attitudes to the French classics is a mixture of admiration and irritation; irritation at what he sees as complacency. They could have made even better wine in Bordeaux, he implies, if they had been a bit more adventurous. At Mondavi's Oakville winery in the Napa, adventure is the keynote. "You will notice that there are changes between vintages in our wines," he said, introducing a tasting. "We try things like picking later for more flavour, then we get too much flavour, so we pull back and pick earlier. What counts is our palates – there are five, six or seven people who taste constantly. We're just learning how to make wine."

The learning involves trying just about every variation possible in wine-making. The small amount of Pinot Noir he makes has gained from storage in small oak casks, and from the abandonment of de-stalking — the grape stalks go into the vat along with the fruit contributing tannin to the wine. The entire winery is a laboratory, a place of unremitting experiment. To allow stem-retention, the crushers which receive the grapes were modified. Now the choice is there; stems or no stems. Each fermentation vat in the winery has a temperature control system, all monitored and run by computer. In contrast, some of the white wines are fermented in small oak casks — another Burgundian practice observed, evaluated and experimented with. Even the yeasts that cause the fermentation are the products of the Mondavi laboratory. The casks too, are no mere barrels; six different coopers, wood from different forests — all have been tried, the results tasted, the knowledge added to the store.

No factor that might contribute to the quality of the wine is left unconsidered. The Mondavi team — two sons and a daughter work with their seventy-year-old father — seems committed to yet further work. The latest project is Opus One, a fabulously expensive red wine made at Oakville in collaboration with Baron Philippe de Rothschild of Mouton. Not even Opus One is sacred. It was planned, the first year the wine was made, to have Merlot wine added to the Cabernet Sauvignon and Cabernet Franc in the classic Bordeaux fashion. But the Merlot was rejected at tasting. "It detracts," said Mondavi at the time, "because it doesn't have a strong enough character. We threw it out." No-one could accuse this wine's maker of not having a strong enough character.

Bob Mondavi

CHÂTEAU MARGAUX

The two men we've met in the last pages have taken essentially ordinary wines and made something special of them. The third winemaker – a woman, or rather two women — would concede that the land, the estate they farm, has more than usual importance. It is Château Margaux, one of the greatest wine estates in the world. The story of Margaux proves how essential is the balance between person and place. Great this patch of land may be, but in uncertain hands it can so easily decline.

Bordeaux's wine trade, like so many businesses world wide, suffered badly from the inflation and slump of the 1970s. Things got so bad that hardly any fine wine was bought or sold in the Médoc in the mid-seventies. The then owners of Margaux were forced by mounting debts to sell. They had had no cash to spare for investment: planting new vines and installing new equipment. For some years, Margaux, on paper equal in rank to the other First Growth châteaux, was slipping behind in the only league that mattered, that of price. Latour was making nearly twice the price per cask as Margaux.

The eventual new owner — it took some time to find anyone to take the place on — was a financier, André Mentzelopoulos. Within two years of the deal, he was dead.

Mentzelopoulos had, however, begun a large-scale investment programme. Things were looking up; whole vineyards had been drained, or had their old tired vines removed preparatory to replanting. The beautiful château itself was being restored. Everyone in the Médoc was watching Margaux with fascination; a great wine estate was being reborn. The 1977 and '78 vintages, the first under the new regime, showed promise. Then came the sudden death of the new proprietor.

Few observers expected that Laura, Andre's 60-year-old widow, would want anything to do with the estate. Fewer still reckoned that their daughter Corinne, then in her early twenties, would become involved. Yet the pair decided to continue the work began by husband and father. They retained Professor Emile Peynaud, a noted wine expert from Bordeaux University, to supervise each vintage. And they brought in a gifted young winemaker, Paul Pontallier, to run the place. Pontallier is even younger than Corinne Mentzelopoulos. She directs the business side of the company — and several others — from an office in Paris. He is on the spot at the Château, taking control of the everyday processes that go to make great wine. The two are in daily touch, keeping tabs on every aspects of the estate.

Pontallier talks of Margaux in terms of detail. "It is difficult to say just one thing in Margaux. It is a lot of small ones. Each makes a difference, if you're trying to make great wine." Details include keeping the whole place — cellars, vineyards, even the gravel paths in the gardens — in top-class condition. Pontallier says — and so seriously one must believe him — "we try to have the most beautiful conditions possible for the wine. We can't just consider the technical, we must look at the aesthetic. That's what makes a first growth."

Laura and Corinne Mentzelopoulos

Margaux is latently great wine; the right grapes growing on the right soil, with centuries of experience in wine-making going into every vintage. What the mother-and-daughter team have given Margaux is time, dedication and money. Lots of money. As an investment, the old financier has been proved right; Margaux wine is back on a par with the other first-growths, and the boom in prices has made the price he paid seem cheap. Yet it is not easy to go on putting money into a large, expensive farm whose produce, a decade ago, was just not in demand. It needs money and a bit of passion too; the desire to be the best, to live up to and exceed that first growth tag on the label.

Chapter Four

WINE MASTERCLASS

TECHNIQUES

The only technique needed to enjoy wine is the ability to open a bottle, and even that is becoming redundant as packs such as wine boxes, casks and cans become common. The only essential implement, once the cork is out, is a glass.

So is all the fuss about decanters, and cellars, and glasses of various shapes and sizes, a waste of time? No, if you want to carry the pleasure in wine beyond the point where it is a mere drink.

A little knowledge, in this case, is a most useful thing. A few techniques and a little care, will allow the wine — which after all is not cheap — to give of its best. Techniques are the wine buyer's way of protecting his investment. They are what this chapter is about.

The steps between the vague idea that a glass of wine would be pleasant, and the right wine being on the table at the right time, in the right condition, are simple enough. It comes down to choosing, storing, opening and serving.

Choosing means more than matching the wine with the occasion, a subject gone into in some detail at the start of this book. It means looking into who sells wine, and buying to the best advantage. It involves a certain amount of discrimination at the time of purchase, a little knowledge of the familiar tricks of the trade, in both senses of the term.

Storing wine can involve anything from a cobwebbed cellar to an upended cardboard carton in the kitchen. It is not so much the environment that matters as the planning: how much wine do you need to keep on hand, how long does it need to be kept?

Opening wine is simplicity itself — until there's an old bottle to be dealt with, complete with worrying sediment; or champagne, with its propensity to go off bang and break windows.

Serving involves pleasurable decisions such as what kind of glasses to use, how much to give people, and in what order to open the wines. It also means considering the temperature at which the wine is served, and making sure it gets to and stays at the temperature when and for as long as needed.

In short, it is perfectly possible to buy wine on the way home, open it as you sit down to dinner, and still enjoy every mouthful. It is equally possible to have the right wine for an occasion ready and waiting at home, to serve it at its optimum in every way — and to save money while doing all these things.

A store of good wine, well looked after, guarantees future pleasure.

CARE IN CHOOSING

It is one thing to decide, with the help perhaps of the pages in this book, on food and wine and with your own experience, that a bottle of Muscadet would be the best thing to drink tonight. But there are about 200 different Muscadets easily available from supermarkets, chain stores, mail order outfits and even direct from the growers. Which one is best? The answer of course is the one you like best at the price you can afford. And who can taste 200 wines before choosing? No-one, not even the most dedicated wine trade professional.

Every wine drinker has to abdicate most of the responsibility for choice to the experts. It is more a question of which expert to trust than which wine. The people who buy wine for sale to us are, in varying degrees, experts. By the very act of walking into one of their shops, we are putting our trust in them to choose our wine. The keen wine drinker has to learn a bit about the wine business, to understand a little about how wine reaches us, before he can pick his expert.

In very broad terms, the choice is between specialists and generalists. It used to be between knowledgeable wine merchants and ignorant grocers, between those who made wine a profession, and those who sold it as a commodity in the same manner as sugar or cheese. The grocers had a bad name: G.K. Chesterton went so far as to write *A Song against Grocers* decrying their habit of selling spirits and wine "not frankly and in fellowship" but in a penny-pinching, underhand fashion. Indeed, "grocer's port" became a byword for the adulterated and tawdry. Wine merchants, on the other hand, cultivated an image of gentlemanly expertise, of fine wines carefully laid down in ancestral cellars.

Neither stereotype is entirely dead. There are still chains of food stores which buy wine in the same "never mind the quality, see the price" attitude as their grocer forebears. There are still be-suited wine merchants whose advice is as good as ever and who offer unrivalled ranges of fine wines. But there are also supermarkets selling good wines from all over the world at keen prices. And there are, alas, traditional wine merchants trading on their image rather than their wines, and sadly ignorant of anything that has happened to the world in the last quarter-century.

Luckily for us, the traditional wine merchants are not the only specialists around these days. If your choice falls on Muscadet, it is possible with a little searching to find firms specializing in Loire wines, who will be knowledgeable about their chosen area and who travel to the Loire and pick their wines with love and care. Often such people will trade by mail order, and a dozen bottles will be delivered to your door with no more formality than a phone call. The same will be true of more or less any other wine region you care to name.

No-one wants to stick to a single wine region. This is where the next level of specialization comes in, the wine clubs and serious wine merchants. The best of the clubs offer a range of the world's wines, carefully chosen by experts and with plenty of tasting notes and other literature to help you make your choice. The same goes for the better shops. Wine shops vary widely in their degree of seriousness about wine. Many small corner shops make their living out of selling cigarettes and beer rather than wine. It is a folorn hope to expect much in the way of good wine from such places. They sell little of it, so what is in stock is quite likely to have stood around for some time, often in the worst of conditions. Harsh lighting, extremes of temperature and an upright position on a shelf (the cork dries out) can harm even the most ordinary of wines. The staff in such a shop will almost certainly know less about their wines than you do. The buyers at head office will probably choose their wines on the basis of price alone, with a fancy label perhaps swinging the balance. Except in emergencies, it pays to avoid these places.

Some "wine merchants" have made the decision to stress the wine side of their business. They are easy to spot; they make an effort. You'll find staff keen to help, if not especially expert. Perhaps there will be helpful labels on the shelves or on the bottles themselves, explaining a little about the wines. There will be price lists to be had, and in some cases a magazine or newsletter for customers. And, of course, the range of wines will be much wider than in the beer-and-tabacco stores. In all the wide choice of places to buy, these shops have perhaps the most to offer to the new or diffident wine drinker. Like the better wine clubs, they will have expert tasters and buyers at head office to select the range of wines.

There is much praise for the smaller firms in the wine selling business, the ones which can and do search out unexpected bottles and carry specialized ranges. But no-one should forget that buying power has its uses — and misuses — too. The really big chains, both wine merchants and food stores, buy so much that they can dictate to the winemakers. Some use this power to knock a few percentage points too many off the price. This inevitably leads to poorer wines; some chains go through periods where the buyer is over-keen, and the wines start to lose character and taste and become shadows of their various appellation stereotypes. Obviously if a buyer is forcing the pace of negotiations with, say, a big Côtes du Rhône cooperative, then the vats of tired, sub-standard wine are likely to find their way into the tanker that goes to that supermarket's bottling plant.

The big buyers have to keep price down and quality up; a not impossible equation. One of the largest UK chains was in the habit of buying vast amounts of cheap wine from Spain. It sold at the very bottom of the price spectrum under a brand name, and did very well. But the white wine, especially, was starting to slip in public esteem compared to other wines. It was overweight, flabby, rather tired to the taste. A typical ordinary Southern European cheap white, in fact. The big chain could have taken its custom elsewhere, but they decided on a creative move; they sent their Master of Wine to Spain with an ultimatum for the winery; install modern equipment, and take our advice on winemaking, or we'll move our business. The Spanish firm had little choice . . . In went the cold fermentation system, the stainless steel tanks replaced the dirty old wooden vats, the grapes were picked earlier

when the acidity was higher. Now the brand-name white is a far better bottle; fresher, crisper and tastier. It is selling well, and the consumers are getting more value for their money.

The only way to know which chains are taking wine seriously is to keep an eye on them, and to try their wines from time to time. Or you could, as with any source of supply, listen to the second-hand opinions of wine writers. We, like any journalists, do stand in danger of getting too close to our subject. It is a fair rule of thumb that writers are at their most reliable when talking about wine in generic rather than specific terms, though there are splendid exceptions; commentators who don't mind arousing the ire of the trade by being rude about particular wines by name. If the columnist on your newspaper is unfailingly uncritical about specific

Browsing is a new way of choosing wine. The old kind of wine store had a counter, and an assistant, and the customers asked for what they wanted. Today's buyers have a far wider choice, and are less sure of what they want. So modern wine shops have open shelves and helpful notes to guide customers.

wines, find another source of advice.

Where writers can help most is in keeping the buyer in touch with the progress, or lack of it, being made by particular regions or wine estates. A well-informed author is in the best position possible to assess and comment on, say, the relative virtues of the Bordeaux châteaux. He, or she will taste the wines, will visit the properties, pick up the gossip, learn who is making good wine and who spends his time and attention on gambling or his neighbour's wife.

Another subject we all need guidance on is vintages. Each year is different, and each year's vintage behaves differently as it matures. No consumer can keep up with all the changes, but the top specialist writers can. You can buy their advice very cheaply in books, magazines and newsletters. Here is the answer to that nagging doubt about when your precious bottle will be ready to drink.

As the choice of wine becomes ever wider, blind tastings are increasingly touted as the answer to the dilemma of choice. There are several annual and periodical publications in most wine-drinking countries which match wines against each other. This is laudable, but there are several ifs and buts which must be stressed. Tasting is inevitably an inexact process. Before you can have confidence in the results, you need to know who was doing the tasting, under what conditions, and to what end.

It has become apparent with blind tastings that rogue results can occur. If there are 30 varied wines on show, and half a dozen tasters, it is often hard to establish a consensus. From experience at these events I must confess that the most obvious or showy wine often comes out on top. It is almost inevitable. The palate very quickly becomes tired, especially when a lot of quite

Far left: *there are many ways to buy wine. The better wine stores have a very wide choice ranging from "dump bins" of cheap special offers (foreground) to fine bottles correctly stored lying down in racks (background). Some stores arrange wine by country – here, for instance, there are shelves for French whites, burgundy and so on — while others group bottles by style. This system gathers together dry whites, dessert wines etc.*

Left: *at the opposite extreme, people living in wine areas can visit the source of the wine and buy direct. Estates and wineries may offer the chance to taste – though few are as sophisticated as this Australian set-up. Many small European growers offer tasting samples straight from the casks in the cellar.*

different wines are on show. Tasters pick on the wines with the strongest characteristics, the ones with the powerful nose or the back-slapping taste, because they naturally stand out. Then the panel has to get together and choose a "best buy". The consensus too easily comes down to the most startling wine, not the best. This perhaps cynical analysis is sometimes used to explain the success of California wines tasted blind against European classics. The New World wines, it is said, are more dramatic, louder, but not necessarily as complex. Whether or not this is true, blind tasting certainly emphasizes the showy not the subtle.

This warning against blind tastings is less apposite when true experts are tasting a restricted range of wines under carefully controlled conditions. This began in the wine trade, where buyers select their house claret, say, from a range of samples. The bastardization of the practice comes when journalists or writers apply it to a range of different wines, in an attempt to find the "best". Picking one from a selection of samples of the same thing is not the same as deciding which tastes nicest, a Mosel or a Chardonnay, from a range of wines all in some abritrary price band. Thus the newsletters and magazines which assemble a tasting of, say, 1982 Médocs, *or* 1983 Napa Cabernets, will probably come up with some useful data. The wider the range, the less use the results.

Another way in which the old-fashioned blind tasting system has been adapted is in wine awards. This burgeoning practice began with laudable aims. The idea is for independent experts to taste the wines of a region, blind. Medals are awarded to the best. Good scheme. It works well, if the judges are indeed expert and if the whole thing is organized conscientiously. Sadly, there are medals and medals. One notorious contest offers entrants a guaranteed medal on payment of a fee, which also covers the cost of the awards dinner. Others, only a little less dishonest, divide the medal catergories up so that some entrants cannot fail to win a prize. There are, for instance, very few Indian whisky distillers, so a Double Gold is a virtual certainty if any of that handful care to enter the Indian Whisky class.

It is therefore not entirely true that wines with "gold medal" on their label are indeed of the best. Some awards can be trusted. The French contests held at Paris and Mâcon are serious affairs. The Germans have local and federal tastings, with the winning wines being awarded prizes which they display as gold, silver or bronze strip-labels on the necks of bottles. Medals awarded at shows in Australia and New Zealand can be relied upon. Watch out for the dates attached to medals; a gold at the Brussels fair in nineteen 0 whatever is no more than evidence that the wine firm has been around for a long time.

The wine-producing countries all have quality control systems: Appellation Controllée and the like. These ensure that the buyer is getting what the label proclaims the wine to be, and that it has met certain minimum standards. But they do not and cannot guarantee a good wine. To return to Muscadet, there are several thousand people making wine there, and several hundred merchants. No official control system can turn all these people into careful, skilful winemakers, though the majority are. Nor can a set of regulations stop hail falling on one vineyard and not the next, or rot from spoiling one person's grapes and not his neighbour's.

In the end, we are all in the hands of the people who trade in wine. Care in choosing one's wine merchant is the first step towards drinking well.

BUYING WINE

No-one should need any advice about buying things. Spending money is all too easy. What does need saying about wine is that planned buying is worth the effort. As soon as wine starts to play anything like a regular part in your life, it becomes worthwhile to have a store of it. There are three good reasons. One you are more likely to have the wine you need when you need it. Two, wine stored for a while often improves — even the modest stuff. Three, buying early, and in bulk, saves worthwhile sums of money.

To take the last first, many merchants will give a discount if wine is bought by the dozen bottles, sometimes even the half-dozen. These deals are negotiable: if you can get together with a friend or neighbour and double the size of the order, a further saving can often be made. The dozen lots need not be of the same wine: some stores will let you mix the case. This is the simplest logic for bulk-buying.

In addition, many people buy wine early in its life, both in order to save money and to ensure that they have what they need. This applies mostly to long-lived wines such as port, Bordeaux or other serious reds. The saving comes from taking on the job of financing stock. There was a time, not so long ago, when accountants were unheard of in the wine business. Merchants used to buy the new wine in cask, bottle it and leave it undisturbed in the cellars until they reckoned it was about ready. Then, two or ten years after the vintage, it was put on sale. The price would be not much more than the cost of replacing the wine with the latest vintage. In other words, the dear old wine merchants were not covering the cost of tying up their capital in stock. Times are tougher now. The accountants are through the door and into the boardroom of any surviving wine merchant. Everyone has worked out that if the wine sits around in the cellars for a decade, it represents money that could be in the bank, earning interest. So prices now reflect this equation, never mind any inflation allowance, contribution to overheads and who knows what else the money-men can dream up.

It is open to the private drinker to ignore the accountants and store up his treasure in his own cellar rather than the bank. This involves buying the wine while it is young and keeping it until mature, not bothering too much about the money thus occupied.

It may not on the face of it make much financial sense, but it is somehow easier to hold onto wine that is not ready to drink than to store up money. It is certainly less painful to drink wine bought at yesterday's prices than today's.

There are other advantages. First among them is that by laying down wine you can be sure of getting the wines you want. There are fewer and fewer merchants holding long lists of mature wines, so if you want ten-year-old Shiraz or Burgundy you may have limited choice as well as high prices to contend with.

Then if you have the wine yourself, you control the conditions it is stored in. Some hints on storing come later, but it is worth noting that the international trade in fine wine is a growing one. I heard only the other day of a consignment of 1982 claret that is on its way from New York to London,

A shop window onto the world of wine. The better wine stores offer the consumer a wide choice of bottles from both traditional and novel wine regions. Chains of such stores have the buying-power to negotiate low prices, and they run strict quality control systems to make sure wine is palatable as well as cheap.

Top right: *Cellar door sales are one way to buy wine without a middle-man.*

having failed to sell in the USA at the inflated prices asked. This wine will thus have crossed the Atlantic twice before it is even remotely mature. Winemakers may be clever these days, but they do not design wines with 12 weeks in a cargo container in mind. It only needs the container to spend a few days in the sun on a Gulf of Mexico dockside for it to be ruined beyond help. The hazards of travel cannot be removed altogether, unless you own the château, but it makes sense to minimize them. This can be done by buying from a reputable merchant, and storing the wine at home or in a place where the conditions are predictable.

Storing can improve wine. And not just the classics, either. Many very ordinary wines benefit from as little as two or three months' rest after purchase. This is really the key reason for buying ahead of our needs for most of us. It adds taste to the wine without adding to the bill.

The reason why so many ordinary wines benefit from rest is that the modern wine trade rushes them through the system so quickly. An ordinary jug red will probably be only weeks away from the bottling plant by the time we get it. This is a good thing for most white wines, though there are exceptions, but nearly all reds will gain (or at least not be harmed) by a little bottle-age. Say a couple of months. Any more is dangerous, as these everyday wines are not designed to mature. All you are doing is giving them a rest, a chance for their chemistry to recover from the shock of bottling and transport.

As soon as the wine gets above the basic quality the arguments for storage get far stronger. I am a great fan of the new red wines from Southern France, made on the small estates which are starting to emerge in the "wine lake" country. It is too much to hope that these wines have been aged in cask or bottle for very long. Ageing wine costs the producer money, just as it does the merchant. Some, but not all, of these wines can gain from cellaring. As to which to keep and which to drink, I'll come to that later.

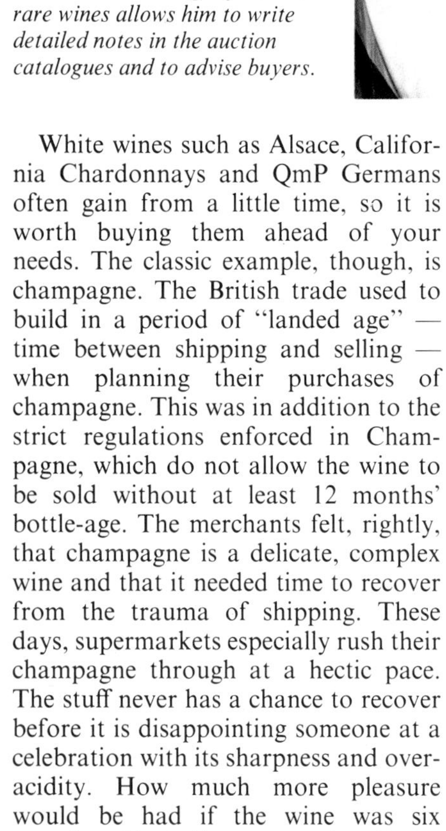

Right: *In an ideal world, we'd be able to taste every wine before we buy. Naturally, few wine stores can offer this facility. Auctions, however, allow prospective buyers to sample the lots before the sale. This tasting is taking place in the Great Rooms of Christie's, the London auctioneers which are as well known for wines as for great works of art.*

Far Right: *Michael Broadbent, Christie's Wine Director, samples the sale lots himself. His unrivalled knowledge of old and rare wines allows him to write detailed notes in the auction catalogues and to advise buyers.*

White wines such as Alsace, California Chardonnays and QmP Germans often gain from a little time, so it is worth buying them ahead of your needs. The classic example, though, is champagne. The British trade used to build in a period of "landed age" — time between shipping and selling — when planning their purchases of champagne. This was in addition to the strict regulations enforced in Champagne, which do not allow the wine to be sold without at least 12 months' bottle-age. The merchants felt, rightly, that champagne is a delicate, complex wine and that it needed time to recover from the trauma of shipping. These days, supermarkets especially rush their champagne through at a hectic pace. The stuff never has a chance to recover before it is disappointing someone at a celebration with its sharpness and over-acidity. How much more pleasure would be had if the wine was six months older! Champagne is often a spontaneous purchase, it's true, but if you can look ahead at all — to a wedding or party in a few month's time, say — it is really worth buying the bubbly now.

The third reason for advance buying is to have the wine you need when you need it. This avoids frantic last-minute purchases, which are all too likely to disappoint. A home wine store of not more than a dozen bottles can achieve this.

There is more to buying than planning ahead. In some parts of the world, mostly in the winemaking districts, it is increasingly common to buy direct from the maker. Growers in some parts of France have seen a dramatic rise in their cellar-door sales as new autoroutes are completed. Chablis, once very much a backwater, is now on the direct route between Paris and Lyon. It is fashionable among Paris winelovers to drive out to Champagne — only a couple of hours away — to load up the estate car with the produce of some small grower. Recently, the southwest autoroute has added the Loire and Bordeaux to the list. The habit of buying direct is also common in Germany, and a positive way of life in the New World winelands of the Cape, the West Coast and Australia. Northern Europeans, too, have taken to buying their wine while on holiday by car in France or Italy.

There are good savings to be made this way, but the most significant gain is in the pleasure of actually seeing the place where the wine comes from and meeting the people who make it. There is no guarantee, of course, that the wine will be any better than the bottles in your local store. In fact you are deliberately doing without the protective shield of a wine-merchant's expertise. The charming grower you stumble upon may be the man the entire wine trade avoids, the one farmer in the village whose wine is fit only for the vinegar factory. Luckily there is an increasing number of reference books listing wine estates and showing whether they accept visitors and sell direct to the public. Some growers do not, of course. They may have an exclusive contract with a merchant, or a series of private customers who order the wine in advance. It is unfair to expect such places to sell wine to casual callers.

Some private buyers build up a long-term relationship with a grower or growers, ensuring that they get the pick of the crop. In places like California, this is the only way there is to get to drink the produce of new, small wineries.

There are other ways of short-circuiting the wine trade, and getting your wine virtually direct from the grower. Two that are increasingly common are door-to-door sales and wine warehouses. It is hard to recommend buying

from visiting salesmen, even those who offer to organize a "wine tasting" for you at home. They will only be selling the wines of one merchant, which limits your choice without gaining the close contact that direct buying offers. The only point of the "tastings" is to make you feel obliged to buy some wine.

Warehouses are a different matter. They import wine direct and also sell off odd parcels of wine. These can be bankrupt stock, bottles with torn labels, wines that are getting old. The rule in a warehouse is thus very much "buyer beware", but among the piled-up cases in these cold, uncomfortable sheds there are bargains to be had. While the warehouses offer basic wines at keen prices, they also list good ones, obscure ones, rare ones. Once you get beyond the cheap stuff, a little knowledge is vital. If you are prepared to take a few risks, and to carry a reference book while you browse, some fine drinking can be had at low prices. Warehouses are very much places of the moment: if there's a glut of champagne (there is, occasionally), or a major currency fluctuation, wines can find their way to them, good and cheap.

Auctions used to be another fertile field for bargain-hunting, but they've gone up-market as wine investment and speculation grow more common. The auctions were once the last resting-place of bankrupt stock, but the warehouses seem to have cornered that market. Auctions are the place to search for older, rarer wines, the sort no longer listed by the big stores.

While wine buying is a much safer activity than it used to be because there is much less really bad wine around, problems do arise. If a wine is "off", take it back, along with the cork, and just about every wine merchant will refund your money. The merchant will send the wine to the supplier, who will probably analyse it to find out what went wrong. It is not fair to take wine back just because you don't like the taste, but complain if it is not what it should be: if it is faded and out of condition, or it is downright rotten. It can happen, and any merchant will accept the fact.

Price is not everything when buying. The old-fashioned merchants used to throw in a complete service with their prices. They would store your young wines, order things for you, give advice, deliver to your door. Today the level of service offered varies widely, not always in parallel with the prices asked. Supermarkets, at one extreme, will not even carry the case of wine to your car. The better merchants will perhaps lend you glasses for a party, deliver free of charge large amounts of wine, store wine for you — at a cost — and offer advice. Tastings are organized for customers, and they'll open an account for you to ease payment. They will even arrange for you to visit their suppliers abroad if you are on holiday.

Whether you want all this service is up to you. You will certainly pay for it somehow. It is worth comparing price and service packages, especially when buying wine in bulk. Some of the clubs, especially, have to be carefully watched. The best are superb, offering great expertise and some splendid deals. The worst are covert ways for lazy wine merchants to shift boring wine at a premium price. Or, even worse, they are run by people with no wine knowledge at all who are just climbing on board the wine boom.

Luckily, the choice both of wines and of ways to buy has never been greater. If choosing bores you, hand the decisions over to a trusty merchant. He'll even plan a cellar for you if you let him. If the thrill of the chase exhilarates you, as it does me, happy hunting.

PLANNING AND INVESTMENT

A drinking plan sounds on the face of it to be the first step towards alcohol poisoning. But it is the action of a prudent man to look ahead a little. A plan for future wine drinking involves spotting which wines, now young, will be good in the future. It means knowing that your daughter will get married in May and buying the champagne the previous November, when it is cheaper and when it will have a chance to gain some bottle-age. It means having enough wine in the house to cater for your planned, and even unplanned, social life.

The great complicating factor in wine is time. Time changes each bottle, for the better if it is good wine to start with. Each vintage is different from its predecessors. So even the wine drinker with fixed tastes has to take account of what time is doing. You may take a fancy to Château Lafite, but if you don't make some study of the ageing and changing of vintages you will either drink your Lafite too young or too old. And even with a great wine, you cannot be sure a mature vintage will be there in your wine-merchant's catalogue every year. Weather disasters happen even in the well-ordered world of Bordeaux, and people do tend to drink wine, making it sadly unavailable for others.

For the less prosperous drinker, an eye on the vintage is even more vital. Good rather than great wines have shorter lifespans, poor vintages are more common.

Time introduces a dimension to cellar planning which some people (myself among them) find somewhat daunting. Planning has started to be useful to you if you do no more than store away the odd bottle. Just putting aside a couple of bottles of a young red which seems to have prospects is an act of cellar planning. You don't need to be a big wheel in the *en primeur* claret market, or a dabbler in Napa futures.

Most wine is sold when it's ready. But quite a few wines reach the shelf too young for optimum enjoyment. This is most true of reds, but some whites, especially Rieslings and Chardonnays, also qualify. Buying these wines, tasting them and then acting on your assessment is cellar planning. You're saying that you will still be drinking wine in a year, and it makes sense to buy at today's prices and drink better wine in twelve months.

There are more intriguing ways of buying ahead, but the main factor must be tackled first: how much will you need? It is important to restrict your planned purchases to a part of your consumption. By this I mean, don't leave out the happy accidents. If you drink two bottles of wine a week, by all means let one of them be the cellared fruits of some long-term planning. But let the other be a new discovery. It could be a chance purchase at a discount store, a supermarket special offer, a wine brought by a friend, something you spot that you've been meaning to try.

The other half of the household consumption can, and indeed should, be planned. If it's a bottle a week that means a plan for just over four dozen a year — say five dozen to allow for parties and holidays. It is easy to imagine getting a year ahead in your buying, so the wines being drunk now will have been in store for twelve months. But, not all wines mature at the same speed. Given careful choice, all the wines in the cellar will be better for a year's age, though some will need more time. The subtlety of planned wine buying is working out how long it will be before the wine is ready. It is possible to draw up endless charts and lists speculating on the lifespan of various wines. But there are too many wines, and too many variables, for this to be much use. So given that your wine cellar contains some age-worthy bottles, how do you know when they are ready?

If you are lucky, other people will be continually opening bottles of wine, and the way to know if your bottles are ready or not is to tap into the news network. The first person to ask is the one who sold you the wine. A well-run wine store will hold tastings of its stock, and will keep in touch with the origin of the wine to get news on how it is coming on. Look at the merchant's annual list: it will often have notes on the state of the various vintages. Magazines and newspaper columns will carry tasting notes and assessments of vintages and individual wines. Several books come out annually with updates on the qualities of vintages. There is no shortage of advice and news, the problem is that some is likely to be contradictory.

Apart from that, the only sure way to see if a wine is ready is to try a bottle. This is fine if you have a dozen: it can be interesting to watch the slow progress of a wine to maturity by trying a bottle every six months or so. If in doubt, you must open that single bottle. Decant it, taste it, and then leave it for an hour or two. Air, in the decanter and the glass, will have the effect of ageing it and bringing on a sort of premature maturity. The important point is that this process does not work backwards: old wine cannot be made young.

It is not worth trying to keep wines that have no keeping qualities. Restrict the long-term cellar to as much as you can afford of the really good stuff and buy everyday wines more frequently.

The mechanics of advance buying used to be the province of the wine trade. Recently, with the upsurge of interest in wine, and the rise in prices, ordinary consumers have joined in. Advance or *en primeur* buying is a habit of the Bordeaux trade, now spreading to other regions. What happens is this. In the spring after the vintage, merchants will go around the châteaux tasting samples of the young wine. It will still be in cask, of course, with anything up to two years' maturing ahead of it before it even sees a bottle, never mind a glass. But the trade buyers will be experienced enough in the quirks of young claret to make a judgment. If the wine is good, they will reserve some. Then, they will try to sell some or all of their allocation to customers.

The ordinary drinker gets the chance, in the summer of the year, to buy some wine *en primeur*. There's no chance to taste, it is a matter of backing the merchant's judgement and reputation, as well as the track records of the various châteaux. Once the choice is made, the merchant will want paying for the wine although it will stay at the château, maturing until being bottled and shipped in a couple of years. The merchant will then deliver the wine to his customer, presenting as he does

Investment can pay off: staggering prices are recorded at auctions of very old and rare bottles. These exceptional affairs apart, the auctions offer a useful way of selling surplus wine and of buying mature vintages unavailable elsewhere. The usual unit of sales is the 12-bottle case, not the single bottle: it pays to keep cases of wine unbroken if you are planning to sell.

another bill for transport and taxes.

Cynics will note that the customer pays for his wine two years or more before he gets it, and that the cash is in effect an interest-free loan to the château or the merchant or both. True. But the customer also gets the wine at the opening price. On past form, the price a year after "opening" — the date when the château first offers it to the trade — will be at least 25% higher. So that should cover the loss of interest on the money.

Buying at opening is a good way to ensure that you get the wine you want. It also makes possible investment and speculation. Wine investment is one of those cyclical financial buzz-words like Australian nickel mines or microchip manufacturers. About once a decade, people with no knowledge of, or interest in, wine start to buy it in the hope of selling at a profit. An equal timespan separates the wine market crashes which lose some or all of these people their money.

The logic behind wine investment is seductive and subtle. There is, the line goes, only so much Latour or Taylors port around. Granted, they make some every year. But people drink it too, and there is no real way that Château Latour could double its production. So pick a well-thought-of year, and the commodity can only get scarcer. Every night, some millionaire or Hong Kong businessman pulls the cork on another bottle of Latour '61. Short of forgery, no-one is making Latour '61 any more. So the price of it has to go up. Thus the investors' logic, which is broadly correct.

The dangers are best illustrated by example. In 1970, especially fine wine was made in Bordeaux. The same was true in 1971. The world was in one of its more bouyant economic moods, and people were spending money. Spending fuelled price rises in Bordeaux as the châteaux saw increased demand for their wines, the price of which had been coasting along for a decade. Inflation, caused by what you will (choose your economist), began to rise, prompting further price rises at the châteaux. The Japanese, for some reason, started to drink claret. Press comment on the two good vintages added to the interest. By late 1972, Bordeaux fever had broken out. Prices jumped as everyone wanted to get hold of some claret. First it was the drinkers, then the speculators, who saw the price curve rising and wanted to join the bandwagon. The '72 wine was poor, although plentiful. But by this time no-one was taking much notice of quality. It was names, famous names on labels, that counted. The '72 vintage was bought as avidly as its forerunners.

1973 and 1974 were not such good years for the world business machine. Oil crises, rampant inflation, slumps on the stock market: the speculators were in trouble. The first thing to go from many peoples' portfolios was wine. It was a marginal investment and it went in the first wave of selling. The selling prompted a little sanity in the marketplace. People started to taste the '72s — and said rude things. 1973 was a little better, not much. Claret prices started to plummet. Distress sales were held at which canny buyers secured parcels of great wines at silly prices. It took until 1979 for the auction prices of claret to catch up with the heady days of 1972.

That was the great Mid-Seventies Claret Crash. It was spiced by some good scandals in Bordeaux, but the fundamental engine was supply and demand. A worryingly similar pattern was being followed in 1983, '84 and '85. Anything can happen.

Investment in wine can and does work. Speculation in wine is very chancy indeed. I'd distinguish the two by saying that an investor can afford to drink his wine, and would be happy to. A speculator, buying on the margin, would probably choke on it. It has been common for some years for buyers to add a few extra cases of wine to their orders, knowing that they are surplus to requirements. When mature, these wines are sold to finance young wine.

Investment would not work without a marketplace. This is provided by the auction houses, especially those in London, which provides a forum for the trading of anything from bankrupt stock Liebfraumilch to 1811 Madeira. If you do want to sell some mature wine, an auction is almost certainly the place to sell. And buyers, too, can find rare, interesting and mature wines which are not stocked by any merchant.

STORING WINE

The best wines in the world are those that never leave the cellars beneath the châteaux where they were made until they are drunk. This truth is commonly recognized by people lucky enough to get invited to dinner at these august places. It isn't just the magic of the surroundings that makes the wines taste better: the traditional château cellar provides ideal storage conditions.

It is nowadays an old wives' tale that wine does not travel. Any well-made wine — and that is a vastly larger percentage than it was — can stand being shipped. What it cannot stand is poor storage at the other end. Good wine changes over time. Up to a certain age, it gets better. Then, after a peak of excellence, it declines. In order to go through this magic process the bottle needs certain conditions. This perhaps makes more sense if the changes are thought of as chemical reactions, which is exactly what they are. Dim remembrances of school laboratories bring to my mind the fact that heat has a lot to do with things. Strange inert powders and liquids sprang to life over the bunsen burner. Temperature is a central factor in the maturing of wine, too. Warm conditions speed up the reactions inside the bottle, cool ones slow them down. Too much heat, too much cold, or too rapid a change between the two, can ruin the whole process.

A lot of chemistry experiments also revolved, I recall, around oxygen or the lack of it. Corks keep oxygen out of the bottle (and the wine in, of course). That is, they do as long as they are moist. Dry corks contract and let in air. This starts a wholly unfortunate chemical reaction: the wine oxydizes. The process is the same as the rusting of iron. The wine takes on a brown colour, be it red or white to start with. It loses all its freshness and a dull, metallic taste pervades it. It is wholly ruined.

Luckily, a moist cork will stop all this, and the way to keep a cork moist is simple: keep the bottle on its side.

It is these two factors which matter most in storing wine: temperature and position. Anywhere that the bottles can be laid horizontally at a moderate (50°-60°F, 10°-15°C) and steady temperature will do. There are lots of other details to consider, but details they are.

Some commercial cellars store wine vertically, by the simple trick of turning the cardboard boxes upside down. This works very well with white wines (you might find it a useful space-saver for home storage) and reds which are not likely to develop a deposit. But any good red wine which might "throw" a deposit needs to be horizontal. It also needs to be undisturbed. If the bottle is left still, the deposit will form along the side of the bottle, making it easy to decant the wine without pouring the deposit off too.

Wine is often described as a living fluid, which is romantic but not quite true. More accurately, it is a complex mixture of living organisms and inert things like minerals and compounds. The living bits include enzymes, which act as catalysts for the biochemical reactions. These involve the alcohol, the various bacteria, tannins, and pigments and a minute trace of oxygen in the wine. This fragment of oxygen is the fuel for all the various activities going

Far left: *the average wine drinker is well served by a rack such as that pictured here. It can be stood on the floor or in a cupboard, or wall-mounted. Note that the bottles are stacked label-upwards.*

Left: *the private reserve storage at a New World winery. The steel and wood racks are a modern version of the traditional brick cellar bins. Because large quantities of the same wine are stored, the bottles can be stacked — there's no need to get at the bottom bottle.*

on. Because it is corked, the contents of a bottle is a closed system; nothing can get in or out, apart from the very tiny amount of air that filters in through the cork and which helps fuel the processes. In the nature of all chemical processes the reactions work themselves out, leading eventually to the state of maturity that is what makes keeping wine worthwhile.

Not every wine goes through this process. Some are so sternly filtered by their makers that they do not have the necessary ingredients for the reactions to take place. Others are pasteurized, killing at birth the living things that might have improved the wine in time – but also eliminating harmful ones that could spoil it.

And it must be stressed that most wines don't have the necessary ingredients to age well. It is only one bottle in a hundred that gains from years of cellaring. The wines that do benefit are those made with age in mind: good clarets, burgundies, Cabernets and other red wines; port; and good sweet whites. These wines have large proportions of sugar, or tannin, which can react with the oxygen. They get these ingredients both from the way they are made and from the place where the grapes were grown. Only the best wine ages, partly but not entirely because it is *made* to age: fermented with the skins, stalks and pips and then aged in wood, Conversely, it is not worth taking this expensive trouble with wine from ordinary vineyards: only the best has the structure and depth to benefit.

Thus the wines that will age in the buyer's cellar have, to a large extent, been chosen for us. Some, though, have more potential than their reputations suggest — this is especially true when remarkably good years confer class and concentration on normally ordinary wines.

There then, in all its biochemical subtlety, is one reason for storing wines: the good ones get better. Indeed, they *need* age: a young Hermitage or Stag's Leap Cabernet is an inky, awkward thing. Give it ten years, though . . .

The other reason, touched on in the pages on buying wine, is that ordinary wines improve too, if over a different timespan and for different reasons. A third, most practical reason to store is that you then have the wine you need when you need it.

Temperature and position are the key factors in wine storage, but other things also help. Low humidity will help to prevent the growth of mould on corks. This is only a problem if you have a very damp cellar and are keeping wines for a long time. What happens is that moulds can grow on the ends of the corks, and can work their way through the cork cells into the wine. A more obvious problem of a damp cellar is that labels fall off bottles, and cardboard boxes rot. This can be a nuisance, not to say a disaster, if you try to lift a box full of bottles with a rotten base. Missing or damp-marked labels make it hard to be sure what's in the bottle, and reduce the value if you ever want to sell the wine.

Light is another enemy of wine, but only strong light, and then it does real harm only to those wines in clear bottles. Vibration is considered bad too, but on what grounds I am not sure. Common sense shows that any shock or disturbance will stir up the sediment in fine wine, but you'll need to have a pretty unstable household for this to be a problem. More to the point, resist the temptation to constantly gloat over your stock of bottles. Lifting them, tilting them, waving them about will disturb the sediment and generally upset the wine. Be strong-minded and keep your hands off.

This list of ideal conditions will lead again and again to a nice dry semi-basement cellar beneath a château — or to any cellar beneath any kind of structure. Cellars, because they are partially or totally below ground, maintain a generally even temperature. They will never get too cold, or too hot, and the rise and fall will be steady. Earth is a great insulator, and the floors and walls of cellars are surrounded by it.

If you have such a cellar, the only problem is to equip it with something to hold the bottles. Quite a few cellars are very damp, but that need not be an obstacle. A friend of mine has a cellar which regularly has six inches of water in it: he's installed a small Japanese electric pump for rainy days, he keeps the bottles well off the floor, and controlled ventilation keeps the humidity at a reasonable level. Cellars can also be very dry, and dryness can cause corks to dry out. A simple way to boost the humidity is a layer of packed sand on the floor, which can be dampened occasionally.

An ideal cellar environment can be achieved, at a price, by the use of air-conditioning. It is most economical to use an insulated cabinet kept at the required temperature. These can be bought, though clever people have been known to adapt wardrobes using refrigerator motors and insulated board. You might even go so far as to consider building on, or under, the house. In hot climates, choose a north-facing wall (south in the southern hemisphere) and erect a well-insulted lean-to structure; a sort of conservatory in reverse. Or it may be feasible to dig down under the garage. The unfortunate experiences of some amateurs leads me to urge that you consult an architect or engineer first.

Most of us, far from digging or building, are hard put to find an unused cupboard in the crowded family home. This is where ingenuity comes in. The bottoms of clothes closets are often under-used and the conditions — darkness, a degree of insulation — will do quite well for wine. Spaces under staircases, lofts or attics (if insulated), old chimneybreasts, under the bed — all

have been tried. A lot depends on how warm your home is. Even with central heating, parts of the house will be cooler than others. A cupboard or alcove on an exterior wall will stay cool, whereas a kitchen will not. Lofts can be used, even if they get too cold, providing the stock of wine is itself insulated. Invest in a maximum-minimum thermometer and take readings for a couple of days in different places.

It is never impossible to find a place for the odd few bottles of wine kept for everyday use. It is the longer-term storage that causes problems. Wines bought by the case are best kept in their cases. They will be easier to stack, and, if the problem is too much warmth, they will keep cold for a surprising length of time due to the insulating properties of the cardboard or wood. It is worth nothing that a large mass of anything maintains heat — or cold — better than small bits. Look at icebergs. So, if you can build up a stack of cases and insulate them (old blankets and newspapers will do) they will say cooler — or warmer — than single bottles.

Once a corner has been found, you'll need some kind of shelf or rack for the bottles. The more expensive French wines sometimes come packed in wooden cases. If you are prosperous enough to afford to buy such wine, don't open the cases until you need to. It is also sometimes possible to scrounge or buy such cases, empty, from wine stores, and you should try to find them with the wooden bottle spacers still inside, and with a lid. These provide very useful racking for longer-term storage.

Old-fashioned cellars had "bins" — sections divided by brick walls and stone-slab bases. The idea was to store several dozen bottles of one wine in a neat, satisfying stack. The butler would then descend every now and again and count them, entering his totals in a ledger for future generations to drool over. Households in those days bought wine by the cask, or the dozen dozen, or some such quantity. Bins, if you have them, are very useful even for the odd bottles or dozens we tend to buy today. But whatever the quantity of wine, some kind of rack will be needed to allow access to individual bottles.

Racks do not have to be single-bottle size. A space a foot or so square, a sort of cubby-hole, is useful as it gives room for a dozen bottles. When stacked one on top of the other, honeycomb-fashion, a dozen takes up less space

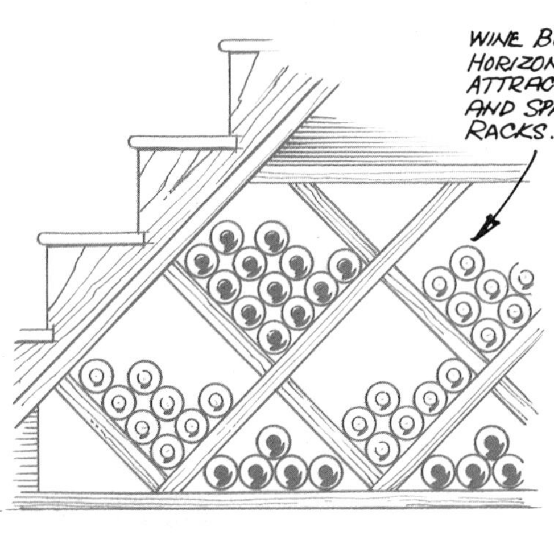

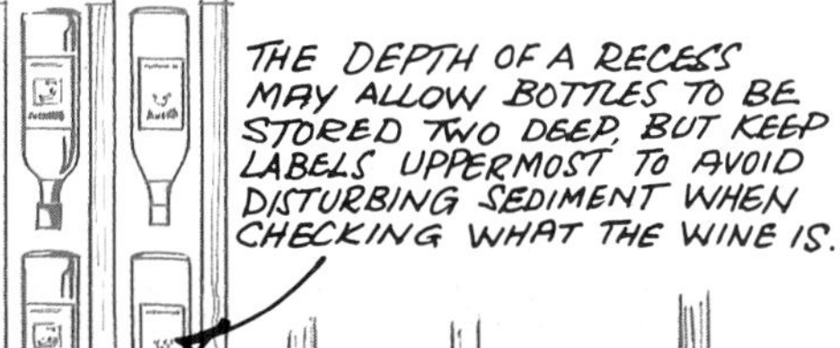

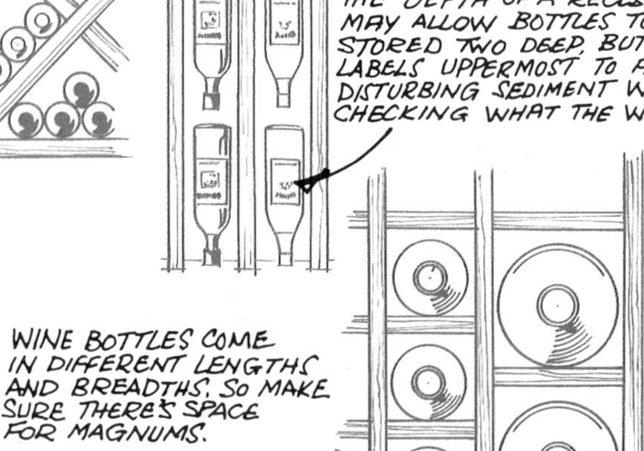

TOUGH CARDBOARD CARTONS WITH DIVIDERS—THOSE MADE FOR SPIRITS ARE THE BEST—MAKE USEFUL CONTAINERS.

Left: *Something to aspire to! The showpiece cellar of a Bordeaux château, where the estate's oldest and most treasured bottles are kept. The square wooden bins on the righthand wall can, however, be copied in a very small space. But there are plenty of cheaper alternatives . . .*

than when in carton or case. Single-bottle racks are useful for those wines we only have one of, which in most people's case will be most of them.

If the space available is awkwardly-shaped, the manufacturers of wine racks will tailor-make them, fitting in spaces in odd corners or making the whole rack in a triangle shape to go under the stairs.

Many people, myself among them, resent spending money on fancy wine racks when it can be spent on wine. Relax: no expenditure is really necessary. Shelfs and bins can be built from scrap timber — the things to spend money on are the plugs and brackets that fix them to the wall. I spoke to someone once whose three-dozen-bottle rack had just fallen off its perch, with horrible results. He was a shocked and bitter man. An even cheaper storage system consists of heavy-duty cardboard boxes begged from a liquor store. Aim for the ones that Scotch or gin come in: they are made of heavy-duty board and are much more rigid than the wine boxes. Lay them on their side and you've got a wine rack. Why pay more?

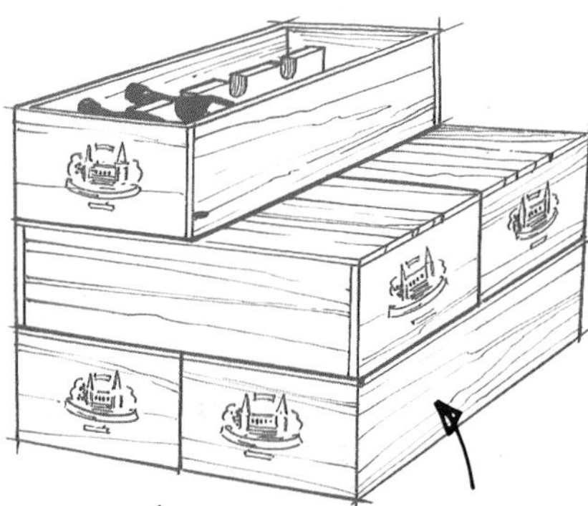

SOME CHÂTEAUX STILL USE WOODEN CRATES FOR PACKING THEIR BOTTLES. THESE MAKE EXCELLENT MINI STORES WITH THEIR WOODEN SEPARATORS TO HOLD EACH BOTTLE IN POSITION. THE CRATES STACK WELL AND ARE EASILY IDENTIFIED BY THE BRAND STAMP AT EACH END.

WHETHER ERECTING OR MAKING USE OF EXISTING SHELVES, ALLOW FOR THE LENGTH OF THE LONGEST BOTTLE. SMALL STURDY BATTENS AT MEASURED INTERVALS ALONG THE LENGTH OF THE SHELF KEEP BOTTLES IN POSITION AND ALLOW FOR EASIER STACKING.

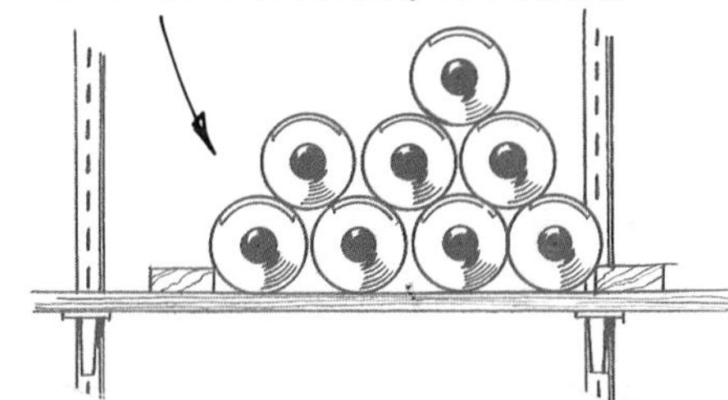

A STURDY AND FIRMLY HUNG WINE RACK OVER A DOOR MAKES ORIGINAL USE OF "DEAD" SPACE.

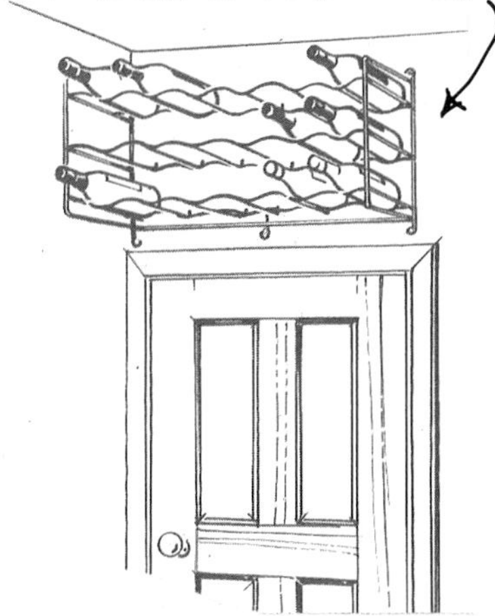

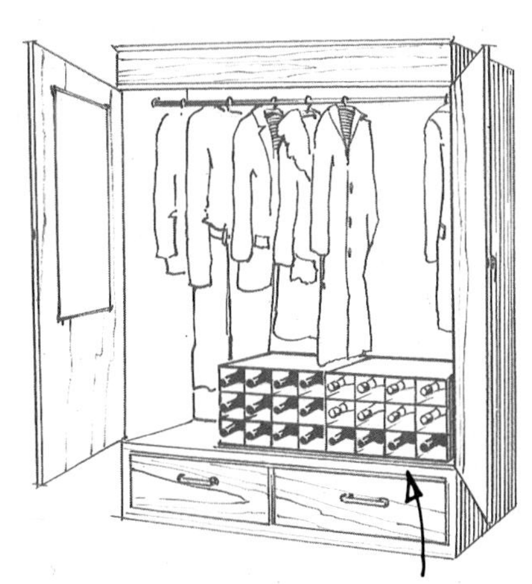

THE BOTTOM OF A WARDROBE CAN ALSO PROVIDE USEFUL ACCOMMODATION.

SERVING

Having gone to all the trouble to choose the most enjoyable wine, and then buy and perhaps cellar it, it's worth taking some trouble over serving it.

The rights and wrongs of serving wine are summed up in the words timing and temperature. When a bottle is opened can have a bearing on the taste, and temperature is crucial to perfect enjoyment. Time also matters because some wines show at their best if given a chance to "breathe", or take in a little air, before being drunk. This is a topic covered in the later pages on the mechanics and philosophy of decanting.

Temperature is easy to get right, and it makes a considerable difference to the flavour of a wine, yet many neglect it. Wines, like people, only function properly in a narrow temperature band. Too cold, and they are dumb, unresponsive and moribund. Too warm, and they are flabby, tired and overblown. This applies to both red and white wines, the only difference is where in the range they should be served.

What temperature does is control the rate at which a wine's aromas and tastes develop. All those chemicals in wine react to heat, and when they are let out of the bottle it is the outside temperature which decides how fast they change. The changes include the transformation from being part of a liquid to a scent. Get this right, and all the scents the wine is capable of show themselves, and all the flavours emerge and mingle in the glass. Too cold, and this is still waiting to happen, and meanwhile the wine has been drunk. Too warm, and the reaction gets overheated — alcohol fumes take over from the lovely, attractive smells and flavours.

Temperature has a bearing on still more aspects on a wine's pleasure quotient. The cooler, the more refreshing. In this respect and in others, white wines are better cooler than red ones, and light wines cooler than heavy ones. Whites need to be cool partly because one of their first duties is to refresh. This brings up another element in the equation: wines can be judged on a simple-complex axis as well as a sweet-dry or red-white one. Simple wines, especially whites, need to be cold. Their charm lies in tartness, briskness — all the refreshing qualities. They have little of that flavour which makes us stop, think and sip. A more complicated white wine has more in it, more to taste. Drink it slightly less cold, to allow the flavours their chance.

It is also true that a deep chill masks the poverty of taste of some wines, and even hides glaring faults. This is why professionals taste even white wines fairly tepid: the truth will then out.

Strangely, the sweeter the wine the colder it needs to be, I have no rational explanation for this, except to observe that a warm sweet wine always tastes cloying, whereas a chilled one adds refreshing notes to the sweetness.

It always used to be said that red wine ought to be served at room temperature. Which room? My comfortable dining room is your dank, draughty cell and someone elses's overheated, stuffy fug. The "rule" was laid down when houses were a good deal colder than they are today. So, if we applied it, we would be drinking wine rather warmer than our ancestors intended. Red wine can be too warm — and often is, especially in restaurants. Between 60 and 65 degrees F (15-18°C) is a good level to aim at.

Red wine should if anything start off too cold. It will be warmed quite quickly by the glasses and perhaps decanter, which will be at room temperature. The drinker's hand on the glass adds further warmth. While a red wine can be gently warmed by the hand, it cannot be cooled. Don't let red wines, specially precious ones, go past their peak of flavour by getting too warm.

Not all reds needs to be warm. There is a tradition in the regions of production of drinking young red wines cellar-cool. This is emulated by all those who refrigerate their Beaujolais Nouveau. Simple red wines are as much about refreshment as whites. They can stand being chilled and it emphasizes their cut and acidity. The better the wine, the less chilled (not warmer) it should be.

Given that temperature matters, how to regulate it? The lucky ones are those with a cellar at 50°F. Their white wines will always be at drinking level and their reds will mature slowly, and can be brought to table a couple of hours ahead in order to warm up. These lucky people however cannot plead the old excuse about how sad it is that the champagne is not cool, otherwise they'd pop a bottle right now. For them, it is *always* cool.

Less well-equipped drinkers resort to the refrigerator if they have planned ahead, and the ice bucket if they have not. Refrigeration will cool a bottle from normal living temperature to drinking condition in about two hours. That is if it is not too full, and if it is left in peace. A busy family, forever opening and shutting the door, will add an hour to the process. Do not, by the way, be tempted to keep wine in the refrigerator for any length of time. A few days is fine, but after that many bottles seem to pick up a rather musty taste.

An ice bucket must contain three things: the bottle, some ice, and a lot of water. Those who forget the last are missing out the most important bit. The reason why a refrigerator takes so long to chill the bottle is that air is a bad transmitter of heat. And all that is happening is that heat is being conducted away from the bottle. If you stick a bottle into nothing but ice cubes all you are providing is a bit of cold air around some ice cubes. Add water, and immediately things start to happen. Water is a far better conductor of heat than air. The cold water transmits the heat away from the bottle, warming itself in the process. This is why an ice bucket will cool a bottle in 10-20 minutes whereas a refrigerator takes a couple of hours.

Ice buckets should ideally be deep enough to take a tall bottle and immerse it up to the neck. If this is not happening, turn the bottle upside-down for the last five minutes. Otherwise the first glass out of the bottle will be warm, even if its successors are cool.

To prolong the cooling of wine on a hot day, use larger lumps of ice. Bear in

mind that when the ice has melted the water will rapidly take on the ambient temperature — and warm the wine back up again.

If the weather is hot, serve the wine a few degrees colder than it should be. It will soon warm up.

The chart shows suggested temperatures for a few representative classes of wine. No rules are fixed, though. The books say drink claret at 65°. But young wines of vintages like 1982, full of fruit and sugar, are delicious ten degrees colder. It is also written that dry sherry should be cold. True, for straightforward fino. But an old dry oloroso — just as dry, but different — would be struck dumb at fino-serving temperature. It needs a little warmth to speak out.

Above: *cool wine in a handsome glass reflects an appetizing gathering of bottles.*

Suggested serving temperatures in degrees Centigrade.

Sparkling	5
Sweet white	5
Rosé	6
Dry sherry	6
Dry white	7
Medium sherry	8
Light red	12
Red Bordeaux	15
Top reds	18

A normal refrigerator is at about 4 degrees. A heated room is about 18–20 degrees.

GETTING THE CORK OUT

Corks have been abandoned for beer bottles, lemonade bottles, every kind of bottle except wine. Why? Because cork, uniquely, lets the wine breathe just a little through its fibres. Unlike plastic, cork is natural and therefore the seal it produces is not quite perfect — to the benefit of the wine. The minute amount of air that gets in allows wine to develop and mature. Wine historians assert that fine wine was only made possible by the discovery of the cork seal in the 17th century. Sufficient to say that today's top wine estates pay over the odds for the best and longest corks.

The adoption of the cork forced someone to invent the corkscrew. Putting it in is no problem; just twist (the only trick is to keep it going straight). Getting it out is tough work: a really strong pull is necessary to budge the cork from the bottle. So inventors have devised subtle gadgets to aid the weary or weak-wristed drinker. The "waiter's friend" employs the lever principle. The Screwpull adapts the old double-action principle, using a long worm with a non-stick coating. For an easy life, choose a corkscrew with leverage or double-action. And pick one with a hollow spiral. Those shaped like a drill, with flanges round a solid shaft, will more likely drill a hole in the cork than pull it out.

1 *Cut or tear away the capsule to expose the cork.*

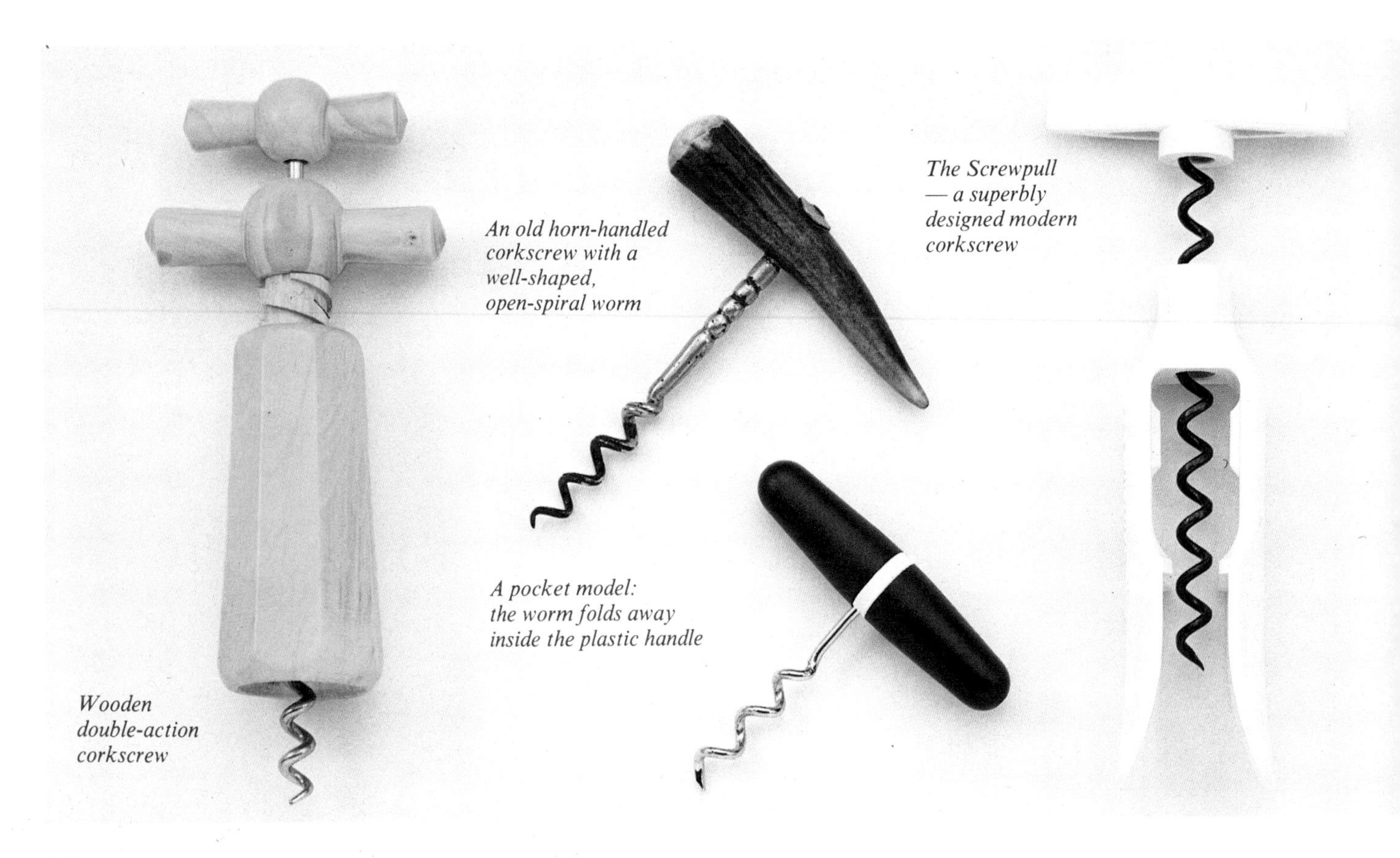

An old horn-handled corkscrew with a well-shaped, open-spiral worm

The Screwpull — a superbly designed modern corkscrew

A pocket model: the worm folds away inside the plastic handle

Wooden double-action corkscrew

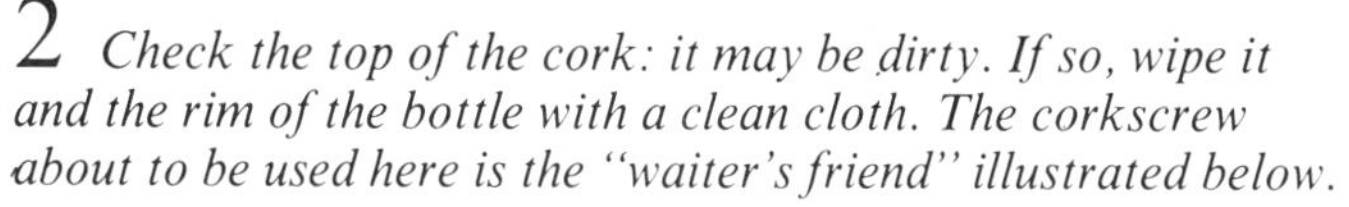

2 *Check the top of the cork: it may be dirty. If so, wipe it and the rim of the bottle with a clean cloth. The corkscrew about to be used here is the "waiter's friend" illustrated below.*

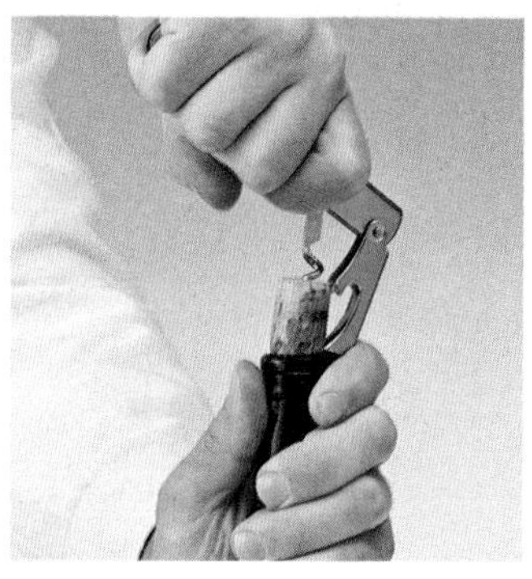

3 *Some corkscrews have off-centre tips, so centre the screw itself, not its end, over the cork for best results. Steady the lever on the bottle's rim, and pull the cork using the leverage.*

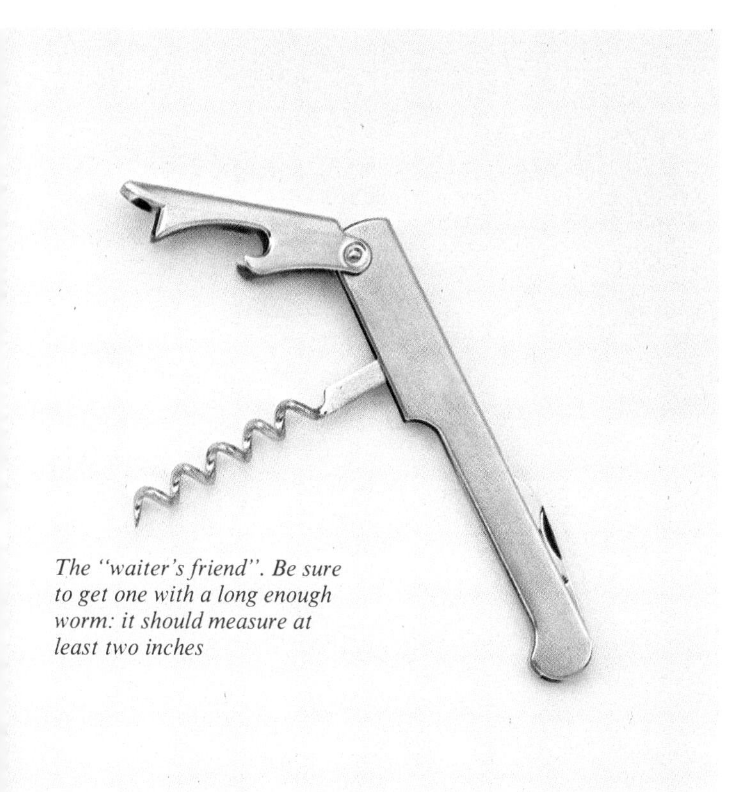

The "waiter's friend". Be sure to get one with a long enough worm: it should measure at least two inches

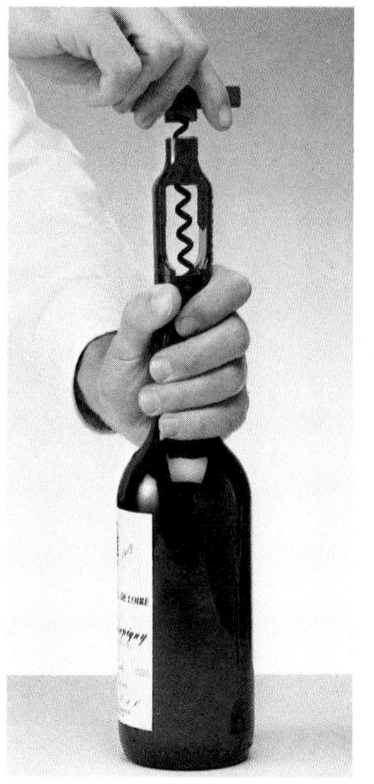

4 *The Screwpull simplifies the process by guiding the worm centrally down into the cork, and by needing only the one action: just keep on turning and the cork climbs out effortlessly.*

Opening Champagne
The pressure behind a champagne cork is formidable: the gas that provides all those beautiful bubbles can also force the cork out at high speed and spray wine across a room. This is dangerous and a waste of expensive wine and it's unnecessary. It takes only a little dexterity to get the wine into the glass without risk or drama.

There are two main steps in the opening of a bottle of fizz. First, get the wire "cage" off the cork, then get the cork out of the bottle. The cage is the modern successor to various bindings of cord and string which used to keep champagne under control. It passes over the top of the cork and anchors around the collar of the bottle. It is secured by a neat little twisted tag. The only problem arises when, as very occasionally happens, the tag breaks. A pair of pliers then comes in useful — but be sure to keep a thumb over the cork.

When removing the cork, the trick is to use the pressure in the bottle to push it out under your control. Don't expect to be able to keep it under your thumb forever — that gas is powerful. But with care you'll be able to ease the cork out by hand with a gentle "phut".

To start with, make sure the wine is cold, and don't shake it about. Have the glasses close to hand to avoid spillage. Open as illustrated, being sure always to point the bottle away from people, or mirrors, or windows . . .

1 *Have the glasses close at hand. Then remove the decorative foil to expose the cork and the wire "cage". Champagne bottles, like guns, should never be pointed at people!*

4 *The second bottle has a stubborn cork: apply more pressure with a thumb or (inset) thumbs. For more force, hold the cork still and turn the base of the bottle instead.*

5 *Pour a little wine into each glass, then top them all up. This avoids over-flowing. Sliding the wine gently down the side of the tipped glass also helps.*

2 *With a precautionary thumb over the cork, untwist the wire tag which holds the cage on. Ease the cage away from the bottle collar and take it off.*

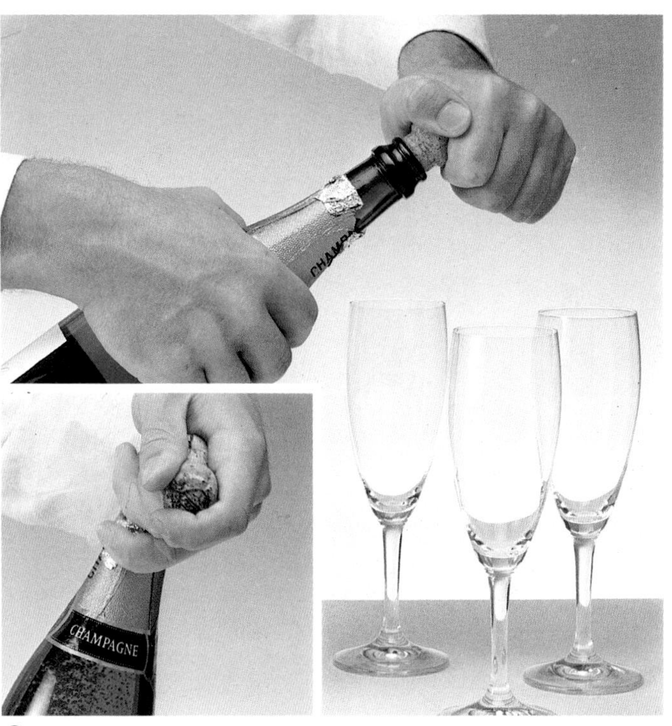

3 *Grip the cork and twist gently. It should start to move up under the pressure of the gas, and pop gently into your hand. The inset captures the escaping gas at the moment of release.*

6 *Fill the glasses three-quarters full to give the bubbles room to show themselves.*

Above: *Tricks of the trade: this is the way professionals pour champagne. It is easier because all the weight of the bottle is in the base. Holding by the neck quickly tires the wrist. The "closer",* ***right,*** *will keep the bubbles in if for some reason you fail to finish the bottle.*

DECANTING

Any container will serve to hold decanted wine, but decanters are traditional and handsome in their own right. Clear glass is best, be it cut, as in the silver-topped claret jug, or plain. The largest of the four is a magnum decanter, big enough to hold a magnum of wine — the equivalent of two bottles.

Antique claret jug — containing claret

Beaujolais in an elegant cut-glass decanter

A magnum decanter which holds two bottles-worth

Tawny port in a modern decanter

Coloured glass can be fun for port — in this case ruby — or liqueurs, but it hides the enjoyable hues of the wine. The old cut-glass decanter shows off the colour of good sherry.

Why decant?
There are two reasons for decanting. First, some wines develop a "deposit" as they age: some of the substances in the liquid turn into solid particles which settle at the bottom of the bottle. Pouring, or decanting the wine into another container allows this deposit to be left behind. The second vessel can be anything from a Georgian heirloom to a jug, a carafe or just a clean bottle.

The second purpose of decanting is to let a wine "breathe". There's much argument about the need for this: most French experts are against it (the "breathing is for people" school of thought). A period in a decanter exposes a young, immature wine to oxygen and "ages" it rapidly. It tastes less hard, and it opens up, releasing scents and flavours which would otherwise be dormant.

The process
When you're decanting to separate wine and deposit, first stand the bottle up for 24 hours to let the sediment sink to the bottom. If such forethought is lacking, the decanting cradle or basket is needed to keep the bottle in the same horizontal position as it was stored, with the deposit lying undisturbed along the lower side.

The candle throws a light upwards through the neck of the bottle, so that you can stop pouring the minute you see the deposit appear. The funnel avoids spillages. This one is silver, but a plastic kitchen funnel will do fine. The cloth is to clean the bottle's neck.

Step one is to remove the cork without shaking the bottle: when using a basket, a waiter's friend or Screwpull ensures a smooth, steady extraction.

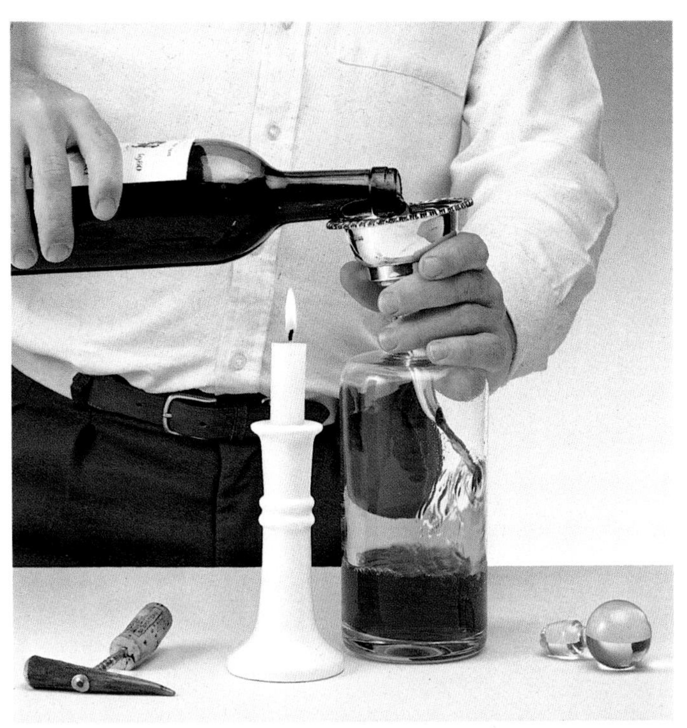

1 *Pour the wine slowly and steadily into the decanter. Don't pause or the wine will slosh back into the bottle and stir up the sediment.*

2 *As you near the end, watch the neck of the bottle — the candle lights it perfectly.*

3 *You'll see the sediment enter the neck: stop pouring and tip the sediment back into the body of the bottle.*

GLASSES

Just as any clean bottle will do duty as a decanter, any glass will hold wine. While bearing this robust truth in mind, it's entertaining to choose and use the most suitable glasses for various wines. The principle of selection is simple: the glass should show off the best of the wine in every way. Clear glass lets the beautiful colour shine through; an in-curved rim holds and concentrates the scent. Thus it's perfectly possible to serve any wine in one style of glass. Of those illustrated below, the large glass second from the left comes close to being an ideal all-purpose wine glass. It is big enough to be only half-filled and yet contains a generous amount. This allows the drinker to swirl the wine gently around, releasing its perfume. The in-turned rim guides this perfume to your nose: a good half of the pleasure of the wine is lost if you miss this. The long stem keeps the warm hand clear of the wine when a chilled white is being drunk. The glass is clear and thin, allowing the wine's colour to show through.

The glass on the far left is almost as good, but perhaps better adapted for white or sparkling wine. The tall-stemmed glass third from the left is the traditional shape for German white

wine. It shows off their subtle colours, but could perhaps do with a turned-in rim.

Cut glass, as in the glass third from the right, attractively reflects facets of light into the wine. Purists demand plain glass, but they miss the delightful play of the candle-light on crystal and on wine. This cut glass does have a long stem and an in-turned rim, so the main attributes of a good wineglass are all there. The next glass is ideal for sparkling wine. The tall shape allows the bubbles to rise attractively, and the narrow top concentrates the wonderful smell of the champagne. (Who on earth designed those boatlike champagne saucers? The contents, not surprisingly, quickly becomes as flat as the glass. If you've inherited some pretty ones, march them down the centre of the table — with night-lights in.) The last in this line-up is another good all-purpose one, though perhaps too small for red wine, which needs space to be swirled about a bit. Where this one wins votes is as a good everyday glass: the heavier weight and that elegant, tapering stem look robust enough to withstand my washing up.

Gewürztraminer—Alsace

Champagne

Sauvignon Blanc—Pouilly Fumé

Professional wine-tasters often use a special glass in the shape of an outsized tulip: it is designed to hold a small amount of wine, which can be swirled about to release aromas and sniffed at through the narrow top. The glass on the far left does duty as a tasting glass but also serves for port or sherry. It has a softened tulip shape, not as exaggerated as the "official" version, but far easier to drink out of. When tasting, pour only a little wine: even less than in the picture.

When enjoying good red wines, especially old ones, the bigger the glass the better (within reason). The large bowl-shaped one second from the left, and the big tulip second from the right, both allow a good measure of wine to be poured but give it space to be swirled. This movement gets air into the wine as well as releasing its bouquet for maximum enjoyment. Clarity is the other requirement for such a glass: the colour of the wine is an important facet of its character, especially when it is old and rare. The big tulip here is perhaps a little too full: in the picture it is being used to serve a young wine which also benefits from aeration but does not call for particular reverence.

The three cut glasses are enjoyable

Cabernet Franc — Saumur Champigny

Gamay — Beaujolais

Cabernet Sauvignon — Claret

containers for port, sherry or madeira, or (in the case of the largest) for red wines.

Carefully-chosen glasses deserve care. It is quite hard to get them properly clean: they seem to pick up odours all too easily, and then transmit them to the wine. Plenty of clean, hot water for rinsing is essential, and finally a polish with a cloth kept specially for the glasses. Store glass upright in a closed cupboard: a cloth draped over them keeps out dust if there's any about. Standing glasses upside down on a shelf keeps them dust-free, but the rim of the glass often seems to pick up a taint from the shelf itself. It is possible to devise ideal systems for hanging glasses from racks by their feet, in a closed cupboard, of course.

However careful you are, a final polish with a clean cloth before use always seems necessary.

There used to be elaborate rules for the placing of glasses on a table. I try to fit in enough for all the wines, plus one for water. If there are two red wines on the table at once, it is helpful to have glasses which can be told apart so people can tell which wine is which.

Ruby port *Pinot Noir — Beaune* *Sherry*

THE CELLARBOOK

It sometimes seems contradictory to keep notes about a passing pleasure such as wine. Yet as soon as you start keeping a little wine in store, and especially when that store contains several bottles of the same wine, it becomes worthwhile. Well-chosen wine gets better with age (we hope) and it is amusing to follow its progress, bottle by bottle, by means of notes. The second purpose of a cellarbook is to keep track of your store of wine. May you own enough to forget how much you've got!

Any notebook can be a cellarbook. Some people use loose-leaf binders, others buy purpose-made ledgers. I manage very well with a hard-backed sketch-book. The plain paper gives flexibility, allowing me to record one bottle or a dozen on the same page. The pages are perforated, allowing their removal when they become irrelevant.

The recording process is in two stages. Log the wine in when you buy it, noting its name, vintage, source of supply and price, and of course the date. Then when it's drunk note down when, and what it was like. Some people add details of the meal and the company, which can be instructive, and will avoid your giving your guests the same wine two dinner parties running. It is then also, of course, a pleasant reminder of happy occasions.

This simple record-keeping can be elaborated endlessly. If you get to own a lot of wine, it is useful to note where the various bottles are. A grid system can be devised, allotting key numbers to the spaces in the wine-rack to ensure orderly storage. A more typical note would be "in spare-room wardrobe" or "under stairs".

It is sometimes quite hard to fit all the details about a wine into purpose-printed cellarbooks, which is another argument for blank paper. Some types of wine are simple: for claret, it is merely château and vintage. For burgundy the vineyard, the grower and (perhaps) the bottler have to be added. German QmP wines have line after line of detail, all of which is relevant to the wine. The simplest way round this is to soak the label off the bottle, but the glue used often defeats the best efforts of a bucket of water. There seems, by the way, to be a reverse correlation between the quality of the wine and the tenacity of the glue: the nastiest wines have the toughest labels.

The hardest side of wine record keeping is logging just how many bottles you've got. If you buy a dozen bottles of one wine, it's worth including a "balance" column in the notes on that page. This should, if conscientiously filled in, tell you at a glance what's in stock. There is probably a way of adding up all these columns in your cellarbook, and discovering how much wine is in store, but I've yet to perfect it. The trouble is that wine comes in as well as out, so any perpetual inventory system has to accommodate movements in both directions. People with personal computers can even buy software to run an electronic cellarbook. But the need to fill in the details remains, and somehow one always forgets to power up the PC, load the cellar archive disk, and enter it all, in the excitement of buying (or drinking) the wine.

A cellarbook becomes a necessity not a luxury when you start to buy the wine *en primeur*, or even order some for delivery by post. It is vital to keep track of whom you have paid for what. Keep the letters, receipts and other documents too: they'll form your title to the wine. A note in the cellarbook allows calculation of which wines will be ready when. It is a pleasant sport to plan years ahead, attempting to estimate the household's likely consumption in the comforting knowledge that a case or two of claret is maturing in the cellar.

CELLAR
BOOK

WINE AND HEALTH

A highly respected wine writer once told me how he was faced with a momentous choice. In his mid-40s he caught a very serious liver complaint. His family doctor, whom he had known since childhood, announced that he would have to give up wine — for good. "I then had to make the most difficult decision of my life," he told me. "After much thought I made up my mind. I changed my doctor." The old gentleman was nearly 80 when, glass in hand, he told me this tale.

Wine and doctors have always had a rather ambivalent relationship. Ever since ancient times medicine has known that wine is a good and useful thing. They have also known that wine — or to be exact the alcohol in it — is a drug, which in excess can be dangerous.

Alexis Lichine, the encyclopaedist of wine, puts the case for wine with typical Gallic eloquence: "The magic of wine is intrinsic and complete. It induces confidence, a sense of well-being and euphoria, thus conditioning a moderate wine-drinking man to be happy and healthy. It disposes him to relax and encourages his appetite." Lichine goes on to point out that wine is too complex to be completely analysed by even the most modern chemical processes. Its many ingredients, some present in tiny amounts, include several of proven worth.

The ponderous techniques of modern science are groping to "prove" what the ancients, and the natives of wine countries since classical times, knew and have always known: wine is both enjoyable and useful. For instance, wine, especially when diluted, has long been known to be a disinfectant. When the water in cities was unsafe — which was most of the time, until a century ago — wine was an essential everyday drink. Recently, researchers have isolated an ingredient in red wine which kills harmful bacteria, including the dysentery bacillus. This is of course not a substitute for prescribed drugs, but it confirms the empirical wisdom of generations. Travellers today find a glass of wine a great help when facing unknown food in a foreign place, for just the same reason.

Before modern medicine, doctors would prescribe wine as a tonic. Again, recent research has disentangled the reasons why. They are several. First, wine stimulates the appetite. It prompts stomach activity, sets in motion the flow of various gastric chemicals, and (perhaps less scientific, this) stimulates the senses of taste and smell. All combine to awaken appetite in those who, because they are tired, stressed or ill, fine little interest in eating. Too much alcohol has the opposite effect, depressing the appetite. A glass 20 minutes before a meal is usually the right amount. Of course, most people drink before a meal for social reasons, but it is pleasant to think that the apéritif has some function as well as pleasure.

It is not just the alcohol in wine which has this appetite-boosting effect. Tannins and acids present in wine appear to contribute to the process.

Wine is also full of useful ingredients which help supplement the diet. Both red and white wines contain iron, in a form which allows the body to readily absorb it. A glass of wine supplies about 10% of the daily intake needed, points out nutritionist Professor Arnold Bender, who comments "so if you do drink, you would do better to stick to beer or wine — at least you would be getting some nutrients along with the calories." Wine also contains several elements which the body needs; phosphorous, calcium, zinc, magnesium, iodine — the list goes on, Vitamins are present too: A, B and C are found, sometimes in useful quantities. The grape sugar, small amounts of which are left behind by fermentation in many wines, is also easily absorbed.

As Professor Bender points out, wine contains calories. Those on a diet or with the need to watch their weight should drink in moderation. There is much debate about calories and weight-loss, and it's a debate I will not enter here. To give two examples of the range of opinion, Professor Bender points out that a glass of wine contains about 70 calories, while Professor Georges Portmann of Bordeaux says wine can be used to replace calories from fat or sugar, because the calories in wine "will not add to the body weight." Take your pick. It's noticeable, by the way, that French doctors seem to cry the virtues of wine in the diet more loudly than do British or American. Maybe it's a case of a little of what you're used to does you good.

Wine acts as a source of energy (which is to say the same thing as wine contains calories, of course). As such it has a role as a tonic both in medical and social terms. It has been discovered that the alcoholic strength of wine — about 12% — is exactly right for this. If the drink is stronger, the energy from the

alcohol is less readily absorbed by the system.

Another medical/social use of wine is as a mild sedative. A small amount is considered by many doctors to be safer than the drugs otherwise used. A series of studies has shown that old people benefit from a small but steady intake of wine. They sleep better, develop more appetite and (as you'd expect) feel happier. This is partly because wine contains among its vast recipe of chemicals some obscure ones that act as a calming influence — anti-anxiety drugs, as it were. These, it seems, are many times more efficient than the alcohol itself.

One of the classic beliefs about wine was that it was a useful part of the diet if oil or fat were also being consumed. The ancient Roman diet consisted fundamentally of bread, olive oil and wine, and this is the basis of many rural Mediterranean diets to this day. Untutored people still talk about the wine "cutting" the fattiness of food — as is so often the case, they are right. Recent research in Lyon has established a connection between drinking wine and lessening the ill-effects of fat in the diet.

What damage can wine do? Different people have very different levels of tolerance to alcohol and to acidity, etc. Some can't tolerate red wine, some can't take white. But it is of course the alcohol that does any real harm. Normally, the liver copes well with wine. If drunk with food, and at a moderate rate, the digestive system of the body should deal with the alcohol as fast as it is drunk. Too much alcohol overwhelms the system and damage, possibly cirrhosis of the liver, can occur. Alcohol abuse leads to other effects which can compound the damage done to the body. Alcoholics tend to have a poor diet, for instance, leading to vitamin and mineral deficiencies. Alcohol taken with food is much more easily absorbed — but problem drinkers tend to drink without eating.

How much is enough? That's a question only a doctor can answer, for it depends to a great extent on the age, physique and general health of the person asking. It also seems to vary with habit; give up drinking for a while and you'll find it harder to cope with an amount whch used to slip down easily. My very cautious advice is that up to half a bottle of wine a day, drunk with food, is unlikely to do you any harm. This may be too much for small people, and for women, who seem for some unfair reason to come to more harm from alcohol than men.

How and when you drink makes as much differences as how much. Always with food, or before meals, is best (but not, obviously, too much if you haven't eaten in ages). Drink water as well — alcohol dehydrates the body rather than quenching the thirst. Stick to wine, or beer. Spirits (I'm biased here) do you more harm and less good. Drink decent wine; there are more good things, and fewer bad ones, in sound, well-made wines than rough, badly-made plonk. And good wine has more taste, which encourages you to drink it more slowly.

I find it sensible to stop drinking altogether occasionally, both to prove that I can and to give the body a change. A week or ten days on mineral water will be good for the bank balance and for the digestion. Try this once every three months or so — and especially after festivals like Christmas which tax the system.

Most people drink very little by the standards of, say, the French, who in rural areas have been known to drink three or four litres a *day*. But it's worth stressing that if you have any doubt about how much is good for you, ask a doctor.

It is also vital to take medical advice about drinking if you are taking some other kind of drug — even aspirin. Some antibiotics and tranquillizers interact with alcohol.

Hangovers

The body has a way of telling you you've had too much. Sadly, it is retrospective; at the time it probably seemed like a great idea to open the second bottle. Likewise everybody knows that the best way to avert disaster is to drink copious amounts of water — as much as you can manage — to dilute the stuff, wash it quickly through the system and lessen the dehydration effects which are what's really going to make you feel bad. Everybody knows — but no-one at the time is in a fit state to remember.

Science has little to offer on hangovers, except to emphasize the obvious in that irritating manner experts have. They have discovered, you see, that the more you drink the worse it gets.

COOKING WITH WINE

One of the most instructive tastings I have been to in ten years featured not a row of bottles but a couple of stews. Perhaps casseroles would be the right word: technically they were *bouef bourguignon*. One had been cooked using an ordinary wine. The other, as the classic recipe for this Burgundian dish insists, with a good Burgundy — in this case a single-vineyard wine from the Côte d'Or. The tasters could certainly spot the difference.

Elizabeth David makes the same point: "a friend once reproached me with having withheld from her some secret in the recipe for a beef and wine stew. She had cooked it, she said, exactly as I had told her but the flavour was not as good and rich as mine had been. In a sense she was right to tax me with inaccuracy, for I had forgotten to tell her that on that particular day I had used a glass of my good Rhône wine in cooking the dish, and it had made all the difference."

The reason why the quality of cooking wine matters is that it isn't the alcohol in wine that is being added, but the taste, Alcohol has a low boiling point and almost always evaporates during cooking. What is left is the flavour, so it follows that the wine had better have some to start with. This is not to suggest a first growth in every pot. The wine must be honest and without faults, and it must taste of something, that is all. If you'd happily drink it, cook with it.

This puts in their place all those odd left-over bottles hanging around kitchens on the "it'll be all right for cooking" principle. It won't be if it is a week old, tired, and oxidized. There is, however, a use for these left-overs: as a marinade. They are often acidic and sour (which is why the bottles were only half drunk) and these qualities can be put to use. Soak tough cuts of meat in wine overnight, then throw away the liquid and cook the meat. Better still, use decent wine to start with and add the marinade in the stew.

Marinading is only one culinary use for wine, but it's perhaps the most important. A marinade, which is mostly wine with a little oil, herbs or aromatics, both tenderizes and adds flavour.

The next most useful attribute of wine is the taste and texture it gives to slow-cooked meat and poultry dishes. You don't need much wine: the rest of the liquid in a casserole can be water, with a good glassful of wine added. Put it in right at the start, then cook the dish long and slowly. The wine combines with the meat and vegetable flavours to form a rich sauce — and it all happens naturally without any further trouble on the part of the cook.

Wine is also useful in fast-cooked sauces and gravies. Say you have roasted a joint or a chicken. The pan juices, once most of the fat has been poured off, are thickened with flour. Then in goes a generous dash of red wine, salt and pepper, a little vigorous stirring and bubbling — and there is an instant and delicious sauce. The same process works with the pan juices from grilled meats, but there you don't need the thickening flour.

Fish can be baked in a sort of bath of wine: solid fishes such as mullet and mackerel do well this way. Just pour the wine and other seasonings over the fish and bake it, uncovered. The same idea works with grilled fish; the wine and herbs go in the bottom of the grill-pan, flavouring the fish by steaming as much as anything, and forming the basis for a sauce. Poached fish, which cook quickly, can use wine too. When the fish is cooked, pour the wine used for poaching into a pan and boil it to reduce and concentrate it. This strong-tasting fish/wine essence goes into the sauce served with the fish.

Just about the only dishes which use uncooked wine are soups and fruit desserts. The tradition of adding a spoonful of sherry to a clear soup is a sound one. Put it in after the soup has been poured out: the heat will release the aromas and the flavours. Madeira will do as well if not better than sherry.

Fruit and wine are a potentially magic combination. The Austrians steep strawberries in wine to make a sort of cross between a pudding and a drink: leave the cut-up fruit, slightly sugared, in the wine for a couple of hours, then pour the wine and the fruit into glasses. Raspberries, peaches or strawberries all work well.

Spirits are also used in cooking, chiefly to flambé or flame dishes. This is more than a trick to impress the customers. If brandy is added to a pan in which meat, say, has been sautéed, and the brandy set alight, it burns off the fat, leaving a sauce composed of the pan juices and the essence of the brandy — but minus the fat. The alcohol burns away, too. Brandy, whisky, Calvados or any other spirit will do. It pays to warm the spirit a little in a pan or ladle, then to light it before pouring over the dish. The flaming process is often done as a last finishing touch to a dish, but it can be done at an earlier stage. For instance, a beef casserole can be enhanced by burning off the fat used to sauté the cut-up meat before the true casserole cooking starts.

Some cooks make much of using the "correct" wine for each dish. Recipes that stem from local traditions always call for the local wine, but they would, wouldn't they? It was all the wine the country cooks knew about. With our modern choice, it is pedantic to insist on Beaujolais in Coq au Vin, or Muscadet in a fish stew. There are many other red wines which can be substituted for the Beaujolais: look for one that has plenty of taste and essence and is not too acidic or harsh. Cider makes a good alternative to white wine in a number of sauces, as well as pork and fish dishes. Vermouths are also good substitutes for wine: all they are is wine with various herbs added, so they add nothing but good tastes. Sherry is useful in sauces, as it too is just concentrated wine. As with vermouth, use less of it than you would wine.

Wine in the kitchen sometimes causes storage problems: what to do with a couple of glassfuls left over? It will go off if kept in the original bottle. This is because wine will go off if in contact with air, and a bit slopping around in a large bottle gets in contact with plenty. A small, full bottle is the solution: keep half-bottles with well-fitting corks, or a small screw-top jar, into which odd ends of wine can be decanted and then stored. They will not keep for ever, but will be fine for a week.

A glass of Bardolino adds its taste to a dish of braised beef. The rest of the bottle can be served with the meal — if the chef can keep off it.

DENOMINAZIONE
CLASSICO
VINO IMBOTTIGLIATO
CASA VINICOLA

KEY FACTS: France

A Bordeaux label. From the top, it gives; the vintage date; the status "grand cru classé 1855" — the château was included in the great Médoc classification of that year; the château's name; its Appellation Contrôlleé — Haut-Médoc; the name of the proprietor and the fact that it was bottled at the Château. The bottle size — 75 centilitres — and the degree of alcohol are also shown.

AREAS

Bordeaux (see page 64)
Uses straight-sided bottle

Red wines — christened "claret" by the English: Médoc, St-Emilion, dry, refined. Quality; from everyday to top-class.
White wines: dry and medium from Graves, Entre-Deux-Mers. Sweet from Sauternes and Barsac. Most wine from a "château" — there are 3,000. Best are "Cru Classé" or "Grand Cru".

Burgundy (see page 72)
Uses slope-shouldered bottle.

The word is the English corruption of the French Bourgogne — the name of the region.
Red wines: Beaujolais, Mâcon: soft, fruity, Côte d'Or reds: perfumed, round, full. Quality: from everyday to top-class.
White wines: all dry to medium. Quality: from everyday to top-class.
"Grand Cru" is the top grade; next is "Premier Cru". Wines with a village name — Pommard, Volnay — rank better than plain "Bourgogne".

Alsace (see page 74)
Tall, slender green bottles.

Mostly white. Grape varieties shown on label. Mostly dry, except "vendange tardive" (late-pickled, riper grapes). Quality: reasonable to very good.

A Burgundy label. The wine is from the commune, or village, of Puligny-Montrachet and from a single vineyard — Les Combettes, a Premier Cru. Grand Crus use their name alone; such a label would just carry the name "Le Montrachet", for instance. The village of Puligny has joined the name of this prestigious vineyard to its own. Straightforward Puligny-Montrachet comes from anywhere in the commune, but not from the Grands Crus. The name of the grower, printed at the bottom of the label, is important in Burgundy.

Champagne (see page 76)

Sparkling wine, a little still wine. Most is non-vintage; vintage is high-quality. *Brut* = dry, *Demi-Sec or Sec* = sweeter, *Crémant* = less sparkling.

Loire (see page 68)
Bottles: various.

Long river: wide range of wines, from Muscadet at one end to Sancerre at the other. All colours, though mostly white; still and sparkling, sweet and dry.

Rhône (see page 70)
Bottles: slope-shouldered as for burgundy.

Red: Côtes du Rhône everyday, others (eg Hermitage, Châteauneuf) better, Good ones age well.
Whites: rare, can be good.

WINE RULES

Geography is the most important factor. Rules specify *where* a wine comes from and *how* it is made. There are hundreds of regional and local *Appellations d'origine Contrôllée* — AoC (literally; names of controlled origin).

Four quality levels:

- ***Vin de Table*** (most basic): no rules about origin
- ***Vin de Pays:*** origin controlled, also grapes used and methods
- ***Vin Délimité de Quality Supérieur:*** being phased out as vins de pays get better — junior version of AoC
- ***Appellation d'Origine Contrôllée:*** origin controlled

LABEL TERMS

Cave	Cellar
Cave coopérative	Growers' joint-owned winery
Cépage	Grape variety
Chais	Cellar
Château	Estate (No guarantee of quality)
Côte or coteaux	Slopes of . . . implies hill vineyard, and thus good wine
Cru Classé	Classed (ie the best) Bordeaux estates
Cru Bourgeois	Bordeaux: second rank (still very good)
Domaine	Wine-making property
Doux	Sweet
Grand Cru	In Burgundy and Alsace, the best vineyards and wine
Marque Déposée	Registered trade name
Mise en bouteille	Bottled at . . .
Moelleux	Soft, sweet
Négociant	Merchant; often bottles own blends
Nouveau	New wine; especially Beaujolais
Perlé	Slightly sparkling
Pétillant	Slightly sparkling
Premier Cru	Burgundy; rank below Grand Cru
Primeur	See "nouveau"
Servir frais	Serve cool
Supérieur	With AoC name; usually with a degree extra alcohol
Villages	With AoC name; implies better wine
Vin doux naturel	Sweet fortified wine

A VDQS label (Vin Délimité de Qualité Supérieure — the rank below AoC). The wine is Gros Plant from the Loire. The producer's name matters on such a wine; there's no estate or other location given — the producer has probably blended the wine from the crops of several small growers.

A Vin de Pays label. These are the lowest grade of wines with a defined origin – in this case the Département (county) of Hérault. It comes from a Cave Cooperative, as do many of these wines from Southern France.

A Vin de Table — the most basic French wine. The name Cherançay is a brand, having no geographical meaning. The wine could have come from anywhere and is as good as its bottler's reputation. This rosé wine has 11° of alcohol. The higher the degree, the higher the price.

KEY FACTS: Germany, Austria, Switzerland

Wine from the Mosel: Qualitätswein rather than QmP; 1980 vintage; Graach is the village, Himmelreich ("Heaven's realm") the vineyard; Riesling is the grape; Trocken means dry; erzeuger-abfüllung equals bottled by the producer; the last line gives the producer's name. The left-hand side of the label is advertisement by the grower, saying he owns the land in the best vineyards in four world-renowned villages.

This distinctive label carries the eagle of the German State Domaines. It is from the Nahe, 1979 vintage. Schlossbockelheim is the village, Kupfergrube the vineyard. Riesling is the grape, Spätlese the status. In the box is the quality level QmP. The small print, compulsary on German labels, gives the number of its official quality testing. The name of the estate is at the bottom.

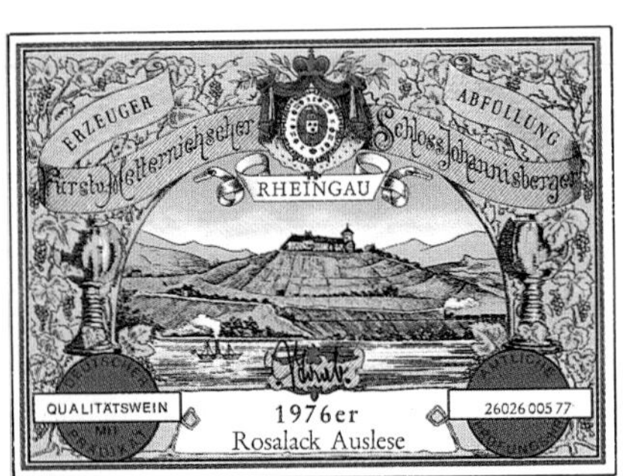

German labels must follow strict rules about the order in which the facts are printed, but the overall design is up to the owner. This is a Rheingau wine, from Prince ("Fürst") Metternich's Schloss Johannisberg estate, which is one of a few top estates which do not have to give a village name on their labels. The vineyard, Rosaleck, and the status Auslese are listed.

GERMANY: AREAS

Eleven quality-wine regions, divided into many smaller zones (see wine rules, below)

Ahr: small red-wine zone; little is exported

Baden: southernmost region. Tasty, solid white wines, some red and rosé. Good value

Franken: wine zone in deepest Bavaria. Uses flagon-shaped bottles for mostly white wines, which are dry and good with food Sylvaner (grape variety) wines are best

Hessiche Bergstrasse: tiny region, white wine, little seen outside locality

Mittelrhein: vineyards of the Rhine Gorge, more romantic than practical. Good Mosel-style wines in warm years

Mosel-Saar-Ruwer: big region of Mosel and tributary valleys. Best wines from Riesling grapes. Can be superb, especially from top estates and in warm years. Saar and Ruwer wines more delicate and fresh. Overall, Mosel wine is lighter and drier than Rhein

Nahe: good wines, especially from Riesling grapes. Less famous than Rhein and Mosel and thus good value

Rheingau: Rhein-bank district specializing in Riesling. Solid, long-lasting wines, the best very good indeed

Rheinhessen: largest region, source of much everyday wine (e.g. Liebfraumilch) and some distinguished ones

Rheinpfalz: makes long-lived, rounded wines in good years. More depth than, say Mosel wine

Württemberg: backwoods region; some red wine, most white, nearly all drunk where made

WINE RULES

Origin, quality level, sugar level — thus sweetness — are all strictly regulated.

Origin: wine can state which "area" it comes from, or from which *Bereich* (district) in an area. Within each Bereich, vineyards are grouped in *Grosslages*, which are used with a village name, ie Wiltinger Scharzberg (see "label terms", below). Individual vineyards are called *Einzellages* — several are grouped to make each Grosslage. Einzellage names are used in the same way as Grosslage names. There are more than 2,500 Einzellages.

Quality: there are three grades:

Tafelwein (most basic): if German, it's called ***Deutscher***. If not so labelled it may well be a blend of wine from other countries. Even Tafelwein has to meet basic quality standards

Qualitätswein eines bestimmten Anbaugebeites: literally: quality wine from a particular region. Usually (and thankfully) shortened to plain Qualitätswein or QbA. Must pass official tests. Can be sweetened. Most (90% +) German wine is QbA

Qualitatswein mit Pradikat: quality wine "with distinction", shortened to QmP. No sweetening allowed. Must pass official tests and be in one of five grades, judged according to level of ripeness of grapes:

Kabinett	*Beerenauslese*
Spätlese	*Trockenbeerenauslese*
Auslese	

Wines in the two last-named grades are made from late-picked, individually-selected grapes infected by noble rot. Both are very sweet and intense; trocken means dry, which refers to the raisiny grapes, not the wine. Auslese is from selected ripe bunches and is less sweet. Spätlese ("late-picked") and Kabinett may not taste sweet at all, due to the acidity balancing the sugar.

There is also *Eiswein*, which means what it says: ice-wine, made from grapes that froze on the vine and thus became even more concentrated.

Another quality level, *Landwein*, is a sub-branch of Deutscher Tafelwein: dry or medium wines from specific regions. Akin to French *Vins de Pays*.

LABEL TERMS

Layout of labels is uniform. In this order come:

Region of origin (see "areas")
Village, often with the letters "er" added to the name (eg Wiltinger). This means "of Wiltingen"
Vineyard name (see "rules")
Vintage
Grape variety (not compulsory)
Quality level eg Qualitätswein (see "rules")
Control number — usually given after letters AP. This shows in code when and where the wine was officially tested
Name and address of maker/bottler

OTHER LABEL TERMS

Abfüllung	Bottled
Bereich	District
Erben	Heirs, successors – used as part of company name
Erzeugerabfüllung	Bottled by producer; estate-bottled
Halbtrocken	Semi-dry
Hock	English term for Rhine wine
Liebfraumilch	Rhine QbA wine of Halbtrocken level, only used in export markets
Originalabfüllung	Estate-bottled
Perlwein	Slightly sparkling
Sekt	Sparkling wine
Trocken	Dry — but see "rules" for Trockenbeerenauslese
Verband Deutscher Prädikatsweinguter	League of quality wine estates
Weingut	Wine estate
Winkellerei	Winery
Winzergenossenschaft	Wine growers' cooperative
Zentralkellerei	Central cooperative

AUSTRIA

Most Austrian wines are white, fruity, full and drier than German. Some sweet wines on German pattern, and soft, light reds. Areas in flux as new rules come in. Rules: as in Germany, though wines tend to be stronger and drier. However, general standard high, value good.

SWITZERLAND

Whites best, especially from French-speaking west of the country. Some light reds, especially in (Italian-speaking) Ticino. Little wine exported.

An Austrian label. The system is similar to Germany's, but the word "Ried" is used for a vineyard. This one comes from the Postaller vineyard in Joching in the Wachau district, as the bottom line states. The maker is the weingut (estate) of Josef Jamek. This wine is from Riesling-Sylvaner grapes — a name in Austria and Switzerland for Müller-Thurgau.

A Swiss label, from the French-speaking west of the country. Swiss labels can be in French, German or Italian. Gamay is the grape, Les Velours the vineyard. Peissy is a hamlet close to Geneva. Swiss wine is dry unless the label says otherwise.

KEY FACTS: Italy, Spain, Portugal

An Italian "table wine" — but a quality one. The Count Tasca d'Almerita has coined the name Regaleali for wine from his estate in Sicily. Vino da Tavola can also be very ordinary table wine.

Barolo, one of Italy's classics. It is DOCG — the highest quality level. Made by Terre del Barolo, a cooperative at Castiglione Falletto. Note the alcohol level: 13.5°, one of the highest for a red wine. The vintage, esential data for a Barolo, is marked on a separate neck label.

In the north of Italy many wines carry grape names as well as a locality. This is from Cabernet Franc grapes grown in the Aquileia DOC zone. The maker is the Tenuta (estate) of Bolani. The extra information in English at the foot of the label has been added by the importer.

ITALY: SOME MAJOR WINES AND REGIONS

Alto Adige: German-speaking northern valley. Brisk, fresh whites, some good reds. Reliable
Asti: sparkling wine centre: most sweet; best ones dry
Barbaresco: lighter cousin of Barolo
Barbera: red grape variety, making wine in north and central Italy
Barolo: classic Italian red from northwest. Needs long ageing
Bardolino: soft, pale, light red from north
Brunello di Montalcino: exclusive, expensive red from central Italy
Carmignano: Central Italy red; cousin of Chianti
Chianti: big zone of red wine; best ones are Classico
Corvo: good everyday estate wine from Sicily
Dolcetto: soft reds from north
Frascati: white, sometimes good, from near Rome
Galestro: soft white from Chianti zone
Gavi: good dry white from north
Lambrusco: fizzy red, usually sweet but can be dry. Also a similar white
Malvasia: grape; makes sweet, usually white, wine
Marsala: fortified, usually sweet, wine from Sicily
Montepulciano: central Italy red; strong and dark
Moscato: Muscat grape; makes scented, fruity wine
Nebbiolo: red grape of Barolo, etc
Orvieto: central Italy white, dry or sweet
Recioto: term means grapes used semi-dried; wine will be sweet
Sangiovese: central Italy grape used in Chianti and elsewhere
Soave: north Italy white; the Classico is best
Spanna: another name for the Nebbiolo grape
Trebbiano: a white grape
Valpolicella: north Italian red; look for Classico or Superiore
Verdicchio: east Italian white; again, look for Classico
Vin Santo: strong wines from dried grapes, usually sweet

WINE RULES

Vino da Tavola: Table wine. Can be a blend, or may carry a regional and/or grape name. Occasionally a DOC-quality wine made with non-DOC grapes and/or methods
Denominazione di Origine Controllata (DOC): Wine of controlled origin. Area of origin is fixed, also production techniques, grapes and, often, ageing. Wine must also meet set standards of alcohol, acidity, etc.
Denominazione di Origine Controllata e Garantita (DOCG): Wines both controlled and guaranteed, ie tasted, tested and approved by official panels

TERMS

Amabile	Semi-sweet
Amaro	Bitter
Annata	Year; vintage
Azienda	Estate, farm
Bianco	White
Cantina	Winery
Casa vinicola	Wine company
Classico	Classic; the central (hopefully, best) heart of a DOC area
Colli	Hills: by implication, good vineyard sites
Consorzio	League of growers
Dolce	Sweet
Fattoria	Farm, estate
Frizzante	Semi-sparkling
Imbottigliato da	Bottled by
Passito	Strong sweet wine from semi-dried grapes
Podere	Estate
Riserva	Grade of DOC wines aged longer than normal. Length of time varies with DOC

Rosato	Rosé
Rosso	Red
Secco	Dry
Spumante	Sparkling
Superiore	Wine meeting higher DOC standards
Tenuta	Estate
Vecchio	Old
Vino da Pasto	Ordinary wine
Vino Novello	"Nouveau" wine

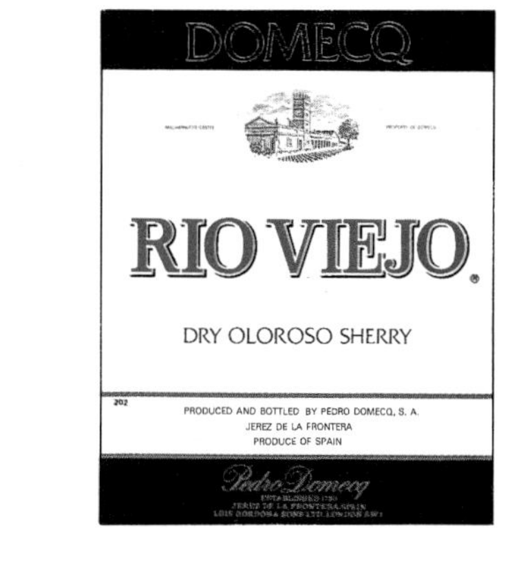

Spain's sherry has simple labels, usually with a brand name — Rio Viejo, here — and the style of the wine, in this case Oloroso. The maker is Domecq.

SPAIN: RULES

Wine zones regulated by *Denominación de Origen* — works like French AoC, though areas are wider and cover much of Spain. Production area, grapes and methods controlled. Each DO has a "stamp" which appears on the label.

TERMS

Año	Year; used to denote age when bottled
Blanco	White
Bodega	Winery
Cava	Sparkling wines made by champagne method
Con Crianza	Matured, aged
Cosecha	Vintage
Dulce	Sweet
Gran Reserva	Matured with both barrel and bottle age for longer than Reserva
Reserva	Matured, for a time specified by DO rules
Rosado	Rosé
Seco	Dry
Sin Crianza	Unaged, non-vintage
Tinto	Red

Rioja, from northern Spain. Often, the only place the word Rioja appears is on the little stamp showing which DO the wine comes from. Imperial is a brand name. Gran Reserva means at least five years old. Compania Vinicola del Norte de España, usually shortened to CUNE, is the bodega or maker. Cosecha means vintage.

AREAS

Alella	Sweet and dry wine region in Catalonia
Duero	Up-and-coming source of dry whites and good reds
Jerez	The sherry region
Jumilla	Solid, tasty reds from central Spain
Malaga	Rich, strong dessert wines, usually sweet
Montilla	Strong, soft wines like sherry, but not fortified
Navarra	Lighter reds, fresh whites
Pénedes	Quality zone in Catalonia
Rioja	Spain's best table wines, red and white. Wide range of styles from unaged to *Gran Reserva*
Valdepeñas	Sound, strong reds

Buçaco, wine from a small vineyard in Portugal, the property of the Palace Hotel at Bussaco. Branco means white, reserva wine of quality. The name of the owner appears in small print at the bottom.

PORTUGAL

Similar rules to Spain; for areas see page 98.

TERMS

Branco	White
Doce	Sweet
Espumante	Sparkling
Garrafeira	Maker's reserve, implies an aged wine
Rosado	Rosé
Seco	Dry
Tinto	Red

KEY FACTS: The New World

Grape names dominate New World labels: this Cabernet Sauvignon is made by Robert Mondavi in California. The vintage and the district — Napa Valley — are given. "Reserve" is the maker's indication that the wine is of superior quality.

The New World of wine has, as yet, little in the way of official regulations. Labels, usually in English, are easily understood. Every country checks and controls the purity of wines as they do other foodstuffs, but the makers are left to make their own mind up about grape varieties, methods and label descriptions of wines.

UNITED STATES: RULES

Very few rules, by European standards. The first Viticultural Areas have recently been registered. These allow wines from specific places to be labelled as such — but there are no tests, no stipulated grapes or methods. What wine tastes like is a matter for the maker alone — but the aim is that regional styles will develop as grape varieties and methods are matched to local conditions.

AREAS

Vineyards in the majority of States; California has by far the largest area. In California, some areas used to describe wine are geographical, some political (counties, etc), some are Viticultural Areas. Generalization is difficult: most kinds of wine are made in most areas.

Napa Valley: prestige region especially for red Cabernet wines
Sonoma: county with several quality regions for good red and white wines
Mendocino: known for red wines
Los Carneros: Pinot Noir/Chardonnay country
Central Valley: mass-production wine district, high-standard everyday wines and some good ones
Santa Barbara: some good-class white wines
Monterey: cool vineyards with Cabernets and white wines.

In Oregon and Washington ("The Pacific Northwest"), good white wines are made, also successful Pinot Noir and a range of others. Other USA vineyards are essentially of local interest: the wine can be top-class, but production is small by standards.

Grape variety and maker's name dominate this label from Washington State. Yakima Valley, the region of production which is named in small print, may one day gain the status of, say, Napa and be used in a more prominent way.

CANADA

Vineyards are expanding in Ontario and British Columbia, and quality is improving.

AUSTRALIA: RULES

Even fewer rules here than in the USA. Appellation by region is just beginning — cross-region blending of grapes and wine still common. Makers set styles: look on the label for show awards, special reserve bottlings, etc.

AREA

Wine districts scattered across Southern half of Australia in five states:

Western Australia: newly fashionable, some vibrant, flavoursome wines from Swan Valley, Mount Barker and Margaret River
South Australia: old-established classic areas like Barossa and Clare still make top wines. Also McLaren Vale, Coonawarra
New South Wales: Hunter Valley and (recently) Upper Hunter have good names for red wines and whites
Victoria: Yarra has good whites, and there is excellent sparkling wine elsewhere in the State
Tasmania: new, small vineyards: cool climate for whites especially

Santa Digna is a brand-name, Miguel Torres the maker, on this Chilean wine. Sauvignon Blanc is the grape variety. The vintage will be on a neck label.

NEW ZEALAND
Informal but useful area name system here. Styles are still being set, and there is much experimentation. Candid and informative labels.

SOUTH AFRICA: RULES
Alone among New World wine nations, the Cape wine industry has a strict system of regulation. Seal of Origin on bottle neck shows area of origin, vintage. Green band shows that wine contains at least 80% of variety stated — "Superior" means 100% varietal. Estate wines are from grapes grown, and wine processed, on a registered wine estate.

AREAS
The better Wine of Origin zones include: Paarl, Stellenbosch, Constantia, Worcester, Tulbagh. "Coastal Region" (seen on labels) is Paarl, Stellenbosch, Constantia plus three other lesser zones. 80 estates, plus cooperative and commercial wineries.

LABEL TERMS

Estate	From grapes grown *and* processed on a registered estate
Landgoed	Estate
Landgoedwyn	Estate wine
KWV	The central cooperative
Pinotage	Grape variety bred by crossing Cinsaut and Pinot Noir
Steen	Local name for Chenin Blanc grape and its wine

In Australia the grape variety gets top billing, with the maker's name second. Clare Valley is the region of origin — a well-known one in South Australia. The estate's owner reckons his name on the label will sell wine. Keen Australian wine drinkers know the reputations of the best winemakers.

New Zealand wine from Montana, the biggest producers. Marlborough is the region, Chardonnay the grape variety. This, like many New World labels, carries interesting extra details about the wine in the small print. This one, we learn, was aged in wood for a short time.

South Africa has strict rules about wine labelling: the term "Landgoedwyn" means estate wine. Groot Constantia is the name of the estate, Cabernet Sauvignon the grape.

INDEX

Page numbers in *italic* refer to illustrations and captions

ACKNOWLEDGEMENTS

T = Top **L** = Left **R** = Right **B** = Bottom
C = Centre **TR** = Top right **TL** = Top left
BR = Bottom right **BL** = Bottom left

BBS Studios, Harlow **12-13, 68, 69B, 71, 75T&B, 76T, 78/79, 84, 86, 87T, 87B, 97, 110, 117TL, BL, TR;** The Anthony Blake Photo Library **27T, 32B;** British Meat **28T&B, 29T, 31T, 37T, 171;** Campbell's Soups Ltd **24T, 33T;** Christie's Wine Department **144/5, 147T;** Cockburn Smithes Ltd **99R;** Comite Interprofessionnel du Vin de Champagne (CIVC) **14, 45TR, 76B, 77, 118, 125TL, 125TR;** The Cookeen Pastry Centre **34T;** Danish Bacon & Meat Council **29B;** The Danish Dairy Board **23, 34B;** Peter Dominic – The Wine Merchants **140;** Chris Foulkes **104, 106;** John Hedgecoe **32T, 153;** Robert Harding Picture Library **136/7;** Homepride Cook-in-Sauces **27B, 31B;** Indage **105;** Italian Trade Centre **80/1, 149;** Krona Margarine **25T&B, 26T, 30B;** Memory Lane Cakes **21;** Jay Moss-Powell **57B, 65, 67, 112, 113** (all), **114/5** (all), **116** (all), **117CR, 125CL, 125BL, 150;** Mitchell Beazley **3, 5, 7, 15, 36T&B, 37B, 41B, 119, 120, 121, 122, 123, 124, 160, 161, 163, 164, 165, 166, 167;** Mushroom Growers Association **24B;** Quinta do Noval **98/9;** Rosemount Estate, Australia **107;** The Savoy Hotel **39;** Scottish Salmon Information Service **26B;** Seagram UK Ltd **91R, 95R;** Silver Spoon **35T&B;** Summer Orange Office **30T;** Syndication International **33B;** Victoria Wine Company **129TL&TR, 139, 142/3B;** Western Australia Department of Agriculture **58BL, 92/3, 94L, 94/5, 126/7B, 128B, 141TC, 143T, 148;** Wine Institute of California **49R, 88, 89T&B, 90;** ZEFA **70T&B, 72L, 73R, 74, 100, 102/3, 112** and Colin Maher **54/55;** H Lütticke **59B;** Klaus Kerth **63, 66, 82/3;** Horst Ebersberg **82/3;** Woebbeking **85;** F Park **93R.**